HUMAN RIGHTS: CONTEMPORARY ISSUES AND PERSPECTIVES

INTERNATIONAL HUMAN RIGHTS AND JUSTICE

HUMAN RIGHTS: CONTEMPORARY ISSUES AND PERSPECTIVES

Additional books in this series can be found on Nova's website under the Series tab.

Additional e-books in this series can be found on Nova's website under the eBooks tab.

HUMAN RIGHTS: CONTEMPORARY ISSUES AND PERSPECTIVES

INTERNATIONAL HUMAN RIGHTS AND JUSTICE

DOUG HODGSON
EDITOR

nova publishers
New York

Library of Congress Cataloging-in-Publication Data

Names: Hodgson, Douglas, editor.
Title: International human rights and justice / editors, Doug Hodgson (dean, School of Law, Fremantle, the University of Notre Dame Australia, Fremantle Western Australia).
Description: Hauppauge, N.Y. : Nova Science Publisher's, Inc., 2016. | Series: Human rights | Includes index.
Identifiers: LCCN 2016003451 (print) | LCCN 2016005531 (ebook) | ISBN 9781634847094 (hardcover) | ISBN 9781634847216 ()
Subjects: LCSH: Human rights. | Justice, Administration of.
Classification: LCC K3239.8 .I577 2016 (print) | LCC K3239.8 (ebook) | DDC 341.4/8--dc23
LC record available at http://lccn.loc.gov/2016003451

Published by Nova Science Publishers, Inc. † New York

CONTENTS

FOREWORD

The Hon. Michael Kirby AC CMG[*]

The years that witnessed the conclusion of the Second World War and the establishment of the United Nations were crucial for international human rights and justice.

The second global conflict in a generation, that caused so much death and destruction, sent a signal that the avoidance of war could only be established on sure foundations if international peace and security were safeguarded alongside fundamental human rights. This message was reinforced by the revelation of shocking cases of genocide and crimes against humanity that appalled human society everywhere. In addition, the detonation of the world's first nuclear weapons indicated clearly that a fresh start to the international order was essential, if the human species and the biosphere were to be preserved.

The *Charter* of the United Nations declared its purposes to be to maintain international peace and security; to develop friendly relations among nations; to achieve cooperation and promote and encourage respect for human rights and for fundamental freedoms without distinctions; and to harmonise the actions of nations so as to attain these common ends. The fact that the pursuit of human rights and conformity with the principles of justice and international law were yoked together in the new global organisation made it clear that the world required a sea change in attitudes as well as actions.

Time ran out for the inclusion of a Bill of International Rights in the *Charter*, as had at first been intended. Thus began the concerted action of the United Nations to endorse the *Universal Declaration of Human Rights* (UDHR) (1948); to adopt the International Covenants on fundamental rights (1966); and to elaborate these notions in a series of treaties, institutions and other initiatives. We are still in the midst of the elaboration of these basic principles. But much progress has been made. This book describes, and itself advances, that progress.

My life has accompanied the building of the United Nations and the new world of human rights. As a small child at kindergarten, I sat on the pavement outside my school to watch Eleanor Roosevelt drive by. She was to become chair of the committee that drafted the UDHR. She passed by the school on her way to open the Concord Repatriation General

[*] Justice of the High Court of Australia (1996-2009); Chair of the UN Human Rights Council's Commission of Inquiry on Human Rights Violations in DPRK (North Korea) 2013-14; Member of the Secretary-General's High Level Panel on Access to Essential Healthcare (2015-16).

Hospital in Sydney. Later as a boy of 9, in primary school, I received a copy of the UDHR. I lived through the Cold War and the widespread fear of atomic bomb tests. My mind was haunted by the black and white newsreels that had recorded the gruesome images of the Holocaust in Nazi Europe and the stream of frightening images of human cruelty, oppression and indifference.

As a lawyer and judge, I attempted to bring Australian law into harmony with universal human rights, as judges in many other countries were doing. And when my judicial service concluded, I found new opportunities to serve United Nations. That service is still continuing. It has given me the rare opportunity to see close up the ongoing attempts to make United Nations treaty law a reality for ordinary people worldwide. This is why I specially welcome this book; praise its authors; and applaud the prospect that it will plant in the minds of new generations the sense of idealism and urgency felt by many of my generation.

Naturally, the United Nations cannot claim to have invented universal human rights. Their classical origins lie in the natural law theory of Greek and Roman philosophers and jurists. The modern legal tradition may be traced to many sources, including the *Magna Carta* of England in 1215 and the original Bill of Rights of England of 1689. These in turn contributed to the natural rights movement reflected in the American and French Revolutions of the late 18th century. But since the *Charter* of the United Nations, a large number of specialised human rights conventions have been superimposed on the basic human rights structure of the UDHR and the two international Covenants. These have provided more specific protections in relation to racial and ethnic minorities; women; children; migrants and refugees; indigenous peoples; and persons with disabilities. Now, moves are underway to recognise and protect another disadvantaged group: defined by reference to minority sexual orientation or gender identity and expression (LGBTI). In terms of expressing specific and meaningful normative content to all these human rights, and ascertaining the relevant scope of the protections afforded by treaty and other law, an impressive body of legal rules, principles and policies has emerged. They constitute one of the most exciting and hopeful of the developments in humanity since 1945.

Adopting treaties and other sources of law is only the beginning of rendering international human rights norms effective. The United Nations has developed a number of mechanisms to render effective the treaties and other sources of law. These include treaty committees; the appointment of special rapporteurs (engaged with thematic issues or specific country concerns); the work of the United Nations Human Rights Council itself, including through the system of Universal Periodic Review and the conduct of Commissions of Inquiry. In many countries, international human rights law and the decisions of international courts, tribunals, committees and other bodies, have been used by municipal decision-makers to influence their reasoning. In Australia, the United States and some other countries, there has been some resistance to this tendency. However, the normative content of the law of international human rights and justice continues to evolve. It displays increasing sophistication and the power of persuasive reasoning and good example.

For all these developments, the contemporary world is full of challenges and difficulties. I have witnessed many of these in my work as chair of the Commission of Inquiry on Human Rights Violations in North Korea. That Commission recommended referral of the crimes against humanity reported in its investigation, to the International Criminal Court. This would require a vote of the Security Council. However, prospects of concurrence on the point were frustrated by the opposition of China and the Russian Federation, both permanent members of the Council and entitled to a veto. Nevertheless, the persuasive power of the report of the Commission of Inquiry continued to influence the evolving view of the international community as to what it should do to respond to the grave human rights violations revealed in North Korea. When, in January and February 2016, that country conducted a fourth nuclear weapon test and launched a long range missile with military potential, the Security Council at last responded strongly. It unanimously agreed upon a lengthy and highly specific resolution (S/RES/2270) condemning North Korea; imposing sanctions; and naming individuals, corporations and vessels subject to such sanctions. This demonstrated at once the possibility of unanimity and the connection between the dual concerns of the United Nations: peace and security and human rights and justice.

Not all cases of international action have been conducive to unanimous outcomes. The Syrian conflict has raged for nearly 5 years. It has wreaked untold damage and misery upon innocent people, mostly civilians, caught up in the conflict. It has resulted in huge migration flows into southern Europe. These, in turn, have endangered border security in the European Union (EU). They have fuelled the growth of extremist political movements within EU member states. The conflict has produced devastating outcomes for human beings, institutions and cultural artefacts of antiquity. These artefacts have included a Roman temple at Palmyra which survived millennia but has now been destroyed – lost forever to the cultural heritage of humanity.

The Syrian and related developments have also presented challenges to the *Refugees Convention* (1951) and Protocol and to the efficiency of contemporary international humanitarian law and its enforcement. The gap between rich and poor countries widens. In some cases, multinational corporations eclipse in wealth, resources and influence the powers of many nation states. Access to basic justice and to the benefits of scientific and technological discoveries is increasingly tenuous. And on top of these challenges, the world's neglected indigenous populations continue to present challenges to humanity's conscience, as well as wisdom for our enlightenment in handling the perils of global climate change and ecological destruction.

This book therefore comes at an extremely important and propitious time for the development of the international law of human rights and justice. It offers a scholarly and varied examination and analysis that will be of interest to legal scholars, practitioners, human rights advocates, international diplomats and others who wish to increase their knowledge of human rights and their potential to address the greatest challenges of our time. The expert contributors come with interdisciplinary talent and experience. They include senior university academics; governmental administrators; human rights researchers and policy makers; philosophers; political scientists, United Nations officials; and representatives from civil society organisations drawn from Europe, North America, the Middle East, Africa and Australia. Their contributions have examined a wide range of human rights applications. They have evidenced the pervasiveness of this body of law and practice.

I predict that this book will be of great interest especially for law students and students of international affairs. I have found, in visits to universities, an increasing engagement of students with the issues of international human rights and justice. I have always emphasised to them, the importance of a deep knowledge about the growing body of applicable law. Passion and commitment are good. But deep knowledge and skills of analysis and the neutral presentation of argument can convert emotion into action. As this book demonstrates, the challenges to international human rights and justice today are so many, so important and so widespread that they require scholarship and descriptive materials of a high order. Converting the growing body of law and policy into effective international action is a great challenge. This book is a good place in which to confront that challenge and to get ready to answering it.

I applaud the authors, editor and publisher for collecting such a stimulating study of diverse themes. But I urge the reader to keep an eye on the overarching question that the individual contributions present. This is how best to achieve adequate supervision and monitoring as pathways to, and determinants of, justice in today's world. This collection is a valuable addition to the library of those who are engaged with the perennial question of how best to internalise human rights ideals. And how to convert them from aspiration to reality.

Typically, that is commonly the challenge faced by those working on human rights in the field and at the United Nations. But it is increasingly of concern to municipal lawyers giving effect to their own national laws. It is therefore, properly, the legitimate concern of the authors. They are to be thanked for the wisdom and experience they have shared with us. Ensuring that the mind, heart and action are all addressed to building a new world order to protect human rights and to attain global justice, represents the noble dream of Eleanor Roosevelt and those who have followed in her footsteps. To us is given the privilege and responsibility of continuing that journey.

18 March 2016

PREFACE

From their classical origins in the natural law theory of Greek and Roman philosophers and jurists to natural rights culminating in the American and French revolutions of the late 18th century, contemporary human rights have been universally recognized by the United Nations in the International Bill of Human Rights compromising the Universal Declaration of Human Rights of 1948 and the Twin Covenants of 1966. A wide array of special human rights treaties protecting racial and ethnic minorities, women, children and persons with disabilities have now been recognized and are monitored in their implementation by treaty committees, special rapporteurs and the UN Human Rights Council. The human rights expansion process continues.

International Human Rights and Justice offers a scholarly and eclectic examination and analysis of topical — and indeed controversial — human rights, equality and protection issues which confront our world today. The intended audience includes legal scholars and practitioners, human rights advocates and students who wish to increase their knowledge of (and passion for) the human rights field. The contributors include senior university academics and administrators, human rights researchers and policy-makers, philosophers, political scientists, United Nations officials and NGO representatives spanning North America, Europe, the Middle East, Africa and Australia. They have examined a wide range of human rights applications which evidence their inherent pervasiveness and dynamism in everyday life. These include:

- The scope of the human right to benefit from scientific progress
- Recent undermining of the protective mechanisms of the *European Convention on Human Rights* (at a time of mass refugee flows into southern Europe)
- Human rights, well-being and the case for equality in the post-2015 development agenda
- Equality of access to justice in American courts as a human right
- The protection of the reproductive rights of African women in a cultural context
- The potential for United Nations human rights norms and protective mechanisms to advance the constitutional recognition of Australian Aboriginal human rights
- Freedom of expression as a fundamental international human right and South African constitutional right
- The destruction of the cultural heritage of humanity in armed conflict as a breach of human rights

- MNCs, governments and the development of human rights infrastructure post-Washington Consensus
- The contribution of cultural practices to ensure greater protection of the human rights of African children
- The reindeer herding right in Norway and Sweden as a protected right under the *European Convention on Human Rights*
- Ensuring justice for the accused in criminal proceedings under the *European Convention on Human Rights* through the delivery of adequate interpretation and translation services

Chapter 1 - The Washington Consensus refers to the global economic ideology, based primarily on free markets and neoclassical economic thinking that has dominated the United States Government and international organizations such as the World Bank and the IMF. The global financial crisis of 2007-2009 and various government interventions to overcome the global financial crisis have very much challenged the relevance of this model and introduce the Chinese concept as the rival model to the Washington Consensus. This chapter provides a conceptual analysis of how governments provide various institutional infrastructures and examines the two models. The author argues that governments in partnership with multinational corporations (MNCs) can help to deal with three key aspects of institutional infrastructure: financial, physical and human rights infrastructure to cope with financial crisis. The chapter addresses the importance of institutional infrastructures, and how multinational corporations and governments can help create the institutional infrastructures that can integrate the MNCs' sphere of influence and responsibility. This chapter also develops further the role of public policy and the role of the state in international business research.

Chapter 2 - There is much talk of inequality. Statistics paint disturbing pictures of growing gaps between the rich and poor. In response, the United Nations has sought to develop an inclusive post-2015 development agenda for poverty eradication and sustainable development. What would the outcome of this global effort look like? What would compel both the privileged and the under-privileged to adopt new behaviours for more even distribution of resources? Fundamentally, the vision is one of happiness, of a life of well-being. One core guidepost is the *Universal Declaration of Human Rights 1948*. This paper affirms the principles of adequacy, duty, and limitations of rights in community. The argument is both rights-founded, invoking accountability under international law on the premise of well-being, as well as utilitarian, demonstrating that the path of adequacy, limitation, duty and community is also a proven path to fulfillment of the promise of human rights and development, that is, individual and collective well-being and happiness.

Chapter 3 - Because political conflicts inevitably become legal conflicts, judicial integrity is an essential element of any system that protects civil rights and civil liberties. Judges must be willing and able to defend the politically powerless from oppression and exploitation. In this chapter, the authors argue that mass inequality in capitalist nations, particularly the United States, poses a substantial threat to judicial integrity. First, the authors document the development of a two-tiered system of civil justice that effectively reserves courtrooms for the haves and prevents have-nots from accessing the courts. Second, the authors maintain that the widespread practice of judicial elections, which appears to make justice a commodity, undermines public trust and potentially corrupts judicial behavior. Finally, the authors note that organized interest groups are beginning to extend their influence beyond the US Supreme

Court by filing amicus curiae briefs in other courts, including state supreme courts, to the detriment of the unorganized masses. For these reasons, the authors believe that growing inequality presents a serious challenge to judicial integrity in capitalist countries and hope to draw attention to this problem.

Chapter 4 - The adoption by the United Nations in 2007 of the *Declaration on the Rights of Indigenous Peoples* marked a watershed in the world-wide recognition of the human rights of Indigenous peoples. Many Australian Aboriginal and Torres Strait Islander leaders believe that international human rights law generally, and the *Declaration* in particular, can be utilised in making human rights advances at the national level. This chapter will begin by tracing the historical and contemporary development of Indigenous human rights norms culminating in the adoption of the *Declaration*. After an examination of the foundational principles of the *Declaration*, the relevant UN norms-development and monitoring mechanisms will be discussed. The chapter will then contextualise the recent history of Australian Aboriginal disenfranchisement, the slow process of legal remedial reform and the prospects for their greater constitutional recognition as "First Peoples" and protection of their human rights as well as the lessons to be learned from the "Northern Territory Intervention." The success, and continuing prospects thereof, of their engagement with the UN mechanisms in order to secure greater justice and recognition of their rights under Australian law and public policy will be evaluated.

Chapter 5 - Interpreting plays a key role in criminal proceedings involving defendants who do not speak or understand the language used by the authorities as well as for the realization of procedural human rights, which are protected, for example, under Articles 5 and 6 of the *European Convention on Human Rights* (ECHR). Often, though, the pool of effectively available interpreters is limited. While often confused by outsiders, translation and interpretation are very different professions. This chapter is only concerned with the work of interpreters. In this chapter, the minimum requirements imposed by Article 5(2) ECHR on interpreters in the pre-court stage of criminal cases will be outlined with special regard to the rights of persons who have already been detained. This norm provides a person who has been arrested with the right to be informed about the reasons of the arrest and of any charges. This has to be done in a way which enables that person to understand his or her situation.

Chapter 6 - Reindeer herding is an important source of indigenous livelihood across the global North and in particular among the indigenous Sámi people. Sápmi, the homeland of the Sámi people, is currently administered by Norway, Sweden, Finland and Russia. In Norway and Sweden, the right to herd reindeer is limited to indigenous persons. The legal nature of this right is still the object of debate from multiple perspectives. While the European Court of Human Rights in Strasbourg has only rarely had the opportunity to deal with questions concerning the human rights of indigenous peoples, the right to herd reindeer is protected under the European Convention on Human Rights. In this chapter, it is shown, using case law from different international human rights bodies, how indigenous peoples have used international human rights litigation to defend and define their rights. While the European Court of Human Rights has played a relatively minor role in the development of indigenous rights in international law, especially when compared to the Human Rights Committee or the Inter-American human rights bodies, it does indeed have a role in protecting the indigenous right to reindeer herding in Sápmi.

Chapter 7 - For many years now the European Court of Human Rights has undergone various reforms in order to enable it to cope more efficiently and briskly with the large numbers of complaints. Protocols 14 and 15 to the *European Convention on Human Rights* amend certain procedures of that judicial body. However, aspects of these changes raise concerns that the protective machinery of the *European Convention on Human Rights* could be undermined. *Protocol 14* introduced, *inter alia*, a new, more exacting, admissibility requirement for individual applications which *Protocol 15*, not yet in force, seeks to make even stricter. *Protocol 15* further provides, *inter alia*, for greater prominence to be given to the principles of subsidiarity and the margin of appreciation and for a reduction in the time-limit within which an application must be made to the European Court of Human Rights. On balance these measures may result in a denial of justice. They have the potential to tilt the balance in favour of the respondent State and weaken the rights of applicants.

Chapter 8 - Cultural property has long been a casualty of war. Buildings and artefacts of cultural property are vulnerable to direct attack, theft and incidental damage as a result of nearby fighting. International humanitarian law (IHL) has sought to protect cultural property during armed conflict – imposing on States both positive obligations to protect and negative obligations to refrain from targeting. This brief commentary will explain the principled basis of the protection of cultural property and discuss the significance of particular incidents of cultural property destruction in the recent conflicts in Iraq and Syria.

Chapter 9 - Our entire social system is pervaded with a myriad of issues relating to freedom of expression, therefore freedom of expression has been established as a key freedom required for sustaining a democracy. However with every right comes responsibility and therein is the need for a limitation on the rights to freedom of expression so as to prevent the destructive and regressive effect it could have. In a system of democracy dedicated to openness and accountability, as ours is, the especially important role of the media, both publicly and privately owned, must be recognized. Freedom of expression is therefore a part of the very definition of self-government: the process of free discussion is required no matter whether the process leads to the truth or not. Freedom of expression is a tool for daily life in modern society.

African human rights, and more specifically freedom of speech, are still weak and indeed in certain areas of Africa in their infancy. Undoubtedly the prosecution of the most serious violations of human rights committed in Africa contributes to the protection and promotion of human rights on the continent. International prosecutions will serve as a deterrent element, and thus contribute to the eradication of the rampant culture of impunity in Africa.

Chapter 10 - The United Nations (U.N.) has long maintained that all persons have the right to share in scientific advancements and enjoy the benefits of scientific progress and its applications. The 2012 *Special Rapporteur* situates this right within the broader field of cultural rights, indicating that what it means to benefit from scientific progress will be context and location-specific. As the U.N. has presented it, the right to science, as it is called, is cast as a positive right—a right that entails actions on the part of some other persons or institutions (e.g., government, institution of education). The *Special Rapporteur* also frames this right as a bridging right—a right that is necessary for citizens to exercise other fundamental rights and liberties. This chapter will explore the limits of government and institutional action that ought to be taken toward enabling this right. The author begins by critically analyzing the idea of progress in science, the kinds of science that can be measured by beneficial applications, and the implications of understanding the right to benefit from scientific progress as a positive, bridging right. Prima facie, this is a demanding right that resource-poor countries would be unable to meet. Moreover, the kind of scientific progress that benefits the citizens of resource-poor countries may not be the kind of science that researchers in developed countries pursue. The author argues that a right to benefit from scientific progress entails a host of other, more fundamental positive rights be met—many of which are necessary for a decent human life, i.e., education/reasoning, personal security, health, etc. Thus, the right to benefit from scientific progress is a positive right that only obtains when more fundamental rights are satisfied. The author argues throughout that a claim that a person has a right to benefit from scientific progress only makes sense if the authors conceive of this right as a bundle theory of rights.

Chapter 11 - Human rights documents enjoin State Parties to ensure that children grow up in a family environment so that they can develop their personality to the fullest. Furthermore, they direct that the responsibility for upbringing of children should be borne by both parents. However, Britwum, Atuguba, Dadzie, Bruce-Catheline, Kuma and Minka-Premo (2004) argued that although the cultural practices of the Akan of Ghana assign responsibilities to fathers to ensure the maintenance of their children, some indigenous practices such as mode of reckoning descent promote parental neglect on the part of fathers. Some authors including Christensen (1954) and Wilson (2011) confirm that the Fantse (a sub-group of the Akan) place a high value on men who socialize and maintain their children as well as those of their sisters. Hence there are social control mechanisms that make men responsive to the maintenance and upbringing of children. Policy-makers have realized that though Ghana has a strong legal framework, there is a need to strengthen the implementation of the laws at the community level and engage all stakeholders and structures at that level in order to ensure that child welfare policies are effective. Considering that Ghana's legal systems are conditioned within the framework of legal pluralism where national laws operate alongside the local customary laws and that laws are more effective when they are in line with the cultural values of a people; policy-makers will be interested in the underlying cultural practices that promote children's rights in Ghana. This chapter examines the literature on the cultural practices of the Fantse and argues that to a greater extent, the cultural values of the Fantse of Ghana ensure the rights of children. It concludes that when the core of Fantse culture is upheld, it will help to overcome the problem of child neglect and the abuse of children's rights. Based on this, it recommends that researchers delve deep into indigenous cultural practices of the various ethnic groups in Ghana in order to educate people and help enforce the laws and policies on children's rights for national development.

Chapter 12 - Though the policy on free antenatal and postnatal care services in Ghana was expected to motivate women to receive maternity care from skilled providers, patronage of the services is low. Instead of addressing this problem, some officials attribute the situation to factors including superstition. Using post-colonial theory to digest the literature on medicalization, medical pluralism, and pregnancy and child-birth, to support the role of culture in health-seeking behaviour, this chapter argues that the targets set for achieving Millennium Development Goal (MDG) Five encourage medicalization; which also promotes super-ordination of biomedicine and subordination of ethnomedicine. Hence, biomedical practitioners overlook the need to improve upon their services and respect for client's rights to choose service providers. The chapter concludes that this super-ordination results in resistance to maternity care from biomedical services and forestalls the achievement of MDG Five. The authors recommend the re-examination of the essence of culture in healthcare for addressing the power relations associated with medical pluralism.

In: International Human Rights and Justice
Editor: Doug Hodgson
ISBN: 978-1-63484-709-4

Chapter 1

THE BOTTOM OF THE PYRAMID COUNTRIES, MNCS, AND HUMAN RIGHTS: WHAT LIES BEYOND THE WASHINGTON CONSENSUS

Ron Berger*

College of Law and Business, Ramat Gan, Israel

ABSTRACT

The Washington Consensus refers to the global economic ideology, based primarily on free markets and neoclassical economic thinking that has dominated the United States Government and international organizations such as the World Bank and the IMF. The global financial crisis of 2007-2009 and various government interventions to overcome the global financial crisis have very much challenged the relevance of this model and introduce the Chinese concept as the rival model to the Washington Consensus. This chapter provides a conceptual analysis of how governments provide various institutional infrastructures and examines the two models. The author argues that governments in partnership with multinational corporations (MNCs) can help to deal with three key aspects of institutional infrastructure: financial, physical and human rights infrastructure to cope with financial crisis. The chapter addresses the importance of institutional infrastructures, and how multinational corporations and governments can help create the institutional infrastructures that can integrate the MNCs' sphere of influence and responsibility. This chapter also develops further the role of public policy and the role of the state in international business research.

Keywords: MNCs, Washington Consensus, Chinese Consensus, institutions, industrial policy, social learning, human rights, infrastructure, governments

* Corresponding author: Email: ronb@clb.ac.il.

INTRODUCTION

The Washington Consensus refers to the global economic ideology, based primarily on free markets and neoclassical economic thinking that has dominated the United States Government and international organizations such as the World Bank and the IMF. The global financial crisis of 2007-2009 has provided a tremendous challenge to the Washington Consensus and its belief in free markets and neoclassical economic thinking. It is a market-centered framework that is slated to deliver faster economic growth and poverty reduction. It promotes the principles of liberalization, privatization, and deregulation, espousing free-market capitalism as its core tenet. In contrast to the Washington Consensus, neoclassical economics paradigm illustrates a growing consensus among social science researchers that institutions are the foundations of economic development and growth (North, 1990, 2005; Christensen, 2008; Ostrom, 2005). The author believes that one of the MNCs' spheres of responsibility is the need for MNCs to be a strong partner with governments in the creation of such institutions that can provide economic and business growth as well as eradicate human rights abuses. Hence the introduction of the Chinese Consensus that promotes a framework based on rights of self-determination of the receiving side. The Beijing Consensus is based on the principles of mutual benefits and non-interference in a nation's internal workings. Dialogue based on equal partnership and effectiveness and efficiency of aid without conditionality are its core characteristics. Shared benefit and proprietorship are core foundations for integrating human advancement and expansion of social prospects.

The purpose of this chapter is to analyze the potential partnership between governments and MNCs in the creation of "institutional infrastructure." I believe that three types of institutional infrastructure are fundamental to national economic success: financial infrastructure, physical infrastructure, and human rights infrastructure. The importance of human rights infrastructure and close link to business ethics values (Svensson and Wood, 2008; Chan, 2008; Michaelson, 2008) also help to define the importance of combining MNCs' sphere of influence with MNCs' sphere of responsibility. This chapter thus argues that governments in partnership with both local and foreign MNCs can help to support these key institutional infrastructures and that foreign MNCs can play a role in the development of such institutional infrastructures. In a sense, I believe that foreign multinational corporations can collaborate with national governments (Rugman and Verbeke, 1998; McGee, 2008; Lenway and Murtha, 1991; Stopford and Strange, 1993) to help develop effective industrial policies for a particular country. This would be going beyond simple tax incentives that most countries use today to encourage foreign direct investment, but constitute a longer term international business partnership which has "institutions" and institutional infrastructure development as one of the key objectives (Valentine and Flesichman, 2008; Zakhem, 2008; Meyer and Peng, 2005).

This chapter is set out as follows. First, it analyzes the Washington Consensus and its free market, non-government, neoclassical economics paradigm. Secondly, the author characterizes the three types of institutional infrastructure that are fundamental to economic development and growth: financial, physical and human rights infrastructure. Thirdly, it analyzes the potential collaboration between foreign multinational corporations, key local players and national governments in developing such institutional infrastructures and the implications for international ethics research in the 21st century.

The traditional definition of global triad competition has tended to take Western Europe, the United States and Japan as the three pillars of this global economic triad. These three representatives of regions in turn were seen to drive global competition and international business strategies through standardized products aimed at sophisticated and high-income consumers. This framework has been used in the majority of research in international business (Levine, 1997). The rest of the non-triad world was seen as either developing or third world countries. Relatively speaking smaller, less developed markets produce no major corporations in global competition and in many cases need economic aid and experience human rights violations. As the bottom of the pyramid economies develop economically, they can be seen as entering the emerging business system. The emerging market business system refers to those regions of the world that seem to be rapidly entering the world business nexus and includes some Asian countries such as China, some Latin American countries such as Mexico, Chile, Brazil, and within Africa, countries such as South Africa and Egypt. In this sense, the nature of emergence can be seen as relatively general, and not specific to any particular national or regional culture. These emerging countries include the 'top layer' of the developing or bottom of pyramid countries of the world.

The Washington Consensus versus the Chinese Consensus

By the late 1980s there was a convergence in the views of the United States Government, the World Bank and the IMF on the nature of economic development and growth. This was termed, by John Williamson (1990), the Washington Consensus. There were three key components of this approach very much in line with traditional static, neoclassical economics: market forces as allocator of economic resources, openness to foreign direct investment and free trade liberalization. Institutions were not a part of this economic paradigm, which was seen to suit all countries. The Washington Consensus implementers believed that emerging or developing countries would benefit from economic and business success and growth if they followed the key principles of this Washington Consensus (Birdsall and de la Torre, 2001). In the late 1990s this model was enriched with various other ideas that broadly fall under "good governance" (Zakhem, 2008; Christensen, 2008; Kuczynski and Williamson, 2003; Easterly, 2001). In some sense, the Washington Consensus was closely in line with the robust economic success of the United States economy in the 1990s. The belief in a single model or paradigm for economic success is not new. In the 1970s, the model that was most widely discussed was Sweden and several other continental European countries. In the 1980s, the researchers' and policymakers' favorite discussion economic paradigm was Japan. In the 1990s, it was the United States model of the Washington Consensus and its broader implications for emerging markets and from 2010 it was the Chinese Consensus.

In the early 21st century three factors facilitated to weaken if not discredit the principles of the Washington Consensus' approach to economic development and growth. Various leading economists, such as the Nobel Laureate Joseph Stiglitz, who became the Chief Economist to the World Bank, alluded to the problems of imperfect information, asymmetric information and market failures in developed economies, which would of course have much greater implications for emerging or developing economies. Other economists from the World Bank, such as William Easterly (2001), looked at the realities of the world, and pointed out that Latin American countries, which probably followed the model of the Washington Consensus most closely, had achieved economic growth rates of only 2% throughout the 1990s and even lower in the 1980s. In contrast, countries such as China, which seemed to be following an industrial policy in direct contradiction to most of the tenets of the Washington Consensus, continued to achieve economic growth rates approaching 10% throughout the 1980s, 1990s and continuing into the 21st century based on a different paradigm called the Chinese Consensus.

Secondly, numerous corporate scandals in the United States in the early 21st century helped to raise the question whether a universal system or a particular type of capitalism should be seen as a single solution to all countries. The well-known corporate scandals of major American corporations such as Enron, Andersen, WorldCom, Tyco and many others helped raise questions within and outside the United States about the U.S. governance model, which had become an integral part of the Washington Consensus. European countries did not suffer from any major corporate scandals which appeared similarly systemic in the late 1990s and the 21st century (Christensen, 2008; Michaelson, 2008; Chan, 2008). The global subprime financial crisis which began in 2008 in the United States raised further questions about the universal virtues of the Washington Consensus approach to global economic policy.

Thirdly, researchers from other social science disciplines began to emphasize the importance of "institutions" and institutional analysis in predicting economic development and growth (Chan, 2008; Christensen, 2008; Kuczynski and Williamson, 2003). Comparative research in corporate finance, international business and corporate governance showed the importance of perhaps two or three models of capitalism, and national business systems, which have been proven to be economically successful and resilient over the last several decades. The Anglo-Saxon model, on which the Washington Consensus is most closely based, was increasingly seen as just one type of system, with strengths and weaknesses like other systems. Other systems with a more collective and Communitarian approach (Bowles and Gintis, 1996) were seen to be the norm in continental European countries, as well as in the developed Asian economies of Japan, Korea, Taiwan and Singapore.

The present meta narrative, the Washington Consensus that is imperfect, is presumed to be substituted by all sorts of supplementary consensuses. The best-recognized alternative meta narrative is the emergent Beijing Consensus that highlights self-development. It is based on rights, sovereignty and equity in aid architecture. The Beijing Consensus with its over-arching agenda signifies a new and substitute aid architecture to that of the Washington Consensus. The Chinese aid architecture, with its concern for ownership and self-directed development with mutual respect, capability deprivation and equity that remains at the forefront of the agenda, takes the traditional aid agenda several steps beyond just encouraging internal and external liberalization. The Beijing Consensus endorses a framework founded on rights and self-determination for societies. The task of aid is to assist recipient countries out of shortage and expand their competencies for supportable development, but they are incomplete, and do not account for individual rights and community sovereignty and needs. Aid recipients that know best their needs and problems are not accorded the opportunity to determine their own development path, to promote local ownership and to support long-term self-determination. Rather, aid is a mechanism for promoting donor self-interests and prolonging aid addiction and it has a history of capabilities deficiency in developing countries. The idea of state power replaces the power of markets as the driver for self-determined development. Currently, aid is quite consciously used to keep aid-receiving countries in line with donors' political and economic interests, with military aid included as necessary. Accepting that poverty decline is good, but societal inclusion is healthier, giving more weight to involvement, voice and rights, leads the author to question the efficiency of present aid architectures. The Chinese model provides non-democratic government involvement, but compromises eclectic process of engagement. This is seen as a mid-way between appropriate mixtures of markets and government functions. What is so central to contemplate is that aid value is limited just to promoting economic development rather than extending itself to its duty of addressing integrating human rights in aid programs, capabilities deprivation, and regenerating development reins in failed states. The contrasts between the Washington Consensus and the newer views on institutions, social science paradigms, and economic development are shown in the figure below.

Institutional infrastructure	Washington Consensus	Chinese Consensus
Develop the key three institutional infrastructures: financial, physical, human rights infrastructures.	Free markets – market forces are superior to government second guessing the market.	Pragmatism involving a commitment to self – directed development and ownership.
A new industrial policy and partnership among government, key local players and foreign MNCs.	Free trade and liberalizing trade in all sectors and industries of a national economy.	Promotes mutual benefits, social and productive sector projects in country needs.
Government-key local players-foreign MNCs select and invest in multiple, related sectors, agglomeration.	Foreign direct investment and the encouragement of any type of foreign direct investment.	Provides more policy space and increase the bargaining power by mutual respect.
Strategy for entry into global competition can differ across countries.	Good governance, legal structures to ensure the protection of property rights, and contract enforcement.	Human rights-driven project design with mutual interests of all parties considered.

Figure 1. Washington versus the Chinese Consensus.

GOVERNMENTS, LOCAL AND FOREIGN MNCS

In this chapter I advocate a conceptual model of industrial policy that requires collaboration among national governments, local MNCs and foreign multinational corporations. This three-way collaboration and knowledge-sharing is fundamental in today's complex global business environment (Zakhem, 2008; Christensen, 2008; Rugman and Verbeke, 1998). High uncertainty and continuous change are fundamental to today's global business environment. Thus, they believe that neither national governments, nor key local players nor foreign multinational corporations, acting alone, have sufficient information or knowledge to choose winners or losers, or to make optimal investment decisions in a complex global environment of high uncertainty. A three-way collaborative knowledge and investment partnership among national governments, key local players and foreign multinational corporations can help to minimize the costs of ineffective investment and business decisions. Hence, I advocate a global economic policy that involves a close partnership among national governments, key local players and foreign multinational corporations. This is shown in Figure 2 below.

The concept of a big push was formulated in the post-World War II 1940s, when regions were separated, and even nations were relatively less interconnected to other nations economically. In the 21st century's global business environment, I believe that the broader model of new industrial policy is more appropriate. This new industrial policy, as discussed, would be a big push initiated by a three-way partnership between national governments, key local players and foreign multinational corporations. The purpose of this three-way partnership among governments, local MNCs and foreign MNCs would be to invest not in a specific product or sector, as a foreign multinational corporation traditionally does, but to invest more broadly in order to maximize agglomeration economies (Ocampo, 2003). Agglomeration economies require investment beyond a specific sector, but often in several interconnected industries. Thus, if a national economy has developed an automobile industry, this also requires investments in numerous parts and components industries as well as financial institutions connected to the automobile industry. Such agglomeration economies have been extensively studied in the international economics and economic growth literature (Hausmann and Rodrik, 2004). I believe that such global economic policies can be developed through an analysis of three institutional infrastructures presented in this chapter.

THREE INSTITUTIONAL INFRASTRUCTURES

In using the term institutional infrastructure, I refer to infrastructure that is well grounded and existing in a national economy on a long-term basis, reflecting a commitment by governments and key local players. However, the differences in institutional infrastructures influence the attractiveness of the environment for other resources such as talented global managers, which in turn increasingly helps to determine the location and joint venture decisions of multinational corporations (McGee, 2008; Michaelson, 2008). I define institutional infrastructure as comprising financial, physical and human rights infrastructure: Institutional infrastructure is defined as a national economy's long-term commitment to three key types of infrastructure: financial, physical and human rights. These three key infrastructures are embedded in local institutions – including informal traditions, norms, and social conventions especially towards the global economy, foreign direct investment and multinational corporations. This is shown in Figure 3 below.

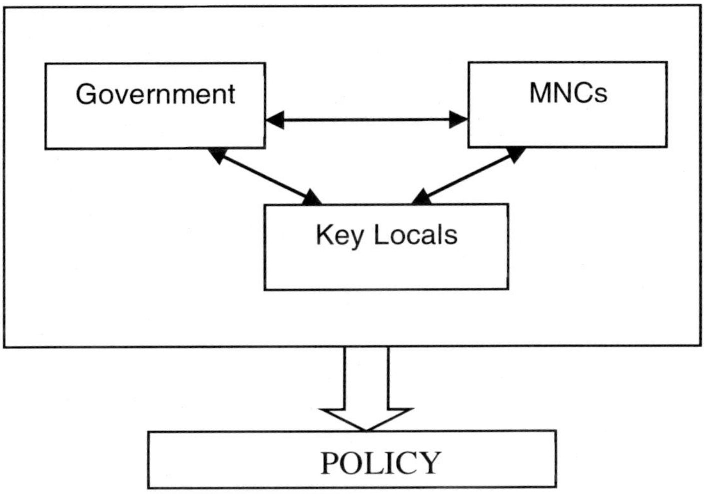

Figure 2. Three-way global partnership: Government – Key Local Players - Foreign MNCs.

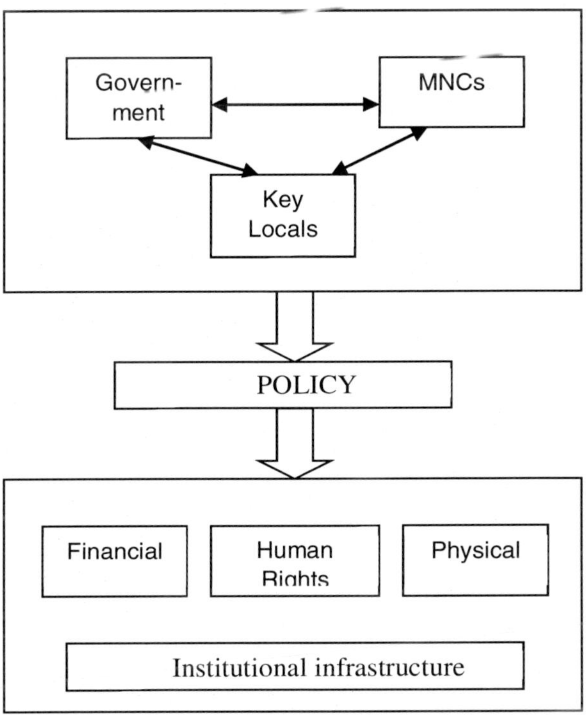

Figure 3. Institutional infrastructures: Financial – Physical – Human Rights.

FINANCIAL INFRASTRUCTURE

The global financial crisis of 2007-2009 that began with the subprime crisis in the United States of America illustrates the crucial role of financial infrastructure in global economic stability. In the growing literature on comparative corporate governance and finance, there have been extensive discussions about the differences between the more stock market-driven financial institutions in Anglo-Saxon countries, and the more bank-driven financial institutions in continental Europe and the developed Asian economies such as Japan and Korea. The conclusions of this research in international business, comparative corporate governance, and corporate finance is that both financial institutions of a stock market-based business system and the financial institutions of a bank-based business system have their relative strengths and weaknesses (Christensen, 2008; Beck and Levine, 2002; Levine, 1997). A general conclusion from these various strands of research is that a national economy's financial institutions are part of a greater picture including other types of institutions (McGee, 2008; Haggard, 2003). The existing literature however has not sufficiently researched the interdependence between a national economy's financial institutions and other types of institutions. The need for a more interconnected view of financial institutions has become more evident even in developed economies as the dramatic changes of the global internet, digital technologies and knowledge-based societies create a new type of dynamic and interdependence between financial and other types of institutions.

A clear example of developing institutional infrastructure, such as financial infrastructure, is the case of China. China, in preparation for full liberalization of its financial services, undertook the stock market listing of its four largest national banks: the Bank of China, the Industrial and Commercial Bank of China, the China Construction Bank, and the Agricultural Bank of China. The strategy for this development of financial infrastructure is a three-way partnership between the Chinese Government, foreign financial MNCs and key local MNCs, including the major Chinese banks. This three-way partnership has led to a three-step strategy that has been carefully followed in China. First, certain foreign multinationals are selected by the Chinese Government as the key strategic investors in the key local players, the Chinese banks. Secondly, two foreign financial multinationals are chosen as underwriters to the upcoming stock market listing. In addition, the policy is that there must be a third underwriter, which must be a Chinese local financial institution. Thirdly, the partnership of government, foreign financial MNC and local financial MNC ensures a successful stock market listing. Since October, 2005, such a three-way partnership led to the successful stock market listing of the China Construction Bank on the Hong Kong stock market. The stock market listing raised $9.2 billion U.S. dollars. It was one of the top 10 largest initial public offerings (IPOs) in global stock market history. This three-way partnership continued in the year 2007 for the stock market listing of the remaining three of China's largest banks, the Bank of China, the Industrial and Commercial Bank of China, and the Agricultural Bank of China.

Physical Infrastructure

By physical infrastructure, the author means not only the creation of basic foundations in transportation industries such as shipping ports, railways and airports, but also the deeper institutional connections to the national economy. Physical infrastructure that is appropriate for a national economy is interconnected (Olson, 1982) to the type of sectors or industries that are globally competitive in that national economy. In turn, this depends on the industrial policy decisions towards particular industries or sectors as decided by knowledge- sharing among national governments, foreign multinational corporations and key local players. Large cross-section of country data have shown a regularity in terms of industry concentration or diversification during different phases of a country's national economic development. Those countries that have successfully moved from emerging or developing country levels to a more developed or OECD level of national incomes have done so by going through a more diversified process in industries and sectors, until they reach such developed economy or OECD level of national income. Once they reach this high level income level, their economies become more concentrated over time (Hausmann and Rodrik, 2004).

For those national economies that have made the successful transition and taken the dynamic path from developing via emerging to developed economy levels, there is thus a "turn around" from focused or concentrated simple economies via diversified complex economies to concentrated complex economies. The projected turnaround point occurs quite late in the development process and at a surprisingly robust level of income per capita. Increased sectoral specialization, although a significant development, applies only to high-income countries. Countries diversify over most of their development path. The implication of this empirical research on a wide cross-section of countries is that for countries to achieve successful economic development, diversification needs to happen at a national economy level. Such diversification is a complex issue, and in turn requires the choosing of winners and losers in the correct sectors and industries across a national economy.

Physical infrastructure then is no longer just about transportation, railways and shipping ports. Physical infrastructure must help reflect a national economy's chosen diversification strategy into various industries and sectors. But such diversification must also take into account the nature of the global business environments, which industries are most competitive, which industries are new and emerging, and the potential interaction with multinational corporations that are market leaders in their industries from various countries. A national "fit" must be created between the physical infrastructure, the national diversification strategy, and the local institutions that can accommodate and not hinder such a complex match. The creation of such institutional infrastructure in turn requires a new industrial policy that includes national governments, foreign multinational corporations and key local players. The best examples of institutional infrastructure development in terms of physical infrastructure can be seen from the successful cases of Latin American industries – especially Chile, Brazil and Mexico (Agosin, 1999; Ocampo, 2003). Chile has experienced great economic and business success in the salmon and forest industries (Clapp, 1995). Brazil's greatest successes have been in steel and aircraft. Mexico has at least two global industries and multinational corporations in car components and personal computers (Melo, 2001).

These successful economic and international business cases from Latin America, Chile, Brazil and Mexico have been based on a close three-way partnership among government, foreign multinational corporations and local MNCs. In the famous case of the salmon industry in Chile, the Foundation Chile, a government agency, worked with major local companies in partnership with multinational corporations from Norway and Scotland. This three-way partnership adapted to the Chilean business environment a technology that had been developed by Norwegian and Scottish multinational corporations. Before this development, Chile had never exported salmon: in 2006, Chile is one of the world's biggest exporters of salmon. Researchers on Latin America have also coined the phrase, that successful economic and business development is a case of "self-discovery" (Hausmann and Rodrik, 2003, 2004).

The author believes that the term "self-discovery" describes well the reality that the global business and economic environment continues to be full of uncertainty in decision-making (North, 2005). Self-discovery also describes well international business collaboration, whereby key local players and entrepreneurs work in partnership with government and foreign multinational corporations to invest and develop in multiple sectors, that are all needed to ensure the development of an industry that is globally competitive.

HUMAN RIGHTS INFRASTRUCTURE

In the 21st century, a human rights infrastructure is fundamental to knowledge-based societies (Christensen, 2008; Chan, 2008; Steensma and Lyles, 2000), especially as an ambition of the world's developed high-income countries. The commercialization of the global internet in the mid-1990s was a fundamentally new driver added to the issue of global communication, and the greater appreciation of global human rights. The global internet and the emergence of digital technology as the foundation of all technology and communications have created an urgent need to develop human rights infrastructure in national economies. Institutional infrastructure, such as human rights infrastructure, requires a closer integration of not only digital technologies and the power of the global internet in communications but also the local nature of knowledge sources. Political economy and development researchers such as Ostrom (2005) have concluded from their analyses that knowledge is normally created at a very micro and local level, at the smallest levels of groups. Even these small groupings of society have their own informal conventions, and other cultural beliefs and values (Valentine and Fleischman, 2008; Elster, 1989; Kolm, 1984) that need to be taken into account in terms of a national economic strategy.

One of the most significant transformations after the late 1990s could be seen in the fusion of two distinct discourses, namely those of human rights and those of development, to form what is entitled the new rights-based approaches (RBAs). The language of rights has also been embraced by a wide range of advocacy movements such as the disabled, women, children, the landless, pastoralist and indigenous peoples. It has been accepted by environmentalist, anti-poverty and human rights groups. The new RBAs epitomized a coalescence of global development and human rights apprehensions, importing liberal thinking about rights. Generally, such small, local groupings and the larger communities play a role in the creation and maintenance of national norms and social conventions. Non-governmental organizations (Teegan, Doh and Vachani, 2004), because of the power of the global internet to connect diverse and small groupings, play an increasingly fundamental connecting role between such local groupings, national governments and local and foreign multinational corporations. Institutional infrastructure such as human rights infrastructure must combine the development of national level strategies on the internet and digital technologies, such as high speed broadband, along with the smaller, local groupings that set the informal norms and social conventions that are also part of any successful national economic change.

Two examples from Asia help illustrate the importance of institutional infrastructure creation in developing a human rights infrastructure. The first example is that of high speed broadband institutional infrastructure development in Korea. In 2008, Korea continues to be the world's leader as a broadband country, with 80% of homes in its population of 50 million people having high speed broadband approaching 20 megabytes in speed. This has helped create various other linked sectors such as internet games and animation. High speed broadband was first developed by the Australian telecom company Telstra in the mid-1990s. However, the Korean Government in collaboration with Telstra and local key players such as Korea Telecom and SK Telecom were the first to commercialize the technology fully in the Korean market in the early 21st century. An interesting aspect of this three-way partnership among the Korean Government, key local players and a foreign multinational corporation was the emphasis on developing the high speed broadband infrastructure in the relatively more rural, agricultural and lower income regions of Korea, before including the more cosmopolitan districts and major cities. The author believes this approach helped to preserve the local knowledge, and norms and social conventions, in turn creating a more balanced national acceptance of the global internet and high speed broadband technologies. This further helped to preserve the human rights of the often neglected rural areas and in many cases made it more competitive.

Another example in terms of human rights infrastructure development is from Taiwan. Taiwan was traditionally an exporter of sugar, but due to changing global competition and restructuring, sugar cane became no longer a viable export for Taiwan's farmers (New York Times, 2004; Taipei Times, 2004). The Taiwanese Government's response has been a partnership between the Taiwanese Government, local key players and foreign multinationals to develop a globally competitive orchid flower industry, leveraging the Taiwanese farmers' capabilities. This three-way partnership has created the human rights infrastructure necessary to jump-start such an industry. The three-way collaboration has created a genetics laboratory, quarantine site, shipping and packing areas, new roads, and privately owned greenhouses. In 2008 they have already achieved substantial export success; and in turn the development of such human rights infrastructure in a rural region of Taiwan has been a positive alternative to subsidizing the depressed sugar cane export industry in Taiwan's rural regions.

Debate on the impact of MNCs on society and, more specifically, on human rights is rife with controversy involving both optimistic voices and critical ones. Optimistic views are generally from a profuse political science standpoint and rely on the idea that MNCs are powerful and wealthy actors that are able to contribute to increased GDP levels, greater respect for human rights and democratization, and these views suggest that multinationals may contribute to advancing the cause of human rights because they bring capital, technologies, management techniques and managers who frequently are eager to introduce social improvement alongside their financial investment. Among the optimistic voices is furthermore a community of practitioners, scholars, and policy-makers who believe that large corporations can improve the living conditions of poor countries through the adoption of voluntary codes of conduct and corporate social responsibility (CSR) policies. MNCs are also considered to be critical for minimizing the harmful impacts of armed conflict and actively contributing to peace-building processes in conflict or post-conflict zones, through the adoption of conflict-sensitive CSR policy frameworks. In parallel with these rather optimistic views, there is a group of critical scholars who question the capacity of MNCs to advance the cause of human rights, not least because there is substantial empirical evidence of human rights abuses in which the complicity of large global corporations has been proven. Some precarious theories of globalization outline MNCs as both vital players in, and beneficiaries of, an unbalanced process causing growing inequality and global injustice, pointing to their being symbols of the "broken promises" of the neoliberal project and identifying their global production strategies as causes of the race to the bottom The reduction in labor, social, and environmental conditions results directly from global competition for jobs and investment. Pessimism about the beneficial impact of corporations on the environment and human rights has been expressed by researchers who refer to environmental righteousness and dependency system theories.

Non-state actors already have some form of human rights responsibilities deriving from international law, international treaties and certain non-binding international instruments. Although there is insufficient enforcement at the international level, human rights scholars believe that a strong domestic legal system is crucial to regulate MNC operations in host nations and to constrain human rights abuses. With increased human rights engagement and greater media scrutiny, firms are beginning to incorporate into their business practices responsibility for the labor practices and human rights abuses associated with their operations. In 2003 the Sub-Commission on the Promotion and Protection of Human Rights of the United Nations Commission on Human Rights adopted the Norms on the Responsibilities of Transnational Corporations and Other Business Enterprises with regard to Human Rights 2003. They were non-voluntary in essence, and intended to directly tie business with numerous human rights responsibilities. They explicitly mention the need to create and reinforce hard national and international mechanisms by which to hold businesses to account for human rights transgressions. The *Universal Declaration of Human Rights* (UDHR) was adopted and proclaimed by the UN General Assembly on December 10, 1948. The *UDHR* is recognized as the founding document of the modern human rights movement. At least 25% of the world's population currently live under state regimes that have not ratified one of the two major binding human rights covenants, namely the *International Covenant on Civil and Political Rights 1966* and the *International Covenant on Economic, Social and Cultural Rights 1966*. Unlike states which are motivated by a given national self-interest, NMCs tend to be primarily motivated by generating shareholder returns. By contrast, NGOs such as Greenpeace, People for the Ethical Treatment of Animals, or Amnesty International tend to be primarily motivated towards resolving or contributing to specific issues that will often be framed as a social good or moral concern. As this is meant to suggest, the global public domain can be conceived as a field within which the three mentioned types of institutional actors interrelate with, and try to influence, each other.

MNCs provide a new and fertile space within which NGOs can further their normative agendas; and that this turn of events has contributed to the emergence of terms such as CSR and corporate accountability. States, by contrast, try to influence the activities of MNCs because MNCs can impact, both positively and negatively, upon their various national interests. Thus, states will commonly try to influence MNCs through constructing rules and regulations at both the domestic and international levels that will maximize their potential benefits (e.g., technology transfer, job creation) and minimize their potential negatives (e.g., environmental pollution). Voluntary codes of conduct (VCCs) contain a diversity of norm types, serve a wide range of purposes, and are embedded in a variety of mechanisms for their interpretation and implementation. Human rights discourse expresses superseding moral concerns and recognizes those interests that trump all other contemplations. Sanctions for human rights abuses represent the policy determination that the sender country cares, for example, more about human rights or racial equality than commercial sales to, and corporate investments in, those countries. They represent the determination that sender nations should obviously care about matters other than trade and investment. The political regime that governs business activity both domestically and internationally stands in stark contrast to the progressive capitalist regime of U.S. international business.

CONCLUSION

The global financial crisis of 2007-2009 has helped to challenge the Washington Consensus approach to free market, neoclassical economics and non-government approaches to globalization in the 21st century. Today, governments and institutions are increasingly seen as fundamental to economic development and continued national economic success (Svensson and Wood, 2008; North, 2005; Nelson, 2004; Ostrom, 2005). This chapter provided a conceptual analysis of the role of institutions, by defining three key types of institutional infrastructure: financial, physical and human rights infrastructures. The author has advocated a global framework that requires a three-way partnership among national governments, foreign multinational corporations and large local firms, organizations, and banks, which are called 'key local players.' This chapter complements the earlier works in international business on the role of public policy and the state and their interaction with MNCs (McGee, 2008; Rugman and Verbeke, 1998; Chan, 2008). The author believes that in the 21st century's complex, global business environment, no single groups of actors, whether they be a national government, foreign multinational corporations, nongovernmental organizations (Teegen, Doh and Vachani, 2004) or key local players, can overcome the complexities of uncertainty, which North (2005) emphasized to be a continuing reality of the global economy, and the dynamic pace of change.

This chapter attempts a theoretical and conceptual integration of institutions and institutional infrastructure in international ethics research. At least two areas warrant further research. First, a comparison of the connection and interdependence among the three institutional infrastructures in high-income developed economies, and emerging and developing economies. Secondly, a further development and analysis of the conceptual framework of this chapter towards the continuing important question of MNCs' sphere of influence and sphere of responsibility in the 21st century.

However, despite the idea that MNCs have distinct obligations with respect to human rights, many VCCs, declarations, and corporate responsibility policies avoid the terminology of human rights. This is perhaps because of a fear of creating new legal liabilities, or because human rights are perceived as the concern of governments, not corporations. Where human rights are mentioned, they are rarely specified in any detail, leaving it uncertain which human rights are regarded as at risk from the activities of MNCs. Human rights discourse is primarily a moral discourse and can therefore be included in voluntary codes without undermining their voluntary nature. While the moral view of human rights is associated with the legalization and codification of human rights that has taken place through domestic bills of rights and the achievements of international human rights law in articulating and monitoring its version of human rights, it is possible to approach human rights as a set of moral imperatives that are not to be identified with any system of positive law. Emphasizing the moral nature of human rights facilitates the development of rule-based concretizations of human rights that have direct relevance to the operations of MNCs rather than those of governments, and are primarily directed at voluntary, rather than coercive, implementation. One of the foremost benefits of a human rights approach to VCCs is that it offers optimism in terms of bringing superior moral vigor to bear through modes of self-regulation.

An effective VCC must resemble rules of best practice in that they deliver the aspects with which to understand more generally framed legal requirements of the laws of host counties. Human rights obligations are relative to opportunities and capacities of those involved. VCCs are voluntary as a matter of definition in that they are adopted rather than imposed on those to whom they apply. In the absence of legal sanctions, what grounds are there for supposing that MNCs will ever take this vision of a MNC bill of rights implemented through specific human rights rules as anything more than a superficial public relations exercise designed to protect corporate reputations at minimal cost? The response to this evident difficulty involves a shift of emphasis from intimal to enteral forces and processes by looking to the contribution of civil society, through public opinion and consumer response and shareholder input. Such external accountability to civil society requires a back-up framework of legal support to enable these bodies to fulfil their monitoring and critical functions effectively. Any such soft law must be accompanied by extremely well-organized publicity by human rights NGOs, using the full force of such naming and shaming as is possible and intimal cultures that generate a routine awareness of the moral dimension of human rights in the strategic management of corporations. Creating social mechanisms to provide a conjunction of self-interested and other directed motivations is essential for engendering conduct that accords with moral standards and provides the best opportunity to make progress towards ethical business conduct.

The United States embodied the principles of natural rights and limited government while China sought to build a Soviet-style planned economy. For each country, a series of political and economic crises drew it away from the extremes and towards the center. Today, these two nations have not just met in the middle of that ideological spectrum, they have passed each other. The US now stands for the aggressive use of the state's tough authority to direct firm conduct towards social objectives that are not scarcely associated to the market. On the other hand, China has sought to reduce such restraints in the name of maximizing economic growth to forestall social unrest. In summary, U.S. law now obligates corporations to pursue the social goals of combating corruption and promoting human rights while the Chinese legal regime permits and even encourages profit-seeking with scant regard for social impact.

REFERENCES

Acemoglu, D., Johnson, S. and Robinson, J. (2001). The colonial origins of comparative development: an empirical investigation. *American Economic Review*, *91*, 1369-1401.

Agosin, M. (1999). Trade and growth in Chile: past performance and future prospects. Department of Economics, University of Chile, *Working paper*: June.

Amsden, A. (1989). *Asia's next giant*. Oxford University Press: Oxford.

Bardhan, P. and Roemer, J. (1992). Market socialism: a case for rejuvenation. *Journal of Economic Perspectives*, *6*, 101-116.

Beck, T. and Levine, R. (2002). Industry growth and capital allocation: does having a market-based or bank-based system matter? *Journal of Financial Economics*, *64*, 147-180.

Belev, B. (2003). Institutional investors in Bulgarian corporate governance reform: obstacles or facilitators? *Journal of World Business*, *38*, 361-374.

Bevan, A., Estrin, S. and Meyer, K. E. (2004). Foreign investment location and institutional development in transition economies. *International Business Review*, 13, 43-64.

Birdsall, N. and de la Torre, A. (2001). Washington Contentious: Economic policies for social equity in Latin America. Washington: Carnegie Endowment for International Peace and Inter-American Dialogue.

Bowles, S. and Gintis, H. (1996). Efficient redistribution: New rules for markets, states and communities. *Politics and Society*, *24*, 307-342.

Brewer, T. L. (1992). An issue-area approach to the analysis of MNE-government relations. *Journal of International Business Studies*, *23*, 295-310.

Chan, G. (2008). The relevance and value of Confucianism for contemporary business Ethics. *Journal of Business Ethics*, *77*, 347-360.

Christensen, S. (2008). The role of law in models of ethical behavior. *Journal of Business Ethics*, *77*, 451-461.

Clapp, R. (1995). Creating comparative advantage: Forest policy as industrial policy in Chile. *Economic Geography*, *71*, 273-296.

Easterly, W. (2001). *The elusive quest for growth*. MIT Press: Cambridge, MA.

Elster, J. (1989). Social norms and economic theory. *Journal of Economic Perspectives*, *3*, 99-117.

Gerschenkron, A. (1962). *Economic backwardness in historical perspective: A book of essays*. Harvard University Press: Cambridge, MA.

Haggard, S. (2003). Institutions and growth in East Asia, University of California, San Diego, *Working paper*.

Hardin, R. (1982). *Collective action*. Johns Hopkins University Press: Baltimore, Maryland.

Hausmann, R. and Rodrik, D. (2003). Discovering El Salvador's production potential, Harvard University, Kennedy School of Government, *Working paper*, August.

Hausmann, R. and Rodrik, D. (2004). Economic development as self-discovery. *Journal of Development Economics*, *72*, 110-135.

Henisz, W. and Swaminathan, A. (2008), Institutions and international business. Special issue of *Journal of International Business Studies*, *39*(4), 537-539.

Hirschman, A. O. (1958). *The Strategy of Economic Development.* Yale University Press: New Haven, CT.

Kogut, B. and Zander, U. (1992). Knowledge of the firm combinative capabilities and the replication of technology. *Organization Science*, *3*, 383-397.

Kolm, S. C. (1984). *La bonne economie*. Presses Universitaires de France: Paris.

Kuczynski, P. and Williamson, J. (2003). *After the Washington Consensus: Restarting growth and reform in Latin America.* Institute of International Economics: Washington, D.C.

La Porta, R., de Silanes, F. L., Shleifer, A. and Vishny, R. (1996). Law and Finance, National Bureau of Economic Research *Working Paper*, no. *5661*.

Lall, S. (2004). Reinventing industrial strategy: the role of government policy in building industrial competitiveness. G-24 *Discussion Paper* no. *28*.

Lenway, S. and Murtha, T. (1991). The idea of the state in the international business literature, Division of Research, School of Business Administration, University of Michigan, Ann Arbor.

Levine, R. (1997). Financial development and economic growth: View and agenda. *Journal of Economic Literature, 35*, 688-727.

Lyles, M. A., Saxton, T. and Watson, K. (2004). Venture survival in a transition economy. *Journal of Management, 30*, 351-375.

McGee, R. (2008). Applying ethics to insider trading. *Journal of Business Ethics, 77*, 205-217.

Mathews, J. (2003). Competitive dynamics and economic learning: An extended resource-based view. *Industrial and Corporate Change, 12*, 115-145.

Melo, A. (2001). Industrial policy in Latin America at the turn of the century. Inter-American Development Bank, Research Department, *Working Paper* no. *459*.

Meyer, K. E. and Peng, M. (2005). Probing theoretically into Central and Eastern Europe transactions, resources, and institutions. *Journal of International Business Studies, 36*, 600-621.

Michaelson, C. (2008). Work and the most terrible life. *Journal of Business Ethics, 77*, 335-345.

Nelson, R. (2004). The changing institutional requirements for technological and economic catch up. Columbia University, Economics Department, *Working Paper.*

North, D. (1990). *Institutions, institutional change and economic performance.* Cambridge University Press: Cambridge, UK.

North, D. (2005). *Understanding the process of economic change.* Princeton University Press: Princeton, New Jersey.

Ocampo, J. (2003). Structural dynamics and economic growth in developing countries, United Nations Economic Commission for Latin America and Caribbean (ECLAC), Santiago, Chile.

Olson, M. (1982). *The rise and decline of nations.* Yale University Press: New Haven, Connecticut.

Ostrom, E. (2005). *Understanding institutional diversity.* Princeton University Press: Princeton, New Jersey.

Rodrik, D. (2004). Industrial policy for the twenty-first century. Harvard University, Kennedy School of Government, *Working Paper.*

Rugman, A. and Verbeke, A. (1998). Multinational enterprises and public policy. *Journal of International Business Studies, 29*, 115-136.

Sabel, C. (2004). Beyond principal-agent governance: Experimentalist organizations, learning and accountability. In: Engelen, E. and M. Ho (editors), *Democracy and the State.* Amsterdam University Press: Amsterdam.

Steensma, H. K. and Lyles, M. (2000). Explaining IJV survival in a transitional economy through social exchange and knowledge-based perspectives. *Strategic Management Journal, 21*, 831-851.

Stopford, J. and Strange, S. (1993). *Rival state, rival firms: competition for world market shares.* Cambridge University Press: Cambridge, UK.

Svensson, G. and Wood, G. (2008). A model of business ethics. *Journal of Business Ethics, 77*, 303-322.

Teegen, H., Doh, J. and Vachani, S. (2004). The importance of nongovernmental organizations in global governance and value creation: An international business research agenda. *Journal of International Business Studies, 35*, 463-483.

UN Sub-Commission on the Promotion and Protection of Human Rights. Economic, Social and Cultural Rights: *Norms on the Responsibilities of Transnational Corporations and Other Business Entities with regard to Human Rights*, 26 August 2003, E/CN.4/Sub.2/2003/12/Rev.2.

Valentine, S. and Fleischman, G. (2008). Ethics programs, perceived CSR. *Journal of Business Ethics*, *77*, 159-172.

Williamson, J. (1990). *What Washington Means by Policy Reform*, Chapter 2 from Latin American Adjustment: How Much Has Happened? Peterson Institute for International Economics.

Zakhem, A. (2008). Stakeholder management capability. *Journal of Business Ethics*, *79*, 395-405.

In: International Human Rights and Justice
Editor: Doug Hodgson

ISBN: 978-1-63484-709-4

Chapter 2

The Premise/Promise of Well-Being: Human Rights and the Case for Equality in the Post-2015 Development Agenda

Alisa Clarke[*]

Human Rights Officer, UN Office of the High Commisioner for Human Rights, President, Global Vision Institute

Abstract

There is much talk of inequality. Statistics paint disturbing pictures of growing gaps between the rich and poor. In response, the United Nations has sought to develop an inclusive post-2015 development agenda for poverty eradication and sustainable development. What would the outcome of this global effort look like? What would compel both the privileged and the under-privileged to adopt new behaviours for more even distribution of resources? Fundamentally, the vision is one of happiness, of a life of well-being. One core guidepost is the *Universal Declaration of Human Rights 1948*. This paper affirms the principles of adequacy, duty, and limitations of rights in community. The argument is both rights-founded, invoking accountability under international law on the premise of well-being, as well as utilitarian, demonstrating that the path of adequacy, limitation, duty and community is also a proven path to fulfillment of the promise of human rights and development, that is, individual and collective well-being and happiness.

Keywords: adequacy, community, development, duty, equality, well-being

Introduction

There is much talk of inequality. National, regional and global statistics paint disturbing pictures of growing gaps between the rich and the poor. Even as we celebrate small victories

[*] Corresponding author: Email: alisa.clarke@globalvisioninstitute.org.

in the achievement of Millennium Development Goals (MDGs), we are cognizant of the shortcomings of income growth for some at the expense of many. In response, the UN has been working towards an inclusive and people-centered post-2015 development agenda to succeed the MDGs, aimed at poverty eradication and sustainable development. This agenda will further promote peace and security, democratic governance, the rule of law, gender equality and human rights for all. Critically, it will now also be a commitment by all nations, including industrialized and traditional donor nations.

What then would the outcome of this global effort look like? What would compel both the privileged and the under-privileged to adopt new behaviours that would effectively involve a more even distribution of resources? What have we learned from the historical experiences of wealth, poverty, economic doctrines and social contracts that could inform this ideal of the human condition?

Fundamentally, the vision is one of happiness, of a life of well-being. And while certainly the components of this state are highly subjective, there are commonalities that are shared by us all. One potential core guidepost of this common understanding is the framework of human rights, broadly conceived, that is, covering all rights and responsibilities, including economic, social and cultural rights as well as civil and political rights. In this respect, the *Universal Declaration of Human Rights 1948 (UDHR)*, the *International Covenant on Economic, Social and Cultural Rights 1976* and the *International Covenant on Civil and Political Rights 1976*, themselves the outcomes of international negotiations on global aspirations, are useful touchstones for a fuller exploration of what we seek.

In particular, this chapter will affirm the often neglected significance and application of the principles of adequacy, duty, and the limitations of rights in community. It maintains that human rights, thus more comprehensively understood, provides the scaffolding around which a model for well-being can be offered, and corresponding obligations and behaviours elicited.

This chapter thus makes the following arguments:

In section "I: The promise of well-being," it contends that the principles of well-being fundamentally include those of adequacy, sharing and community.

Section "II: The premise of well-being" demonstrates that the above principles are also enshrined in human rights instruments and jurisprudence.

For section "III: Inequality," it is asserted that the redistribution of resources engendered through application of the above principles can mean greater equality.

In section "IV: Well-being and development," the chapter explores how particular policies of the well-being agenda can therefore be usefully included in the post-2015 framework, notably given its espoused focus on reducing inequality, with a view to a truly transformative global agenda.

The chapter concludes with an assessment of the implications of this more comprehensive conceptualization of the human rights framework for achieving well-being and related equality in a new global development agenda.

I. The Promise of Well-Being

As a primary motivator of human behavior, understanding of the mechanics of well-being is fundamental to designing effective and widely acceptable frameworks for action, including action at community, national and global levels.

The State of Well-Being: Factors and Implications

This chapter uses the terms happiness and well-being inter-changeably[1] as descriptions of life satisfaction. The state of happiness has been the subject of growing research, notably since the work of Richard Easterlin in 1974. He used data on subjective measures of happiness in nineteen countries to examine the relationship between income and happiness. His findings yielded a paradox whereby within-country evidence showed that for a given point in time, those in higher income groups were happier on average than those in lower income groups; however, over time and across countries the link between income and happiness weakens. [Easterlin, pp. 89 -121]

More recent research distinguishes between emotional well-being (experiences of joy, stress, sadness, anger, etc.) and life satisfaction (thoughts people have about their life). In one 2010 U.S. study [Kahneman, D. and Deaton, A., pp. 16489–16493], it is determined that life evaluation rises with income, but that for emotional well-being, happiness does not increase beyond an annual income of $75,000, representing a decreasing marginal utility of income from this income level.

Additional growing research tests assumptions of the economic approach and the understanding of utility in economics, the implications of differences in experienced utility, and possibilities for public policy. [Frey, B. and Stutz, A., p. 679]

Such studies are among those that informed the 2012 World Happiness Report [Helliwell J., Layard R. and Sachs J.], presented on the occasion of the UN High Level Meeting on Well-being and Happiness in 2012. The Report examines the factors facilitating well-being, presents data on happiness levels globally and related methodologies, and suggests directions for policy. Among the key external factors identified are income, work, community, governance, values and religion, and, at the individual level, mental and physical health, family experience, education, gender, and age. The Report contends that:

> "raising incomes can raise happiness levels, especially in poor societies, but fostering cooperation and community can do even more, especially in rich societies that have a low marginal utility of income. It is no accident that the happiest countries in the world tend to be high-income countries that also have a high degree of social equality, trust, and quality of governance." (p. 7)

The document suggests that new indices of a nation's well-being should be considered beyond Gross Domestic/National Product for economic stability that better capture community cohesion, support to the most vulnerable, ethical standards and environmental sustainability. While securing basic living standards is essential for happiness, beyond this baseline, policy goals should include high employment and decent work; a strong, inclusive and participatory community with high levels of trust; improved physical and mental health; support for family life; and universal good-quality education.

In this vein, one exploration of the relationship between social capital, in the form of social trust, and income inequality, in the case of the U.S., demonstrated considerable evidence of social capital being a significant equalizer. [Ram, R., p. 89]

---

[1] The Merriam-Webster dictionary defines happiness as 'a state of well-being or contentment' http://www.merriam-webster.com/dictionary/happiness, accessed on 21 August 2015.

New studies also scientifically validated the principle of human psychology that people are happier when they spend money on others rather than on themselves (as well as on experiences, treats, time and deferred consumption). [Dunn, E. and Norton, M., pp. 105 - 134]

The above findings all underscore the elements of a development model as promoted in this chapter under the human rights rubric, where adequacy and limitations may be equated with a particular income range and related opportunities, goods and services, and where the notion of community and interdependence is emphasized and promoted, with attendant duties and benefits.

II. The Premise of Well-Being - Well-Being and Human Rights

In some of the theoretical literature, human rights and well-being are presented as conflicting philosophical frameworks. This derives from the juxtaposition of welfarist consequentialism or utilitarian perspectives on the one hand, according to which consequences are assessed based on maximizing some measure of overall well-being [Singer, P., pp. 229 - 243], and traditional rights theories on the other hand, which are concerned with choices independent of consequences, and whereby individuals are entitled to exercise a kind of veto over policies aimed at benefitting a majority or achieving overall well-being, so that individual rights are unrelated to well-being, as asserted for instance by Immanuel Kant. [Cronin C. and De Greiff P. Eds., p. 165 - 201]

Several other scholars attempt to demonstrate that human rights may not maximize well-being [Sen, A.] or minimize violations of individual rights [Nozick, R.], to the extent that there are necessary trade-offs in the exercise of individual and collective rights in specific instances when the two cannot readily co-exist. James Griffin [Griffin, J.] concludes that rights cannot be adequately based on deliberations of well-being, but should be understood as being grounded in the requirements of normative agency, while Judith Jarvis Thomson [Thomson, J. J., pp. 149 - 175] refers to the notion that infringements of rights can be justified by considerations of well-being.

William Talbott [Talbott, W.] and others attempt to reconcile the apparent conflict by placing the two types of theories on two different levels. This second-order consequentialism defends first-order rights by redirecting the focus of consequentialist assessment from acts to rules or institutions or social practices. He further contends that there are two ways that consequentialist considerations can play an important role in most non-consequentialist theories of human rights. First, a negative role, in allowing the possibility of making at least minor exceptions to human rights norms because of the bad consequences of not infringing them. Secondly, the positive role of including some sort of right to well-being. In this latter respect, while non-utilitarian in principle, Talbott suggests that the capabilities approach of Amartya Sen [Sen, A.] and Martha Nussbaum, [Nussbaum, M.] notably as applied to UN development indictors, approximate well-being, including as they do "capabilities to lead the kind of life [people] value—and have reason to value" [Sen, A., p. 18] and recognizing the importance of assessing social arrangements by their consequences for well-being. [Sen, A., p. 60]

This chapter presents another perspective, in asserting that the above potential conflict is based on a limited framing of the human rights regime, one which neglects the dimensions of adequacy, duty, community and limitation, as articulated in the *UDHR* and elsewhere. Rights theories *per se* are thus not negated, but viewed as part of a more comprehensive approach. The notion of limitation under this rubric admits as legitimate concern with potential tradeoffs in reconciling individual and collective rights.

The argument being posited here further suggests that there is a false dichotomy between individual and collective well-being, in that individual well-being is shown to be a function of collective well-being, asserted in the section above on the promise of well-being. Utilitarian perspectives are also thus not negated, notably when inclusive of distribution beyond average utility, as accommodated in Parfit's triple theory. [Parfit, D.]

These positions are explored further below, with respect to the premise of well-being. The overall argument is therefore supportive of both rights theories and distributive utilitarianism, and goes some way to eroding the distinction between them.

The Premise of Well-Being in International Human Rights Law

Adequacy

Adequacy in International Law

Article 25 (1) of the *UDHR* states that 'Everyone has the right to a standard of living adequate for the health and well-being of himself and of his family, including food, clothing, housing and medical care and necessary social services'

In contrast, the *International Covenant on Economic, Social and Cultural Rights (ICESCR)*, an international treaty with 161 State Parties, while invoking the *UDHR* in its preamble, makes no specific reference to well-being. Article 11 of the *ICESCR* recognizes 'the right of everyone to an adequate standard of living for himself and his family, including adequate food, clothing and housing.' The content of this right under the *ICESCR* is more fully articulated in the general comments (4, 7 and 12; also in 5, 6, 14, 15) on the *ICESCR*, wherein various standards are also established.

However, the key concern here is with the notion of adequacy *per se*. The term necessarily implies the question – 'Adequate for what?'[2] Since no explicit response to that question is offered in the *ICESCR* but is given in the *UDHR*, invoked in the preamble, and is not available in any other preambular reference, can we not reasonably infer that 'the health and well-being of himself and of his family' is implied? Well-being thus becomes the need or purpose to be satisfied by the desired standard of living.

Further, Article 11 of the *ICESCR* recognizes 'the right of everyone to an adequate standard of living for himself and his family, including adequate food, clothing and housing, and to the continuous improvement of living conditions.'(emphasis added). Here the task of

[2] The Merriam-Webster dictionary defines 'adequate' as 'enough for some need or requirement,' while the Oxford dictionary defines adequate as 'enough in quantity, or good enough in quality, for a particular purpose or need' Merriam-Webster Online Dictionary http://www.merriam-webster.com/ Accessed 6 March 2014, and Oxford dictionaries http://www.oxforddictionaries.com/definition/learner/adequate/ Accessed 18 October 2015.

reconciling the *UDHR* and *ICESCR* provisions expands. A coherent reading of Article 25(1) of the *UDHR* could rationally lead one to the conclusion that there is a point at which the satisfaction of certain needs effectively serve a person's well-being. Once these standards are met, the rights of the person are fulfilled. An individual's entitlement beyond that point is not assured within this framework of understanding. It may well be that one can avail oneself of circumstances that surpass these standards, but it is not an explicit entitlement.

What then is meant by 'continuous improvement of living conditions'? The right in question is still the singular right to an adequate standard of living. This is made clear by the sentence immediately following this phrase, such that the whole of Article 11 states:

> The States Parties to the present Covenant recognize the right of everyone to an adequate standard of living for himself and his family, including adequate food, clothing and housing, and to the continuous improvement of living conditions. The States Parties will take appropriate steps to ensure the realization of this right, recognizing to this effect the essential importance of international co-operation based on free consent. (emphasis added)

Since reference is being made to the totality of the one right to an adequate standard of living, 'continuous improvement of living conditions' can only mean the ongoing enhancement of living conditions, all of which nonetheless serve the purpose of satisfaction of well-being, which is itself the limiting condition of the entitlement.

Adequacy in International Jurisprudence

The legal obligations of States under the *ICESCR* cover the duty "to take steps, individually and through international assistance and co-operation... to the maximum of its available resources, with a view to achieving progressively the full realization of the rights recognized in the present Covenant by all appropriate means" (Article 2, 1).

In determining the roles to be played by various State Parties in international co-operation towards fulfilling this duty, the concept of adequacy *per se* is already implicitly being applied. The Concluding Observations of the UN Committee on Economic, Social and Cultural Rights (CESCR) concerning the fourth periodic report by Japan, for example, notes that "The Committee, while acknowledging the contribution of the State party to official development assistance, encourages it to expeditiously increase the level of its contribution with a view to achieving the international standard target of 0.7 per cent." [UN CESCR, para. 32] The same recommendation is made for Austria [UN CESCR, para. 10] and Belgium. [UN CESCR para. 9] No such recommendation is made, however, in the Concluding Observations for Rwanda, [UN CESCR] Ecuador [UN CESCR] or Azerbaijan. [UN CESCR]

The international standard target of 0.7 per cent of Gross National Product referred to by the CESCR derives from the pledges made by high-income countries since 1970 in forums from the UN General Assembly (GA), the Third UN Conference on Least Developed Countries and the 2002 UN International Conference on Financing for Development. The evident criterion for adequacy being applied, through which the duty for official development assistance (ODA) is assessed, is that of national income or GNP.

The nature of State Party obligations, as spelled out in General Comment 3 of the CESCR, also entails the obligation to recognize, respect, protect and fulfill the associated human rights. These duties encompass both negative duties, such as the prevention of violations by third parties e.g., forced evictions, and positive duties, such as legislative, judicial, institutional, administrative, policy, budgetary, economic, social and educational measures, and associated strategies.

In addition, as noted above, the content of the ICESCR right to an adequate standard of living is more fully elaborated in General Comments 4, 7 and 12 also in 5, 6, 14, and 15 of the CESCR. They provide a broad outline of the contours and substance of the notion of adequacy as it applies to the right to an adequate standard of living.

General comment 4 on the right to adequate housing posits that 'While adequacy is determined in part by social, economic, cultural, climatic, ecological and other factors, the Committee believes that it is nevertheless possible to identify certain aspects of the right that must be taken into account for this purpose in any particular context.' [UN CESCR, para 8] It further identifies these aspects as legal security of tenure; availability of services, materials, facilities and infrastructure; affordability; habitability; accessibility; location; and cultural adequacy. General Comment 7 relates to forced evictions.

General Comment 12 [UN CESCR] on the right to adequate food determines that the content of the concept of adequacy implies the availability of food in a quantity and quality sufficient to satisfy the dietary needs of individuals, free from adverse substances, and acceptable within a given culture, as well as the accessibility of such food in ways that are sustainable and that do not interfere with the enjoyment of other human rights.

Reference to an adequate standard of living is also made in CESCR General Comment 5 on Persons with Disabilities. Here the right specifically includes access to adequate food, accessible housing, adequate clothing and support services.

Similarly, in General Comment 6 on the economic, social and cultural rights of older persons, the CESCR attaches great importance to the UN Principles for Older Persons, which provides that older persons should have access to adequate food, water, shelter, clothing and health care through the provision of income, family and community support and self-help.

CESCR General Comment 15 on the right to water notes that the right to water clearly falls within the category of guarantees essential for securing an adequate standard of living, particularly since it is one of the most fundamental conditions for survival. The content of the right entails availability; quality; accessibility in terms of physical accessibility, economic accessibility, and without discrimination; as well as information accessibility.

Community and Duty

Another fundamental principle of human rights is that of community, notably as it relates to duty. Article 29 (1) of the *UDHR* states that 'everyone has duties to the community in which alone the free and full development of his personality is possible.' Interdependence and mutuality are thus posited as the primary ground of our very being and subsistence.

The prominence of community in cultural life is reflected in the degree to which this dimension is incorporated into the human rights systems of different geographical regions and corresponding cultures. This is demonstrated with the *African Charter on Human and Peoples' Rights 1981* [Organization of African Unity] which most comprehensively enshrines communal entitlements. Its Article 27 states that every individual shall have duties towards his family and society, the State and other legally recognized communities and the international community, and that the rights and freedoms of each individual shall be exercised with due regard to the rights of others, collective security, morality and common interest. Its Article 28 further itemizes elements of duty, encompassing, *inter alia*,

- To work for the cohesion and respect of the family;
- To serve his national community by placing his physical and intellectual abilities at its service;
- To pay taxes imposed by law in the interest of the society;
- ... and, in general, to contribute to the promotion of the moral well being of society

The *American Convention on Human Rights 1969 [*Organization of American States] in its Chapter V on Personal Responsibilities establishes the relationship between duties and rights, such that every person has responsibilities to his family, his community, and mankind. Importantly, 'the rights of each person are limited by the rights of others, by the security of all, and by the just demands of the general welfare, in a democratic society.' (Article 32, 2.)

For its part, in its Preamble, *the Charter of Fundamental Rights of the European Union 2000* [European Union] declares that enjoyment of the rights so referenced entails responsibilities and duties with regard to other persons, to the human community and to future generations.

In a similar vein, *the Human Rights Declaration 2012* of the Association of South East Asian Nations, while not having the legal status of an international treaty as the charters above, nonetheless upholds that 'the enjoyment of human rights and fundamental freedoms must be balanced with the performance of corresponding duties as every person has responsibilities to all other individuals, the community and the society where one lives.' [ASEAN, para. 6]

Evolving Notions of Duty: Business and the Environment

As the private sector has assumed an increasing role in the global economy, notably with the rise of transnational organizations and globalization from the late 1990s, their impact on the enjoyment of human rights has become the subject of growing attention. Questions of child labour, workers' rights, land rights, the rights of indigenous persons and of migrants, among others, are ever more viewed as pertinent to the conduct of business. As such, in 2005 the UN Secretary-General appointed a Special Representative with a mandate to identify and clarify international standards and policies regarding business and human rights, culminating in the 2008 framework "Protect, Respect and Remedy: A Framework for Business and Human Rights" and its endorsement in 2011 by the UN Human Rights Council as the *Guiding Principles on Business and Human Rights*.

The *Guiding Principles* outline the duty of States to protect human rights, and go further in establishing the responsibility of companies to respect human rights, encompassing both the legal obligation to comply with national law, as well as the responsibility to respect the of relevant international instruments where national law is absent, inclusive of the *UDHR*, *ICESCR*, *ICCPR* and the eight fundamental International Labour Conventions. The *Guiding Principles* also determine that both states and companies should provide remedies to victims of abuses attributed to companies. Notwithstanding the fact that these guidelines do not have the status of international law, and the distinction between duty and responsibility, this development is illustrative of the widespread acceptance of the concept of duty towards the larger community. This is all the more striking by virtue of the fact that it extends such responsibilities to non-State actors, who are traditionally not cast as duty-holders under international law. While operationalization of the guidelines and growing knowledge on the challenges of its application are ongoing, [Buhman, K., p. 206] its approval as a normative framework, notably through a process of consultation involving governments, NGOs and businesses alike, gives credence to consideration of its implementation among a number of companies in the future.

The *Guiding Principles* assume particular importance with respect to development concerns and well-being, notably in so far as they intersect with human rights standards. Here considerations regarding the right to health have been especially relevant, drawing attention, for example, to the duties of pharmaceutical companies to ensure access to medicines. [Hunt, P. and Lee, J., p. 220]

Similarly, duties with respect to the environment are gaining ground as a factor in human rights discourse, including through the actions of businesses. One example of this is the right to water and sanitation, affirmed as a legally binding human right by the UN Human Rights Council in 2010. A business may impact on the enjoyment of this right, though, for example, polluting activities, as documented for the Niger Delta. [Gaughran, A., p. 52]

More broadly, the thinking underlying the relationship between the environment and human rights is based on the idea that the enjoyment of human rights is fundamentally dependent on the functioning of our ecosystems, with evident linkages to sustainable development. With respect to climate change, this dependence is expressed through, inter alia, landslides and flooding and corresponding displacement and further marginalization of the poor. [Humphreys, S. pp. 37 - 42, 320 - 330] In this context, the international community is mired in an acceptance of the notion of duty that is articulated in terms of common, but differentiated, responsibilities between developed and developed countries, which has not proven productive to consensus or action in countering these effects, as in the UN *Climate Change Convention* meetings. In response, some scholars point to the customary international law principle of “do no harm,” which requires states to ensure that activities within their jurisdiction or under their control do not cause damage to the environment of other states, and that could thus serve as an obligatory component of multilateral environmental agreements and human rights. While questions have been raised over the effectiveness of litigation [Tully, S., p. 213], at least one study identifies a duty of "due diligence" to ensure that states' policies, actions, or possible neglect do not impede the realization of human rights elsewhere. [McInerney-Lankford S., Darrow, M.]

Limitation

As ascertained in the *American Convention* mentioned above, and in the theoretical literature previously outlined, an extension of the notion of community and duty is that of limitation. We are more forcefully aware than ever in history of the impact of our individual actions on others, as every kind of media feeds our growing collective awareness. This awareness implies expanded consideration of the implications of our choices on the general welfare of others, and a thoughtful circumscribing of our actions to accommodate that knowledge.

In this respect, and notably in alignment with the assertion of the principle of the indivisibility of human rights, whereby rights cannot be ranked, Article 29 (2) of the *UDHR* claims that ‘everyone shall be subject only to such limitations as are determined by law solely for the purpose of securing due recognition and respect for the rights and freedoms of others and of meeting the just requirements of morality, public order and the general welfare in a democratic society.’

This concept is more fully articulated, for example, in General Comment 10 of the Committee on Civil and Political Rights regarding the right to freedom of opinion as enshrined in the *International Covenant on Civil and Political Rights*. [UN CCPR] The Committee notes that Article 29 stresses that the exercise of the right to freedom of expression carries with it special duties and responsibilities and for this reason certain restrictions on the right are permitted which may relate either to the interests of other persons or to those of the community as a whole. While such restrictions can only be imposed by a State subject to certain conditions (of necessity, as provided by law, for respect of the rights or reputations of others, or for the protection of national security or of public order, or of public health or morals) the premise of limitations in the interest of larger considerations, notably at the individual level, signify that human rights may be exercised only to the degree that they allow for the exercise of human rights by others and the larger community.

Examinations of the challenges and dilemmas posed by these possible tradeoffs point to the need for a heightened appreciation of the specific context, legislative framework, actors, and approaches to determining facts, [Tran, C., p. 257]; concern for the comparative implications of different courses of action [London, L., p. 11]; as well as consideration of the balance of forces of sovereignty and accountability. [Debeliak, J., p. 422]

III. Inequality

Equality is a cornerstone of human rights, enshrined in Article 1 of the *UDHR*. The operationalization of this principle takes myriad forms in, *inter alia*, international, regional and national law, institutions, policies and programmes.

The *Declaration on the Right to Development*, adopted in 1986, is one of the clearest applications of the principle of equality to the international arena. The right to development is a concept that goes some way to addressing the above -mentioned principles of duty and community, where community may be viewed as the community of nations. It is concerned, *inter alia*, with asserting the need for redress of historical human rights violations that have wrought dependence and poverty, especially in former colonies. It further invokes the responsibility for development, in alignment with Article 29 of the *UDHR*, as well as the duty to cooperate to promote observance of human rights by all. Official Development Assistance may be viewed as one facet of fulfillment of the right to development.[3]

In a similar vein, stronger calls are being made for cooperation between developed and developing countries with the recognition of rising inequality within and between nations. The report of the UN High Level Panel of eminent persons on the post-2015 development agenda, the Open Working Group Proposal for Sustainable Development Goals, [UN General Assembly] and the outcome document of 2015 intergovernmental negotiation "Transforming Our World: The 2030 Agenda For Sustainable Development"[United Nations] make addressing inequality a prominent theme. In this respect, the call is made for the end of

---

[3] "Since 2010, the year it reached its peak, ODA has fallen by 6.0% in real terms. Disregarding 2007, ...the fall in 2012 is the largest since 1997. ...The financial crisis and euro zone turmoil led many governments to implement austerity measures and reduce their ODA budgets. Despite the current fiscal pressures, however, some countries have maintained or increased their ODA budgets in order to reach their set targets." OECD. (2013). Development Co-operation Report 2013: Ending Poverty OECD Publishing (2013).http://dx.doi.org/10.1787/dcr-2013-en.

extreme poverty by 2030, [Un Panel of Eminent Person on the Post-2015 Development Agenda] a goal also adopted by the World Bank. The Panel vision encompasses the end of extreme poverty regardless of status so 'no one is left behind,' sustainability, inclusive growth, peace and responsive governance, and, notably, a new global partnership of mutual accountability. The proposed framework thus also brings into play the principles of duty and community. It further tacitly gives a nod to the notion of limitation, in advocating swift reduction in corruption, illicit financial flows, money-laundering, tax evasion, and hidden ownership of assets.

In thus invoking the above principles, the legal authority of human rights and related international instruments can be brought to bear in further ascertaining the nature and degree of entitlements and obligations regarding the right to a standard of living adequate for well-being, both individually and at national and international levels.

While the justiciability of economic, social and cultural rights is in its nascent stages, the evidence base can draw on a growing number of cases and decisions. These include the 2012 Committee on the Elimination of Discrimination Against Women ruling on gender discrimination in the area of employment in Turkey [CEDAW]; the 2012 judgement by the Botswana High Court to overturn a customary law preventing women from inheriting the family home [Botswana/High Court of Botswana]; the 2012 ruling issued by Mexico on the human right to water and sanitation [Second Tribunal Cuernavaca, Morelos, Mexico]; the 2012 judgement by the Durban High Court in South Africa to provide permanent housing for poor families that had been evicted from an informal settlement in order to allow for the construction of a road [Durban High Court]; the 2013 Supreme Court of Justice ruling in Honduras ordering health services for public hospital patients [Honduras, Supreme Court of Justice]; and the 2013 decision of the European Committee of Social Rights against Greece on its failure to mitigate the impact of large-scale pollution on the health of citizens [European Committee of Social Rights]; as well as a body of case law on the right to adequate housing [UN General Assembly, Special Rapporteur on Adequate Housing, paras. 55 - 63].

The entry into force in 2013 of the *Optional Protocol to the ICESCR*, establishing an individual complaints mechanism, also lends enhanced credibility and weight to efforts at justiciability in the realm of economic, social and cultural rights.

In further placing new dimensions of development under the rubric of international law, a new layer of accountability is thus established. This can conceivably add critical new substance, jurisprudence as well as accountability to the post-2015 development architecture and the related quest for equality.

IV. Well-Being and Development

The concept of development successfully conveys the sense of progress towards a higher level of functioning. For many it is a beacon that lights the way from situations of deprivation to employment, goods and services that more reliably ensure their enjoyment of human rights.

Development suffers, however, from being interpreted as open-ended, and is often a synonym for unchecked wealth accumulation with none of the dimensions of adequacy, interdependence, or limitation identified above as significant for well-being. This may be linked to the more widespread acceptance of the capitalist model of economic growth following the end of the Cold War and the demise of communism in the east, moving from one extreme to the other as we experimented with the social contract that would best express the optimal equilibrium between our individual and collective identities.

Against this backdrop, the global economic and financial crisis of 2008, that reverberates still, has perhaps compelled us to acknowledge that the pendulum may have swung too far, and that any economic model must admit of a place for other players beyond concentrated privilege, for a sense of sufficiency beyond greed, and for restrictions of the field of play. [Ghent, A., p. 246] It is perhaps in that space of experience of the limitations of economic growth and development that we may find the greatest openness for designing our ideal global development agenda.

The efforts of the Government of Bhutan, and in recent years the Governments of Britain, Canada and France, to make happiness operational in its policy approach has thus spawned and supported a growing body of evidence and practice on this subject.

The Bhutanese Government frames well-being and happiness in terms of 'integrated material, relational and spiritual development' and counters the yardstick of Gross Domestic Product with its own Gross National Happiness index. The index covers nine domains – living standards, health, and education, the use of time, good governance and ecological resilience, psychological well-being, community vitality, as well as cultural diversity and resilience.

In France the 2008 Commission on the Measurement of Economic Performance and Social Progress sought, *inter alia*, to identify the limits of GDP as an indicator of economic performance and social progress and to assess the feasibility of alternative measurement tools. Among the recommendations was a shift in emphasis from measuring economic production to measuring people's well-being. [Stiglitz, J. and Fitoussi, J.P.]

Similarly, the UK government in 2010 requested its Office for National Statistics to develop measures of well-being and progress. [Dolan, P., Layard, R. and Metcalfe, R.]

At the regional level, the Organization for Economic Cooperation and Development (OECD) also undertook an initiative on 'Measuring the Progress of Societies,' further publishing an experimental set of measures comparing evidence on well-being in developed countries and several non-member countries. [OECD] Also taking the effort forward are the EU Sponsorship Group on "Measuring progress, well-being and sustainable development" and the European Commission's "GDP and beyond."

Internationally, at the UN, Bhutan sponsored the 2011 GA resolution on 'Happiness: Towards a holistic approach to development' and the subsequent 2012 Meeting 'Wellbeing and Happiness: A New Economic Paradigm.'

The meeting promoted a vision of balance among all aspects of national and global wealth including natural, human, economic, social, and cultural wealth. Among the outcomes of the meeting were policy recommendations, whose criteria were ecological sustainability, fair distribution, efficient use of resources and contribution to the well-being of all life and to human happiness. These included removal of fossil fuel subsidies and chemical agricultural inputs, technology transfer, investment in sustainable infrastructure, small-scale local production and consumption, incorporation of traditional knowledge in agriculture and research, creation of common assets such as oceans, regulation of advertising, fair trade systems, increased progressivity of taxation, valuing of non-market natural/social/cultural assets and services through accounting systems and indices such as the GNH index and the UN Human Development index, frameworks to reward sustainable practice and penalize unsustainable practice, increased financial and fiscal prudence, and working towards international consensus including through the process for determining the post-2015 development agenda. Importantly, recommendations were also made for inclusive societies and governments; for the new economic paradigm to be fully aligned with UN principles and conventions that include human rights, the rule of law and a rights-based approach; and for the promotion of compassion and altruism. [Royal Government of Bhutan]

The concept of development as happiness has also been examined from the perspective of cultural values. The results of a values assessment in Bhutan indicated that although the Bhutanese people have a Gross National Income per capita of less than US $2,000, the level of anxiety and fear that is present in the culture of Bhutan is extremely low and the level of cultural alignment between the values of the people, and the values they experience in their daily lives in the culture of Bhutan, is high. Additionally, in one 2007 study, [White, A., pp. 17 - 20] Bhutan ranked eighth out of 178 countries in subjective well-being and was the only country in the top twenty happiest nations with a low level of GDP per capita. In remarking on this, and on the Bhutanese ideals largely reflected in the GNH index domains, Barrett [Barrett, R., p. 17] argues that in measuring happiness, consideration must also be given to values, in that people only experience happiness to the degree to which they are able to experience what they value. Surveys and policies should therefore also incorporate measures of values in the population, and acknowledge that the beliefs and values in a person's family, organization, community or nation can either limit or support the person in meeting their needs based on their values. Such an approach would seem a natural corollary to the standards proposed by the CESCR for cultural acceptability. It also responds to concerns raised by other scholars on the limitations of culturally subjective interpretations of happiness. [Duncan, G., p. 16]

Caution is also advised from some quarters regarding the use of happiness as an exclusive measure of progress. In addition to citing concerns with measurement and the short-term nature of data gathered, the point is made that happiness should not be promoted as an indicator at the expense of human rights indicators. [Stewart, F.]

CONCLUSION

A comprehensive application of the human rights framework to development, and more specifically to inequality in development, thus brings to bear civil and political, economic, social and cultural rights, and the right to development. It also calls upon the principles of duty and community, at individual, local, national and international levels. And importantly, this paper argues that new attention can be given to the concepts of adequacy and limitation in the respect, protection and fulfillment of the right to a standard of living adequate for well-being, with implications for the application of international law and justiciability of new principles.

The argument being submitted is in alignment with both rights theories, in invoking obligations and accountability under international law on the premise of well-being, as well as with utilitarianism, in demonstrating that the path of adequacy, limitation, duty and community is also a proven path to fulfillment of the promise and purpose of human rights and development, that is, individual and collective well-being and happiness.

The implications for policy are significant and diverse, and draw upon the significant momentum of well-being approaches in public policy circles at all levels. While specific economic prescriptions are beyond the scope of this paper, among these are conceivably consideration of national well-being indices for both developed and developing countries that incorporate community and the environment in addition to economic growth. Another useful indicator could be the optimal income level for a given society or nation beyond which marginal utility begins to decrease, suggesting the range for adequacy and limitations of income levels. Values assessments would further assure cultural acceptance and adequacy. Greater investment could thereby be made in sustainable infrastructure and technology, development of local markets, traditional knowledge, common assets, fair trade systems, frameworks for participatory decision-making and monitoring of development efforts, and the promotion of compassion and altruism.

Addressing inequality then also becomes a more holistic, dynamic, inter-dependent and mutually satisfying enterprise. We grow to see the task as involving the use of finite resources in keeping with an understanding of the more modest material needs required for our well-being, while also fundamentally reorienting our motivations around how much is to be gained by greater distribution among our neighbours as conceived along local, national and global dimensions. In thus expanding and renewing our understanding and application of human rights, we further energize the impetus towards its universal enjoyment, and its expression in the post-2015 development agenda.

References

Association of South East Asian Nations. (2012). ASEAN Human Rights Declaration, Phnom Penh, 19 November.

Barrett, R. (2012). Love, Fear and the Destiny of Nations: The Impact of the Evolution of Human Consciousness on World Affairs Fulfilling Books. Botswana/High Court of Botswana. (2012). 12 October 2012, *Mmusi and Others v Ramantele and Another, inheritance*, [2012] BWHC 1.

Buhman, K. (2012). 'Damned if you do, damned if you don't? The Lundbeck case of pentobarbital, the guiding principles on business and human rights, and competing human rights responsibilities' *Journal of Law, Medicine and Ethics*, *40*, 2, (Summer 2012) 206.

Cronin, C. and De Greiff, P. Eds. (1998). 'Kant's Idea of Perpetual Peace.' *The Inclusion of the Other.* Cambridge, Mass.: MIT Press, 165–201.

Debeliak, J. (2008). 'Balancing rights in a democracy: the problems with limitations and overrides of rights under the Victorian Charter of Human Rights and Responsibilities Act 2006.' *Melbourne University Law Review*, 32.2, 422. Dolan, P., Layard, R. and Metcalfe, R. (2011). *Measuring subjective well-being for public policy*, Office for National Statistics (UK).

Duncan, G. (2005). What do we mean by "happiness"? The relevance of subjective wellbeing to social policy. *Social Policy Journal of New Zealand*, *25*, 16.

Dunn, E. and Norton, M. (2013). *Happy Money: The Science of Smarter Spending*, New York: Simon and Schuster.

Durban High Court. (2012). 19 September 2012, *Mchunu and Others v Executive Mayor of eThekwini and others*, Case No. 13904/2011.

European Committee of Social Rights. (2013). 23 January 2013, *International Federation for Human Rights (FIDH) v. Greece, Decision on the merits Complaint n° 72/2011.*

European Union. (2000). *Charter of Fundamental Rights of the European Union*, 18 December.

Easterlin, R. (1974). Does Economic Growth Improve the Human Lot? Some Empirical Evidence. In Paul A. David and Melvin W. Reder, eds., Nations and Households in Economic Growth: Essays in Honor of Moses Abramovitz, New York: Academic Press, Inc.

Frey, B. and Stutz, A. (2010). "Recent advances in the economics of individual subjective well-being." *Social Research*, *77*, 2, 679.

Gaughran, A. (2012). Business and human rights and the right to water. *Proceedings of the Annual Meeting-American Society of International Law*, *106*, 52.

Ghent, A. (2011). The happiness effect: emerging from the worst economic crisis in decades, more governments than ever are measuring health and happiness as well as gross domestic product. But how will the study of well-being shape new policies? *Bulletin of the World Health*, *89*, *4*, 246.

Griffin, J. (1986). *Well-Being*. Oxford: Clarendon Press, 1986.

Helliwell, J., Layard, R. and Sachs, J. (2012). World Happiness Report. New York, April.

Honduras/Supreme Court of Justice. (2013). 23 October 2013, Mario Catarino Rivas of San Pedro Sula, San Felipe and Tegucigalpa School and Hospital Atlantis vs. Honduras, healthcare for patients in public hospitals, writ of amparo.

Humphreys, S. Ed. (2011). *Human Rights and Climate Change*. Cambridge, New York: Cambridge University Press.

Hunt, P. and Lee, J. (2012). 'Human rights responsibilities of pharmaceutical companies in relation to access to medicines' *Journal of Law, Medicine and Ethics*, *40*, 2, 220.

Kahneman, D. and Deaton, A. (2010). 'High income improves evaluation of life but not emotional well-being' in *Proceedings of the National Academy of Sciences of the United States of* America, September 21 vol. *107*, no. 38.

London, L. (2008). 'Confinement in the management of drug-resistant TB: the unsavoury prospect of balancing individual human rights and the public good' *South Africa*, *1.1*, 11.

McInerney-Lankford, S., Darrow, M. and Lavanya R. (2011). *Human Rights and* Climate *Change: A Review of the International Legal Dimensions.* Washington DC: World Bank.

Nozick, R. (1974). *Anarchy, State, and Utopia*. New York: Basic Books.

Nussbaum, M. C. (2000). *Women and Human Development: The Capabilities Approach.* New York: Cambridge UP.

Organization of African Unity. (1981). *African Charter of Human and Peoples' Rights*, Banjul, 27 June.

Organization of American States. (1969). *American Convention on Human Rights*, San Jose, 22 November.

Organization for Economic Cooperation and Development. (2011) *How's life? Measuring well-being*, Paris: OECD.

Parfit, D. (2011). *On What Matters*. Volume *1*. New York: Oxford UP.

Ram, R. (2013). 'Social capital and income inequality in the United States.' *Atlantic Economic Journal*, *41.1*, 89.

Royal Government of Bhutan. (2012). The Report of the High-Level Meeting on Wellbeing and Happiness: Defining a New Economic Paradigm. New York: The Permanent Mission of the Kingdom of Bhutan to the United Nations. Thimphu: Office of the Prime Minister.

Second Tribunal Cuernavaca, Morelos, Mexico. (2012). 19 April 2012 amparo en revisión 381/2011.

Sen, A. (1970). *Collective Choice and Social Welfare*. San Francisco: Holden-Day.

Sen, A. (1999). *Development as Freedom*. New York: Alfred A. Knopf.

Singer, P., (1972). 'Famine, Affluence, and Morality. ' *Philosophy and Public Affairs, 1*, 229–243.

Stewart, F. (2014). 'Against happiness: A critical appraisal of the use of measures of happiness for evaluating progress in development.' *Journal of Human Development and Capabilities*, *15*, 4, 293-307

Stiglitz, J., Sen, A. and Fitoussi, J. P. (2009). *Report by the commission on the measurement of economic and social progress*. Paris: OECD (2009). Retrieved from http://www.stiglitz-sen-fitoussi.fr/documents/rapport_anglais.pdf.

Talbott, W. (2013). 'Consequentialism and human rights' in *Philosophy Compass*, *8*, 11 1030 – 1040.

Thomson, J. J. (1990). *The Realm of Rights*. Cambridge, Mass.: Harvard UP.

Tran, C. (2012). 'Facts and evidence in litigation under the Charter of Human Rights and Responsibilities Act 2006 (VIC) and The Human Rights Act 2004 (ACT)' *Melbourne University Law Review*, *36*, 1, 287.

Tully, S. (2008). 'Like oil and water: a sceptical appraisal of climate change and human rights.' *Australian International Law Journal*, *15*, 213.

UN CESCR. (2013). Concluding observations concerning the fourth periodic report of Japan, 10 June 2013, E/C.12/JPN/CO /3.

UN CESCR. (2013). Concluding observations concerning the fourth periodic report of Austria, 13 December (2013) E/C.12/AUT/CO/4.

UN CESCR. (2013). Concluding observations concerning the fourth periodic report of Belgium, 23 December 2013. E/C.12/BEL/CO/4.

UN CESCR. (2013). Concluding observations concerning the fourth periodic report of Rwanda, 10 June 2013, E/C.12/RWA/CO /2-4.

UN CESCR. (2013). Concluding observations concerning the fourth periodic report of Ecuador, 13 December 2012, E/C.12/ECU/CO/3.

UN CESCR. (2012). Concluding observations concerning the fourth periodic report of Azerbaijan, 5 June 2013, E/C.12/AZE/CO /3.

UN CESCR. (1990). General Comment 3- The nature of States parties obligations, Geneva, 14 December.

UN CESCR. (1991). General Comment 4- The right to adequate housing, Geneva, 13 December.

UN CESCR. (1994). General Comment 5- Persons with disabilities, Geneva, 9 December.

UN CESCR. (1995). General Comment 6- The Economic, Social and Cultural Rights of Older Persons, Geneva, 8 December.

UN CESCR. (1997). General Comment 7- The right to adequate housing: forced evictions, Geneva, 20 May.

UN CESCR. (1999). General Comment 12- The right to adequate food, Geneva, 12 May.

UN CESCR. (2003). General Comment 15- The right to water, Geneva, 20 January.

UN Committee on Civil and Political Rights. (1983) General Comment 10 – the right to freedom of expression, Geneva, 29 June.

UN Committee on the Elimination of Discrimination Against Women. (2012) Views of February 24, 2012. *R.K.B. v. Turkey***.** Communication No. 28/2010.

United Nations General Assembly. (2014). Full Report of the Open Working Group of the General Assembly on Sustainable Development Goals, issued as document A/68/970, New York: United Nations, available at http://undocs.org/A/68/970.

United Nations. (2015). Transforming Our World: The 2030 Agenda For Sustainable Development. New York, United Nations. Available at https://Sustainabledevelopment. Un.Org/Content/Documents/7891transforming%20our%20world.Pdf.

UN Panel of Eminent Persons on the Post-2015 Development Agenda (2013) Report of the UN High Level Panel of eminent persons on the post-2015 development agenda, New York, 30 May 2013.

UN General Assembly. (2008). Optional Protocol to the International Covenant on Economic, Social and Cultural Rights, Resolution A/RES/63/117, 10 December.

UN General Assembly. (2008). Report of the Special Rapporteur on adequate housing as a component of the right to an adequate standard of living, and on the right to non-discrimination in this context. A/63/275. 13 August 2008 (paras. 55-63).

White, A. (2007). A Global Projection of Subjective Well-being: A Challenge to Positive Psychology? *Psychtalk.*, *56*, 17-20.

In: International Human Rights and Justice
Editor: Doug Hodgson

ISBN: 978-1-63484-709-4

Chapter 3

INEQUALITY, ACCESS TO THE COURTS, AND JUDICIAL INTEGRITY

Barry Edwards[1,*]***, Allison Trochessett***[2] ***and Tyler Yeargain***[3]

[1] JD, PhD, Lecturer, Department of Political Science,
University of Central Florida, Orlando, FL, US
[2]Ph.D, Candidate, Department of Political Science,
University of Georgia, Athens, GA, US
[3]Undergraduate Student, Department of Political Science,
University of Central Florida, Orlando, FL, US

ABSTRACT

Because political conflicts inevitably become legal conflicts, judicial integrity is an essential element of any system that protects civil rights and civil liberties. Judges must be willing and able to defend the politically powerless from oppression and exploitation. In this chapter, we argue that mass inequality in capitalist nations, particularly the United States, poses a substantial threat to judicial integrity. First, we document the development of a two-tiered system of civil justice that effectively reserves courtrooms for the haves and prevents have-nots from accessing the courts. Second, we maintain that the widespread practice of judicial elections, which appears to make justice a commodity, undermines public trust and potentially corrupts judicial behavior. Finally, we note that organized interest groups are beginning to extend their influence beyond the US Supreme Court by filing amicus curiae briefs in other courts, including state supreme courts, to the detriment of the unorganized masses. For these reasons, we believe that growing inequality presents a serious challenge to judicial integrity in capitalist countries and hope to draw attention to this problem.

[*] Corresponding author: Barry Edwards. E-mail: barry.edwards@ucf.edu.

INTRODUCTION

Because political conflicts inevitably become legal conflicts, access to a fair, independent judiciary is essential to upholding civil rights and civil liberties. Judges must be willing and able to defend politically powerless members of society from oppression and exploitation. International human rights norms recognize the human right to equality and non-discrimination before the courts and the right to fair and public hearings by independent, competent, and impartial tribunals. The *Universal Declaration of Human Rights 1948*, which represents the classic international statement of human rights, endorses equality before the law and the right to have civil rights claims and criminal charges fairly adjudicated by competent courts[4]. Under international soft law, judicial independence requires, at a minimum, that judges decide matters impartially, without being improperly influenced, and that the method of selecting judges safeguards against improper appointments[5].

In the United States, access to an independent judiciary is seen as "conservative of all other rights ... the foundation of orderly government"[6]. Courts potentially serve as a great equalizer; money and power may dominate ordinary politics, but no man is thought to be above the law. Indeed, the US Supreme Court has declared: "There can be no equal justice where the kind of trial a man gets depends on the amount of money he has"[7]. While there is much to applaud in the modern judiciary's defense of civil rights and civil liberties, we believe economic inequality presents a serious challenge to judicial integrity and hope to draw attention to several dimensions of this problem.

By almost any measure, economic disparity between economic elites and the masses is significant and increasing in the US and in most industrialized nations (Bartels, 2009; Piketty and Saez, 2014). This ominous trend has important implications for the judicial process: economic inequality affects which cases judges hear, which interests are heard, and the incentives judges have to make particular decisions.

These problems are particularly severe in state court systems with elected judges. What happens to the administration of justice when resources are limited and judges are elected? Judges cannot devote their full attention to all cases; they must prioritize the resolution of some cases over others. As we discuss in this chapter, there is some evidence that judicial integrity is compromised by electoral incentives. Viewed from the perspective of electoral value (rather than legal merit), some cases have more electoral value than others do and some decisions are more politically popular than other decisions are. To maximize return on limited judicial resources, courts endeavor to please their best clients, rather than defend the most

---

[4] *Universal Declaration of Human Rights 1948*, G.A. Res. 217, U.N. GAOR, 3d Sess., U.N. Doc. A/810 (1948), Art. 7, 8, and 10. The international community also recognizes the rights to equality and non-discrimination and to have claims heard by impartial judges in the *International Covenant on Civil and Political Rights 1966*, 999 United Nations Treaty Series 171, Art. 2(1) and 14(1), the *European Convention for the Protection of Human Rights and Fundamental Freedoms 1950*, European Treaty Series 5, Art. 6(1) and 14, and the *American Convention on Human Rights 1969*, Organization of American States Treaty Series, No. 36, Art. 8 (1), 24, and 25(1).

[5] *Basic Principles on the Independence of the Judiciary*, adopted by Seventh United Nations Congress on the Prevention of Crime and the Treatment of Offenders, U.N. Doc. A/CONF.121/22/Rev.1 (1985), endorsed by G.A. Res. 40/32, U.N. GAOR, 40th Sess., Supp. No. 53, at 204, U.N. Doc. A140/53 (1985). See particularly Art. 1, 2, 4, 6, and 10.

[6] Chambers v. Baltimore and Ohio R.R., 207 US 142, 148 (1907).

[7] *Griffin v. Illinois*, 351 US 12, 19 (1956).

vulnerable members of society. Increasingly, courts are operated like a for-profit business rather than a public service.

In this chapter, we argue that economic inequality poses a substantial threat to access to the courts and judicial integrity. First, we document the development of a two-tiered system of civil justice that effectively reserves courtrooms for the haves and prevents have-nots from having their claims fairly heard. Second, we maintain that the widespread practice of judicial elections, which appears to make justice a commodity, undermines public trust and potentially corrupts judicial behavior. Finally, we note that organized interest groups are filing more amicus curiae briefs in state supreme courts to the detriment of the unorganized masses.

TWO-TIERED CIVIL JUSTICE SYSTEM

In this section, we outline the contours of a two-tiered system of justice in the United States. A number of relatively recent developments have limited the ability of ordinary citizens and consumers to exercise their traditional right to have their cases heard by judges and juries. Having civil disputes resolved by the judicial system is increasingly a privilege reserved for economic elites. The great mass of ordinary cases is now subject to an array of devices that preclude litigation or compel individuals to settle in the shadows of the legal system.

Some of the implications of economic inequality on access to justice are relatively well documented, particularly with respect to criminal justice. It has been shown that poor defendants frequently stay in jail awaiting trial because they are unable to post bail; as a result, they cannot assist in the preparation of their defense and are more like to be convicted and sentenced (Neubauer and Meinhold, 2012). Public defenders are chronically underfunded, poorly supervised, and crushed by staggering caseloads (Udell and Diller, 2007). As a result of these and other factors, "it is often better to be rich and guilty than poor and innocent" (Rhode, 2001, p. 1790). Without discounting the seriousness any of these issues, we want to draw attention to some of the implications of inequality on civil justice, such as limited access to legal representation, the proliferation of mandatory arbitration provisions, and procedural devices to manage judicial workload.

Although the US has more lawyers than other country in the world, the legal needs of most Americans are not served. It is estimated that four-fifths of the civil legal needs of poor Americans is unmet as is roughly half of the civil legal needs of middle class Americans (Rhode, 2001; Udell and Diller, 2007). It is hard to reconcile the fact that many recent law school graduates are unemployed with the fact that most individuals pursue claims without representation, unable to hire attorneys (Hadfield, 2010). This mismatch between the supply of and demand for lawyers has profound consequences for daily living. "For people of limited financial means," Udell and Diller (2007, pp. 1129-1130) "access to an attorney can be the difference between losing a home or keeping it, suffering from domestic violence or finding refuge, succumbing to illness or obtaining a cure, remaining hungry or securing food, or languishing in prison or reuniting with family and community." Most people face these crises alone. As the economic standing of the middle class erodes, we should expect these unmet legal needs to increase.

Although states are required to provide attorneys to poor criminal defendants, indigent civil litigants have no comparable right to an attorney (Rhode, 2001). For example, poor parents are not entitled to court-appointed attorneys when the government files suit to terminate parental rights and take their children away from them (although it is hard to imagine a more severe state sanction)[8]. According to the Supreme Court, due process may require appointing counsel in very specific circumstances, but it recently held in *Turner v. Rogers* that an indigent defendant is not entitled to counsel when he faces incarceration as a result of contempt of order to pay child support[9]. Some states provide poor parties counsel in select civil cases, even though not required to do so by federal law; nevertheless, the right to counsel in civil cases is not widely recognized at the state level (Davis, 2012).

Access to quality legal representation plays a particularly important role in responding to domestic violence. Legal representation can help victims achieve some measure of safety and security in order to leave their abusers. However, victimization is generally regarded as a private, civil matter for which there is no right to an attorney. According to Abel and Rettig (2006), New York is the only state that guarantees counsel in domestic violence proceedings. In fact, in domestic violence cases, *abusers* are entitled to legal representation (despite minimal risk of incarceration) while *victims* are expected to navigate the legal process alone (Rhode, 2001). In some jurisdictions, legal aid may be available to assist in filing a temporary protective order, but legal aid budgets are limited and legal aid lawyers, limited by restrictive regulations.

As discussed above, middle and working class individuals frequently must represent themselves in court. Self-representation is on the rise, but judges show reluctance, and even hostility, toward *pro se* litigants. In courts of limited jurisdiction, like specialized courts for housing disputes and small claims courts, most parties are self-represented, but even these courts, Rhode (2001, p. 1804) observes, "have been designed by lawyers, and courts have done far too little to make them accessible to the average claimant." According to Rhode (2001, p. 1806), "[s]ome courts are openly hostile to unrepresented parties, whom they view as tying up the system or attempting to gain tactical advantages." Judges lose patience for *pro se* litigant's rambling statements and unfamiliarity with standard courtroom procedures (Engler, 1999; Goldschmidt, 1998; Van Wormer, 2007). Based on an extensive study of a specialized housing court in Baltimore, Engler (1999, pp. 2015-2016) observes, "some judges do not simply deter unrepresented litigants, they silence them." Proceeding *pro se* in a family law matter involving domestic violence is particularly challenging because judges view these cases as toxic with no practical, legal solutions. Even judges who are sympathetic to the plight of unrepresented parties may be reluctant to antagonize lawyers by improving *pro se* assistance; judges may view the support of local lawyers as critical to re-election campaigns and professional advancement (Rhode, 2001). Civil litigation, for Americans of ordinary means, is an overwhelming burden.

Another factor limiting access to courts is the proliferation of binding arbitration provisions in agreements frequently entered into by individuals. Traditionally confined to specialized industrial agreements, arbitration provisions are now found in a wide variety of contracts. According to Sternlight (2005), mandatory arbitration terms spread into all types of contracts as a result of a series of favorable Supreme Court decisions in the 1980s and 1990s.

[8] See *Lassiter v. Dept. of Social Services*, 452 US 18 (1981) (poor, incarcerated mother not entitled to attorney when state seeks termination of parental rights).

[9] 131 S.Ct. 2507 (2011).

It is estimated that over twenty-five percent of the US workforce and more than a third of significant consumer transactions are now subject to mandatory arbitration (Demaine and Hensler, 2004). When a consumer or employee signs an agreement with a binding arbitration provision, he or she gives up the right to trial and consents to have any claims arising out of the agreement resolved by a private company (typically selected by the author of the agreement) before any dispute or disagreement actually occurs.

Arbitration is not necessarily inferior to litigation. It is particularly appealing when parties knowingly agree to it after a dispute arises. For example, in the domestic relations context, arbitration can help parties limit risk, protect privacy, and reduce costs compared to traditional litigation (Edwards, 2008). The "creeping" use of binding arbitration in standard consumer and employment agreements is problematic insofar as it creates a lesser system of civil justice for consumers and employees. Researchers have documented repeat player advantages in arbitration (Colvin, 2011). Arbitration provisions may also limit the remedies available to injured parties. For example, mandatory arbitration agreements now frequently include collective action waivers. When collective action waivers are used, the individual gives up his or her right to join with others to pursue a collective remedy (Udell and Diller, 2007). This practice is particularly troubling with respect to consumers' rights because collective action may be the only way to effectively overcome the cost of arbitration. The Supreme Court recently endorsed the use of collective action waivers in mandatory arbitration provisions so we can expect to see them in greater use[10]. These terms may seem unfair and unreasonable, but individuals have no real power to bargain over terms when they sign up for phone service or start a new job (Sternlight, 2005). The individual's only option is not to engage the corporate marketplace, but the consolidation of wealth and market share in our winner-take-all economy makes that option increasingly unrealistic. The only real limitation on mandatory arbitration provisions imposed by corporations is a rarely-enforced probation on unconscionable terms[11]. For these reasons, we should view mandatory arbitration as one of the main features of a two-tiered civil justice system.

Rather than adequately fund state courts or reduce the volume of criminal prosecutions, most states have implemented procedural barriers to make it more difficult for individuals to have civil cases heard by a judge or jury. The US Constitution guarantees criminal defendants the right to a speedy trial but no such right exists in civil cases. An injured person, defrauded consumer, or parent seeking child support may not have their complaints heard for months or even years (Grossi, Mills and Vagenas, 2012). Procedural devices designed to manage judicial workload may appear to promote efficiency, but closer examination reveals that they significantly burden ordinary individuals' access to courts. We'll look at two examples: tort reform and mandatory mediation.

Responding to a perceived "litigation crisis," most states have enacted tort reform legislation (American Tort Reform Association, 2015). Among the most significant reforms are heightening the requirements for filing certain personal injury claims, particularly medical malpractice actions. In many states, prospective plaintiffs are now required to retain expert witnesses to testify by way of affidavit before conducting any discovery in order to commence a lawsuit (Brown and Lomurro, 2014; Papailiou, 2013). These pleadings

[10] See *AT&T Mobility, LLC v. Concepcion*, 131 S.Ct. 1740 (US 2011).

[11] See, for example, *Washington Mutual Finance Group v. Bailey*, 364 F.3d 260 (5th Cir. 2004), where the Court held that illiterate individuals have a duty to read small print arbitration terms or have them read to them to independently verify bank employees' assurances they were just signing "insurance and finance papers."

requirements significantly raise the cost of pursuing claims, forcing many individuals to settle for modest recovery or abandon their claims entirely.

Another procedural requirement that falls particularly hard on ordinary individuals is the widespread adoption of mandatory mediation in state courts. In many jurisdiction, parties are required to attempt to settle their disputes by working with a neutral, third-party mediator (usually paid by the parties) before they can bring their dispute to trial. The cost of mediation to private parties is significant. How much does it cost to produce a mediated settlement? According to Edwards (2013), private parties in a typical Georgia state court mediation program paid approximately $1,850 per session (including average mediation and attorney hourly rates). While the cost of mediation may be relatively small in the context of complex, corporate litigation, it is significant in ordinary civil matters. Eaton, Talarico, and Dunn (1999) found that the median award in civil jury trials in Georgia was $7,859 and in bench trials, $17,606. The private costs of mandatory mediation may represent 10-25% of the total expected value of a typical tort case. Given the roughly 50% chance of mediated settlement, typical settlements may not warrant the expected private cost of mediation. As a result, many parties decide the price is too high after receiving a notice to mediate and are forced to settle (Edwards, 2013). In some cases, requiring mediation is a monetary sanction on parties who wish to pursue legal recourse (Dayton, 1991).

The problem is that mediation in state courts is frequently both mandatory and expensive[12]. If courts were to encourage voluntary mediation or provide mediation services at no cost to parties, the danger of coercing settlement by raising litigation costs would be lessened. A court's order to mediate as a precondition to trial limits parties' access to the court system and forces them to negotiate privately, largely unfettered by the rules of law.

The Cost of Judicial Elections

State courts have never seen quite the level of independence granted to federal courts. From the very beginning, judges were essentially subservient to the wills of the executive and legislative branches of state governments, which had appointed them to office in the first place (Croley, 1995). If judges issued rulings contrary to the taste of state legislators, it was not uncommon for the legislature to respond by removing judges from office, cutting their terms of office, or even charter new courts (Shugerman, 2012).

In the 1830s, the State of Mississippi, seeking in part to reduce the dependence of judges on the legislative and executive branches, transitioned from a purely appointive method of judicial selection to a purely elected method. By 1860, twenty-one out of thirty states in the Union elected their judges. This, Hall (1983) writes, was not done out of "emotional" support for democratic principles, but because moderates at the time felt strongly that judicial elections, if properly regulated, would enhance the "power and prestige" of the judiciary.

Judicial elections have evolved significantly since then. Progressives, eager to trim the power of "party bosses," pushed the idea of nonpartisan judicial elections, which was an idea quickly embraced by a number of states. Concerns about voters' ability to make an informed

[12] Alternative dispute resolution in the federal court system is different than ADR in state courts. Referrals to ADR are often voluntary in US District Courts, or made on a case-by-case basis. Frequently, federal magistrates serve as mediators, which substantially reduces the cost borne by litigants.

decision without partisan cues, however, persuaded a few states to move back to partisan elections. An apparent solution was discovered in 1940, when the State of Missouri implemented a method of selection that merged appointment and elections—while judges would be appointed, they would also face retention elections every few years. The idea was to combine judicial independence and democratic accountability in one system (Streb, 2007).

Today, we face a complex map of state judiciaries that serves as a telling metaphor for federalism—different states, acting with their constitutional authority to develop different systems, have developed different methods of selection and retention for judges. Thirty-nine out of fifty states utilize some method of judicial election, which represents ninety percent of all state judges. Even within judicial elections, there is a great deal of variety—nonpartisan, partisan, and retention elections—which gives states the ability to concoct a combination of multiple selection methods (Streb, 2007).

The nature of contemporary judicial elections leaves much to be desired—uncontested elections, pervasive voter apathy, and third-party expenditures all threaten the fabric of judicial elections, and in turn, the integrity of the judiciary. Levenson (2014) argues that when voters have no way to make an informed decision, they "tend to vote based on factors that have little or no bearing on a candidate's qualifications," specifically calling attention to anecdotal examples of "qualified sitting judges with foreign-sounding last names being defeated by less-qualified or unqualified challengers with Anglo-Saxon sounding names."

Over the last few decades, spending on judicial elections has increased substantially. The Brennan Center for Justice reports that campaign fundraising, which was $83.9 million from 1990 to 1999, increased to $206.9 million from 2000 to 2009. Where has most of the money gone? Television advertisements. From 2000 to 2009, $93.6 million was spent on television advertisements alone, more than was raised in the entire preceding decade (Sample, Skaggs, Blitzer, and Casey, 2010). A subsequent report noted that a large part of the explosion in spending in judicial elections was driven by independent expenditures, which, they note, often led to "less transparent and more negative races" (Bannon, Velasco, Casey and Reagan, 2013).

What is particularly troubling about the rising cost of judicial elections is that judges' decisions appear to be swayed by the necessities of modern judicial campaigns. "In too many states," observed Former Supreme Court Justice Sandra Day O'Connor, "judicial elections are becoming political prizefights where partisans and special interests seek to install judges who will answer to them instead of the law and the Constitution" (Sample et al., 2010, p. 4). Consistent with O'Connor's observation, there is mounting evidence that elections undermine the integrity of the judiciary; as one might expect, judges appear to act in manner that advances their ability to raise campaign contributions and win re-election:

- The *New York Times* found that Ohio Supreme Court justices voted in favor of contributors approximately seventy percent of the time, with one justice voting in favor of contributors over ninety percent of the time (Liptak & Roberts, 2006).
- A 2008 study found that in cases where there was a single donor appearing before the Louisiana Supreme Court, justices voted for their contributor approximately sixty-five percent of the time. When both parties before the Court were campaign contributors, the justices were significantly more likely to take the position of the party who had given them more contributions (Palmer & Levendis, 2008).

While democratic accountability is frequently viewed as a virtue of judicial elections, the electoral connection potentially undermines a judge's ability to protect vulnerable members of society from oppression and exploitation. High court justices who issue controversial rulings on divisive social issues oftentimes see electoral retribution following public campaigns against them. California Supreme Court Justice Rose Bird serves as one of the first (and best) examples of this occurrence. Bird, who was appointed to the Supreme Court by then-Governor Jerry Brown, was strongly opposed to capital punishment, and consistently struck down death penalty sentences. When she faced a retention election in 1986, television advertisements featuring the parents of murder victims were used against her. In the end, she—and two of her colleagues—were removed from the Supreme Court by an overwhelming majority of California voters (Lindsey, 1986). Tennessee Supreme Court Justice Penny White, like Bird, faced electoral consequences for her tenure on the Court, but unlike Bird, only issued one ruling that voters found problematic. In *State v. Odom*, White ruled to uphold the defendant's conviction, but struck down the death penalty sentence[13]. The response was swift—in a retention election held later that year, she was targeted by conservative interest groups and the state's Republican politicians, and ended up losing her seat (Bills, 2008).

To win elections, judges frequently run on platforms that emphasize their "tough on crime" attitude (Thompson, 2014). These campaign promises are troubling because they commit judges to a course of action rather than judging each case on its individual merits[14]. Consistent with these expectations, the influence of elections on judicial behavior is perhaps most evident in the field of criminal law where judges are expected to perform the often unpopular task of upholding the rights of particularly powerless members of society.

- Huber and Gordon (2004) found that as elections draw closer, sentencing of defendants becomes significantly more severe.
- A study conducted by the American Constitution Society for Law and Policy, in conjunction with the Emory University School of Law, found that, as the amount of television advertisements airing in high court elections increases, "the less likely justices are on average to vote in favor of criminal defendants" (Shepherd & Kang, 2014).
- The Equal Justice Initiative found that, in Alabama, judges are significantly more likely to sentence criminal defendants to death, overriding jury decisions that would have sentenced the defendants to life imprisonment, in election years (Equal Justice Initiative, 2011).

Regardless of whether one supports getting tough on crime, the impact of elections on judges' behavior is disturbing for two reasons. First, elections produce inconsistency. The length of a defendant's sentence depends on the electoral calendar, rather than the seriousness of the crime, defendant's criminal history, or other legitimate sentencing factor. At a minimum, judicial integrity requires consistency. Second, legislatures already express the

[13] 928 S.W.2d 18 (Tenn. 1996).

[14] According to former Supreme Court Justice John Paul Stevens, "[a] campaign promise to 'be tough on crime,' or to 'enforce the death penalty,' is evidence of bias that should disqualify a candidate from sitting in criminal cases" (Bright, 1997).

public's desire for tough criminal sanctions. It is important that the judiciary check and balance the legislature to maintain the rule of law.

The US Supreme Court addressed some of these issues in *Caperton v. A.T. Massey Coal Co.* in 2009[15]. In 2002, Caperton was awarded $50 million in compensatory and punitive damages by a jury in West Virginia. Massey appealed the ruling to the West Virginia Supreme Court of Appeals immediately thereafter, but before the Court could hear the appeal, several of its members were up for re-election in 2004. One of the justices was Warren McGraw, who was opposed by private practice attorney Brent Benjamin. Massey formed a political action committee to support Benjamin's candidacy, and spent nearly $3 million on television advertisements attacking McGraw for allegedly being "soft on crime." The campaign to unseat McGraw worked—Benjamin ended up defeating him with 53% of the vote and took his seat on the Supreme Court of Appeals. Then, when hearing Massey's appeal, Benjamin joined a 3-2 majority on the Court to reverse the jury's settlement against Massey. Caperton filed several motions to have Benjamin disqualified, but in a twist of irony, Benjamin himself reviewed the motions and denied all of them (Todt, 2011).

Caperton filed an appeal to the United States Supreme Court, which granted certiorari and heard the case. In a 5-4 opinion authored by Justice Anthony Kennedy, the Court held that it was a violation of the Fourteenth Amendment's Due Process Clause for a judge with a demonstrated conflict of interest to not recuse himself. According to Kennedy, "There is a serious risk of actual bias … when a person with a personal stake in a particular case had a significant and disproportionate influence in placing the judge on the case by raising funds or directing the judge's election campaign when the case was pending or imminent"[16].

While it is difficult to prove that someone like Brent Benjamin is actually biased in favor of campaign contributors, there is something unsettling about marketing and promoting judicial values to raise campaign contributions and win elections. Research suggests that the "political prizefight" nature of modern judicial elections, prominently featuring negative television advertising, tends to corrode public confidence in the judiciary (Gibson, 2008, 2009). We believe that judicial elections, which are almost unknown outside of the United States, tend to degrade judges' integrity, reducing justice to a commodity beholden to opinion polls and campaign contributions[17].

INTEREST GROUP INFLUENCE

When a case is heard by a state supreme court or the US Supreme Court, the focus is typically on the parties named in the lawsuit. However, there are often third parties operating in to influence the outcome of the case. These parties are called amicus curiae, or "friends of the court." These "friends" can range from interest groups, to states, to government officials who are either asked by the court or choose on their own to file a brief in a case.

Amicus Curiae, translated to be "selfless servant of the court," like most of American legal traditions, evolved out of early English common law (Flango, Bross and Corbally, 2006, p. 181; Samuels, 2004). Samuels (2004) reports evidence of amicus participation in Ancient

[15] 556 US 868 (US 2009).
[16] 556 US at 884.
[17] Some Swiss cantons elect judges and Japanese Supreme Court justices face periodic retention elections.

Rome, where the briefs were used for informational purposes. The first amicus brief to be submitted to the United States Supreme Court was filed in a dispute over land titles on behalf of the State of Kentucky by Henry Clay (Samuels, 2004). The Court did not permit *private* interest groups to submit amicus briefs until the 1900's (Samuels, 2004). It was also during this transitional time that amicus briefs became more adversarial and less neutral (Krislov, 1963). During the 1940's special interest groups such as the NAACP and the ACLU began to promote their causes in the courts as both litigants and amici. For example, in *Brown v. Board of Education*, 347 US 483 (US 1954), there was an amicus brief that used social scientific data to describe the ills of racial segregation (Samuels, 2004).

Amicus participation at the Supreme Court of the United States (SCOTUS) has increased by over 800% in the past 50 years (Kearney & Merrill, 2000). There have been similar increases in state courts of last resort (Corbally, Bross and Flango, 2004). The rise in amicus brief filings in state supreme courts is significant because state courts are becoming centers of policy due to their status as courts of last resort for many litigants. Interest groups, and other groups with policy agendas, are realizing this importance and acting accordingly by participating at greater rates as amicus curiae.

The primary purpose of amicus briefs is to provide courts with additional information of some type (Comparato, 2003; Flango et al., 2006; Munford, 1999; Spriggs & Wahlbeck, 1997). According to Flango et al. (2006), amicus amplify or supplement the legal and factual arguments presented by the litigants, emphasize the broader consequences of the potential ruling, and their mere presence emphasizes the importance of the legal issue at hand. Amicus curiae participation also alerts courts that certain cases are politically, socially, or economically significant (Caldeira & Wright, 1990). In her in-depth analysis of amicus curiae briefs in right to privacy cases, Samuels (2004) asserts that amici effectively supplement information parties provide to courts. Unlike the litigants, the amici may be willing to take the political or tactical risk of making a particular argument that one of the legal parties declines to make. Highly technical arguments may be given more credibility if presented by an amici with expertise in a particular field.

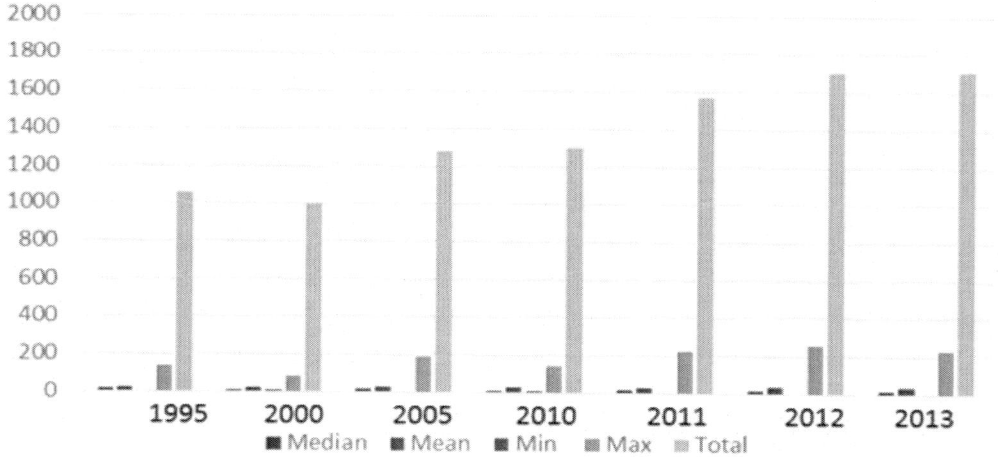

Note: Volume of filings measured by number of cases containing at least one amicus brief; median, mean, min, and max refer to level of activity in individual states.

Figure 1. Amicus Filings in State Supreme Courts, 1995-2013.

If amicus filings by interests groups simply helped courts better understand complex issues, their growing influence in appellate litigation at the state and federal levels would not be troubling. Like lobbyists in the nation's legislatures, however, organized interest groups file amicus briefs to influence courts to make decisions in their favor (Banner, 2003; Collins, 2007; Collins & Martinek, 2010; Samuels, 2004). Not surprisingly, amicus briefs are often filed on behalf of organized business interests that can afford to file them (Caldeira & Wright, 1990). As a result, the information presented to courts by way of amicus briefs may be leading and lopsided, advancing the particular interests of vested economic interests rather than the cause of ordinary individuals.

Although existing research on amicus activity in state high courts is limited, scholars have analyzed the levels of participation, the key players involved, and amici influence on judicial decision-making (Comparato, 2003; Corbally et al., 2004; Epstein, 1994; Flango et al., 2006; Songer & Kuersten, 1995).

The available evidence suggests amicus briefs filed by interests groups do influence state supreme courts:

- Songer and Kuersten (1995) studied the success of litigants who are supported by amicus at the merits stage, comparing judges' votes in similar cases with and without amicus support. Their results indicate that amicus support does have a significant influence on litigant success at the merits stage.
- Samuels (2004) finds that even though amicus participation in the state courts is considerably lower than in federal courts, amicus briefs filed in state courts are frequently cited.
- Based on a survey of Chief Justices and appellate court clerks, Flango et al. (2006) report that amicus curiae briefs at the state court level are generally viewed favorably.

While the direct influence of amici on judicial decision-making is striking, it is important to note that these interests groups may also exert a powerful indirect influence on judicial decisions. As discussed in the preceding section, many high court justices are elected in highly contested partisan races. As a result, state supreme court justices, concerned with their electoral support, will tend to support those litigants and third parties who control their livelihood (Comparato, 2003). Interest groups donate large sums of money to judicial candidates. It is rational to assume that individual justices who receive campaign donations from amicus curiae, in either a selection or retention election, will be more likely to side with these amici as well as include amicus language in their judicial opinions. Justices may be ethically obligated to recuse themselves from hearing a case if they have received significant campaign donations from a party, but no such prohibition applies to interest groups participating as amicus curiae. The presence of amici in a case can be used as a surrogate for salience, or the importance of the case to the general public, a measure that is hard to find when comparing across the states. The presence or absence of an amicus brief in a case, as long as the state filing requirements are taken into consideration, can offer the state court justices a measure (even if informal) of the potential impact and reach of a particular ruling.

While these indirect effects of interest group activity are somewhat speculative and are subject to ongoing research (Trochesset, 2014, 2015), we think there is some evidence that interest groups are leveraging judicial elections to influence state supreme courts. If judicial elections make some high courts particularly susceptible to interest group influence, interest groups should concentrate their amicus filings in jurisdictions with judicial elections. Consistent with this view, states with the lowest amicus participation are also from states without partisan elections of their justices. For instance, three states with political appointments have a mean amicus participation rate of just one or two cases with amicus per year. It is notable that of the top ten states for amicus participation, four are states where judges are selected via partisan elections (Michigan, Ohio, Pennsylvania, and Texas). Although these do not claim causation, they do highlight the possible variables at play in the role of interest group influence on state courts of last resort. In this light, increasing interest group activity by way of amicus curiae briefs in state supreme courts is a troubling development for individual appellants. When parties of ordinary means are able to overcome numerous obstacles and have their claims heard by a state supreme court, there may be an outside interest group working to tip the scales in favor of organized, business interests.

CONCLUSION

In this chapter, we have attempted to draw attention to several problems economic inequality raises for access to justice and judicial integrity. In our view, these problems undermine our capacity to protect civil rights and civil liberties.

It seems unrealistic to suggest that the answer to these problems lies in eliminating economic inequality or fully funding the right to counsel in all cases. Rather than eliminate inequality to solve its effects on the judicial system, we ought to focus on ways to reduce how much of a difference wealth and income make on court outcomes. One of the main problems is that court-based processes are too costly and complicated for most individuals to navigate. States should make procedures for frequently litigated claims as simple and straightforward as possible and consider amending rules regulating the unauthorized practice of law (Barton & Bibas, 2012; Hadfield, 2008). To some extent, alternatives to traditional litigation, like arbitration and mediation, were intended to provide simpler, more efficient dispute resolution methods, but they are quickly becoming second-rate solutions for ordinary individuals. Courts should consider whether these alternatives are fair in practice or impose unreasonable, coercive costs on individuals.

We would also suggest reducing the unsavory influence of money on judicial selection and decision-making. One possible solution is the abolition of judicial elections in favor of nomination commissions and merit appointments (Riggs & Gillette, 2015). Another possible solution is public financing of judicial elections to eliminate any special interest influence (via campaign contributions) on the elected judges. With respect to interest groups influencing appeals courts through amicus curiae briefs, courts should consider actively soliciting input from non-profit organizations to counterbalance the influence of special interest groups, or perhaps requiring prospective amici to demonstrate the need for their participation in a given appeal.

We cannot provide definitive solutions to the problems that economic inequality presents to access to the courts and judicial integrity. There are multiple contributing factors and the problem affects different types of cases at multiple levels of the judicial system. Although our contribution is primarily to draw attention to several aspects of the problem that have not been widely discussed, we hope our work adds to this important topic.

REFERENCES

Abel, L. K., and Rettig, M., (2006). State Statutes Providing for a Right to Counsel in Civil Cases. *Clearinghouse Review: Journal of Poverty Law and Policy* 40, 245-270.

American Tort Reform Association. (2015). State Reforms. from http://www.atra.org/legislation/states.

Banner, S., (2003). Myth of the Neutral Amicus: American Courts and Their Friends, 1790-1890, *The Constitutional Commentary* 20, 111-130.

Bannon, A., Velasco, E., Casey, L., and Reagan, L., (2013). The New Politics of Judicial Elections 2011-12. In: L. Kinney and P. Hardin (Eds.). Washington, D.C.: Brennan Center for Justice at New York University School of Law.

Bartels, L. M., (2009). *Unequal Democracy: The Political Economy of the New Gilded Age*. Princeton, NJ; Princeton University Press.

Barton, B. H., and Bibas, S., (2012). Triaging Appointed-Counsel Funding and Pro Se Access to Justice. *University of Pennsylvania Law Review* 160, 967-994.

Bills, B. D., (2008). A Penny for the Court's Thoughts? The High Price of Judicial Elections. *Northwestern Journal of Law and Social Policy* 3, 29-61.

Bright, S. B., (1997). Political Attacks on the Judiciary: Can Justice be Done Amid Efforts to Intimidate and Remove Judges from Office for Unpopular Decisions? *New York University Law Review* 72, 308-336.

Brown, A., and Lomurro, J., (2014). The Qualification of Experts in Medical Malpractice Cases after Nicholas v. Mynster. *New Jersey Lawyer* (Aug.).

Caldeira, G. A., and Wright, J. R., (1990). Amici Curiae Before the Supreme Court: Who Participates, When, and How Much? *The Journal of Politics* 52(3), 782-806.

Collins, P. M., (2007). Lobbyists before the US Supreme Court Investigating the Influence of Amicus Curiae Briefs. *Political Research Quarterly* 60(1), 55-70.

Collins, P. M., and Martinek, W. L., (2010). Friends of the Circuits: Interest Group Influence on Decision Making in the US Courts of Appeals. *Social Science Quarterly* 91(2), 397-414.

Colvin, A. J., (2011). An Empirical Study of Employment Arbitration: Case Outcomes and Processes. *Journal of Empirical Legal Studies* 8(1), 1-23.

Comparato, S. A., (2003). *Amici Curiae and Strategic Behavior in State Supreme Courts*. Westport, CT: Greenwood Publishing Group.

Corbally, S. F., Bross, D. C., and Flango, V. E., (2004). Filing of Amicus Curiae Briefs in State Courts of Last Resort: 1960-2000. *Justice System Journal* 25(1), 39-56.

Croley, S. P., (1995). The Majoritarian Difficulty: Elective Judiciaries and the Rule of Law. *The University of Chicago Law Review* 62(2), 689-794.

Davis, M. F., (2012). Participation, Equality, and the Civil Right to Counsel: Lessons from Domestic and International Law. *Yale Law Journal* 122, 2260-2281.

Dayton, K., (1991). The Myth of Alternative Dispute Resolution in the Federal Courts. *Iowa Law Review* 76, 889-957.

Demaine, L., and Hensler, D. R., (2004). 'Volunteering' to Arbitrate Through Pre-Dispute Arbitration Clauses: The Average Consumer's Experience. *Law and Contemporary Problems* 67, 55-74.

Eaton, T. A., Talarico, S. M., and Dunn, R. E., (1999). Another Brick in the Wall: An Empirical Look at Georgia Tort Litigation in the 1990s. *Georgia Law Review* 34(3), 1049-1154.

Edwards, B. C., (2008). Comprehensive Arbitration of Domestic Relations Cases in Georgia. *Georgia Bar Journal* (August), 20-29.

Edwards, B. C., (2013). Renovating the Multi-Door Courthouse: Designing Trial Court Dispute Resolution Systems to Improve Results and Control Costs. *Harvard Negotiation Law Review* 18, 281-347.

Engler, R., (1999). And Justice for All-Including the Unrepresented Poor: Revisiting the Roles of the Judges, Mediators and Clerks. *Fordham Law Review* 67, 1987-2070.

Epstein, L., (1994). Exploring the Participation of Organized Interests in State Court Litigation. *Political Research Quarterly* 47(2), 335-351.

Equal Justice Initiative. (2011). The Death Penalty in Alabama: Judge Override. Montgomery, AL: Equal Justice Initiative.

Flango, V. E., Bross, D. C., and Corbally, S., (2006). Amicus Curiae Briefs: The Court's Perspective. *Justice System Journal* 27(2), 180-190.

Gibson, J. L., (2008). Campaigning for the Bench: The Corrosive Effects of Campaign Speech? *Law and Society Review* 42(4), 899-928.

Gibson, J. L., (2009). "New-Style" Judicial Campaigns and the Legitimacy of State High Courts. *Journal of Politics* 71(4), 1285-1304.

Goldschmidt, J., (1998). How Are Courts Handling Pro Se Litigants? *Judicature* 82, 13-18.

Grossi, P., Mills, J., and Vagenas, K., (2012). Crisis in the Courts: Reconnaissance and Recommendations *Future Trends in State Courts*. Williamsburg, VA: National Center for State Courts.

Hadfield, G. K., (2008). Legal Barriers to Innovation: The Growing Economic Cost of Professional Control over Corporate Legal Markets. *Stanford Law Review* 60(6), 1689-1732.

Hadfield, G. K., (2010). Higher Demand, Lower Supply-A Comparative Assessment of the Legal Resource Landscape for Ordinary Americans. *Fordham Urban Law Journal* 37(1), 129-156.

Hall, K. L., (1983). The judiciary on Trial: State Constitutional Reform and the Rise of an Elected Judiciary, 1876-1860. *The Historian* 45(3), 337-354. doi: 10.1111/j.1540-6563.1983.tb01236.x.

Huber, G. A., and Gordon, S. C., (2004). Accountability and Coercion: Is Justice Blind when It Runs for Office? *American Journal of Political Science* 48(2), 247-263.

Kearney, J. D., and Merrill, T. W., (2000). The Influence of Amicus Curiae Briefs on the Supreme Court. *University of Pennsylvania Law Review* 148(3), 743-855.

Krislov, S., (1963). The Amicus Curiae Brief: From Friendship to Advocacy. *Yale Law Journal* 72(4), 694-721.

Levenson, J. A., (2014). Why Voters Shouldn't Be Electing Judges, Op-ed. *Los Angeles Times*. Retrieved from http://www.latimes.com/opinion/op-ed/la-oe-levinson-end-judicial-elections-20140509-story.html.

Lindsey, R., (1986). The Elections: The Story in Some Key States; Deukmejian and Cranston Win as 3 Judges are Ousted. *New York Times*. Retrieved from http://www.nytimes.com/1986/11/06/us/elections-story-some-key-states-deukmejian-cranston-win-3-judges-are-ousted.html.

Liptak, A., and Roberts, J., (2006). Campaign Cash Mirrors a High Court's Rulings. *New York Times*. Retrieved from http://www.nytimes.com/2006/10/01/us/01judges.html?pagewanted=all&_r=0.

Munford, L. T., (1999). When Does the Curiae Need an Amicus? *The Journal of Appellate Practice and Process* 1(2), 279-284.

Neubauer, D., and Meinhold, S., (2012). *Judicial Process: Law, Courts, and Politics in the United States*, 6th Ed. Boston, MA: Cengage Learning.

Palmer, V. V., and Levendis, J., (2008). The Louisiana Supreme Court in Question: An Empirical and Statistical Study of the Effects of Campaign Money on the Judicial Function, *Tulane Law Review* 82, 1291-1314.

Papailiou, A. P., (2013). Making Sense of the Linchpin to Medical Malpractice Litigation: Expert Medical Witness Qualification. *Arizona Law Review* 55, 539-555.

Piketty, T., and Saez, E., (2014). Inequality in the Long Run. *Science* 344(6186), 838-843.

Rhode, D. L., (2001). Access to Justice. *Fordham Law Review* 69, 1785-1819.

Riggs, R. W., and Gillette, W. M., (2015). Process for choosing judges in Oregon must change: Guest opinion. *The Oregonian*. Retrieved from http://www.oregonlive.com/opinion/index.ssf/2015/01/process_for_choosing_judges_in.html#incart_river.

Sample, J., Skaggs, A., Blitzer, J., and Casey, L., (2010). The New Politics of Judicial Elections, 2000-2009: Decade of Change. In: C. Hall (Ed.). New York City: Brennan Center for Justice at New York University School of Law.

Samuels, S. U., (2004). *First Among Friends: Interest Groups, the US Supreme Court, and the Right to Privacy*. Westport, CT: Greenwood Publishing Group.

Shepherd, J., and Kang, M. S., (2014). Skewed Justice: Citizens United, Television Advertising and State Supreme Court Justices' Decisions in Criminal Cases. Retrieved 5/28/2015, 2015, from http://skewedjustice.org/#results.

Shugerman, J. H., (2012). *The People's Courts: Pursuing Judicial Independence in America*. Cambridge: Harvard University Press.

Songer, D. R., and Kuersten, A., (1995). The Success of Amici in State Supreme Courts. *Political Research Quarterly* 48(1), 31-42.

Spriggs, J. F., and Wahlbeck, P. J., (1997). Amicus Curiae and the Role of Information at the Supreme Court. *Political Research Quarterly* 50(2), 365-386.

Sternlight, J. R., (2005). Creeping Mandatory Arbitration: Is It Just? *Stanford Law Review* 57, 1631-1675.

Streb, M. J., (2007). The Study of Judicial Elections. In: M. J. Streb (Ed.), *Running for Judge: The Rising Political, Financial, and Legal Stakes of Judicial Elections* (pp. 1-14). New York: New York University Press.

Thompson, C., (2014, Dec. 11). Trial by Cash. *The Atlantic*.

Todt, J. H., (2011). Caperton v. A.T. Massey Coal Co.: The Objective Standard for Judicial Recusal. *Notre Dame Law Review* 86(1), 439-468.

Trochesset, A., (2014). *Supreme Courtships: Amicus Curiae Influence on State Courts of Last Resort*. Paper presented at the American Political Science Association Annual Conference, Washington, D.C.

Trochesset, A., (2015). *Influential Interests: Amicus Curiae Influence on State High Court Opinions.* Paper presented at the American Political Science Association Annual Conference San Francisco, CA.

Udell, D. S., and Diller, R., (2007). Access to the Courts: An Essay for the Georgetown University Law Center Conference on the Independence of the Courts. *Georgetown Law Journal* 95, 1127-1154.

Van Wormer, N. I., (2007). Help at Your Fingertips: A Twenty-First Century Response to the Pro Se Phenomenon. *Vanderbilt Law Review* 60, 983-1019.

In: International Human Rights and Justice
Editor: Doug Hodgson

ISBN: 978-1-63484-709-4

Chapter 4

THE STRATEGIC USE BY ABORIGINAL AUSTRALIANS OF INTERNATIONAL HUMAN RIGHTS NORMS AND UNITED NATIONS MONITORING MECHANISMS TO SECURE GREATER JUSTICE AND RECOGNITION OF THEIR RIGHTS UNDER AUSTRALIAN LAW AND POLICY

Doug Hodgson*

Dean, School of Law, The University of Notre Dame Australia, BA, LLB, LLM, FAAL
(Fellow of the Australian Academy of Law)

ABSTRACT

The adoption by the United Nations in 2007 of the *Declaration on the Rights of Indigenous Peoples* marked a watershed in the world-wide recognition of the human rights of Indigenous peoples. Many Australian Aboriginal and Torres Strait Islander leaders believe that international human rights law generally, and the *Declaration* in particular, can be utilised in making human rights advances at the national level. This chapter will begin by tracing the historical and contemporary development of Indigenous human rights norms culminating in the adoption of the *Declaration*. After an examination of the foundational principles of the *Declaration*, the relevant UN norms-development and monitoring mechanisms will be discussed. The chapter will then contextualise the recent history of Australian Aboriginal disenfranchisement, the slow process of legal remedial reform and the prospects for their greater constitutional recognition as "First Peoples" and protection of their human rights as well as the lessons to be learned from the "Northern Territory Intervention." The success, and continuing prospects thereof, of their engagement with the UN mechanisms in order to secure greater justice and recognition of their rights under Australian law and public policy will be evaluated.

* Corresponding author: Email: doug.hodgson@nd.edu.au.

Keywords: Aboriginal Australians, International Human Rights Law, United Nations Declaration on the Rights of Indigenous Peoples, Constitutional Recognition, Human Rights Compliance Monitoring, Racial Discrimination, Indigenous Customary Laws and Cultural Protection

INTRODUCTION

There are approximately 370 million Indigenous persons in the world today which comprises five per cent of the world's population; yet they are over-represented as a percentage of the world's poor [Carino]. They reside in some 90 countries and "retain social, cultural, economic and political characteristics that are distinct from those of the dominant societies in which they live." They are descended from a people who inhabited a region when new settler arrivals "became dominant through conquest, occupation, settlement or other means" [United Nations Permanent Forum on Indigenous Issues (2006)].

The past 50 or so years have been marked by the emerging recognition of Indigenous peoples and their rights as special subjects of concern and importance within the United Nations international human rights law framework [Anaya and Williams]. While the human rights of Indigenous peoples are co-terminous with the human rights of all peoples and human beings, there has been growing recognition that certain human rights assume greater importance for them in light of their history and current circumstances and that accordingly most widely accepted human rights must be tailored specifically in their meaning and application to Indigenous peoples [McBeth, Nolan and Rice].

There is currently no formal definition of "Indigenous peoples" which has been adopted in international law or any international legal instruments. However, in a seminal report on Indigenous peoples, José Martinez Cobo, the then Special Rapporteur of the Sub-Commission on Prevention of Discrimination and Protection of Minorities (of the Commission for Human Rights), developed the following working definition [Cobo]:

> Indigenous communities, peoples and nations are those which, having a historical continuity with pre-invasion and pre-colonial societies that developed on their territories, consider themselves distinct from other sectors of the societies now prevailing on those territories, or parts of them. They form at present non-dominant sectors of society and are determined to preserve, develop and transmit to future generations their ancestral territories, and their ethnic identity, as the basis of their continued existence as peoples, in accordance with their own cultural patterns, social institutions and legal systems.

The United Nations Permanent Forum on Indigenous Issues has articulated some characteristics which contribute to a contemporary understanding of what comprises "Indigenous peoples." These include a continuing historical connection or continuity with pre-colonial society, a special relationship with ancestral lands, distinctive cultural, legal, linguistic and knowledge systems, a non-dominant group position within society, perpetuation of cultural identity, and self identification (both as an Indigenous person and as a member of an Indigenous people) [International Law Association]. In relation to the final characteristic, under international law a person's identity as a member of a particular racial or ethnic group is based on the notion of "self-identification" [United Nations Committee on the

Elimination of Racial Discrimination (1990)]. Indigenous peoples identify according to their 'race' as that term is interpreted for the purposes of the *International Convention for the Elimination of All Forms of Racial Discrimination* (hereinafter referred to as the *ICERD*). In other words, they identify according to a commonly held "colour, descent, or national or ethnic origin" [*ICERD* Article 1]. Aboriginal and Torres Strait Islander peoples constitute the Indigenous peoples of Australia.

The recent elevation of Indigenous peoples' rights squarely on the human rights agenda of the United Nations is perhaps a response to seemingly intractable problems which continue to beset Indigenous communities world-wide. McBeth, Nolan and Rice have graphically described the historical circumstances which have conspired to produce these problems [McBeth, Nolan and Rice]:

> The history of indigenous peoples from the seventeenth to the twentieth centuries is principally one of colonialisation, subjugation, assimilation and genocide. It is a history of widespread and deliberate denial and violation of what we now recognise as human rights. Indigenous peoples have been the victims of more powerful peoples who have entered and taken over their land, most commonly European invaders of land in Africa, the Americas and Australasia, although the subjugation and displacement of indigenous peoples has been a world-wide phenomenon.

This shared history of the world's Indigenous peoples has resulted in discrimination, denial of political representation and participation in decision-making and policy formulation, denial of access to economic and social benefits, an undermining of their ability to maintain their identity through their language, culture and traditions, and interference with their use of traditional ancestral lands and natural resources [United Nations Permanent Forum on Indigenous Issues (2006)]. Consequently a large number of different and sometimes controversial human rights issues now confront the world's Indigenous peoples: the right to self-determination, the rights to preserve and enjoy cultural practices and customary legal systems, the right to land ownership and native title recognition, the rights to health, education and development, and ownership and exploitation of cultural knowledge. Indigenous claims to such rights challenge both the sovereign State and powerful and influential national and international private profit-driven interests such as multinational pharmaceutical companies [McBeth, Nolan and Rice]. In relation to the intellectual property rights of Indigenous peoples, Article 8(j) of the United Nations *Convention on Biological Diversity 1992* affirms Indigenous peoples' rights over their "knowledge, innovations and practices" as well as their right to be involved in, and share the benefits from, their application.

Within an Australian context, the major contemporary challenges to Aboriginal and Torres Strait Islander peoples and communities include social exclusion, poverty and homelessness, health (particularly differentiated life expectancy and infant mortality rates), education, protection of cultures and languages, disproportionately high incarceration rates among Aboriginal youth offenders, the protection of women and children, the racial vilification of Indigenous sportspeople, systemic discrimination, disempowerment and lack of meaningful participation in governmental decision-making. This chapter will plot the historical development of Indigenous peoples' rights at the international level, particularly in relation to the promulgation of an international human rights normative framework and the creation of monitoring and implementation mechanisms by the United Nations. It will then examine recent Australian history in relation to the trend towards a steady, albeit grudging, recognition under Australian law of the rights of Aboriginal and Torres Strait Islander peoples as well as canvass the vexed question over the proposed constitutional recognition of their human rights and their status as the "first peoples" of the Australian continent. The track record of successive Australian governments' engagement with the United Nations and the relevant United Nations protective mechanisms will be assessed before the venturing of concluding thoughts on how the United Nations and Australian governments can better secure the long-term security of these rights.

THE HISTORICAL AND CONTEMPORARY DEVELOPMENT OF INDIGENOUS PEOPLES' HUMAN RIGHTS

International engagement with the issue of Indigenous peoples' rights can be traced back to at least 1923 when Chief Deskaheh travelled to Geneva, Switzerland to present a grievances petition to the League of Nations on behalf of the Six Nations of the Iroquois in relation to complaints against Canada. Although the League did not offer any redress in this instance on the ground that the complaints were deemed to be within the exclusive jurisdictional competence of Canadian domestic law, it set a precedent for an increasing and more systematic engagement with the League's successor, the United Nations [Gooda (2013); Anaya (2004)]. The contemporary international Indigenous human rights movement gained traction in the 1960s and 1970s when Indigenous peoples in the Americas and Australasia (comprising Australia and New Zealand) began to press demands for their continued survival as distinct historically-based cultures as well as their entitlement to ancestral lands. These demands were supported by scholars and national and international non-governmental organisations (NGOs) [Anaya and Williams]. In 1972, the United Nations Sub-Commission on Prevention of Discrimination and Protection of Minorities commenced work on the *Study on the Problem of Discrimination Against Indigenous Populations* (widely known as the Cobo Study after the name of the report's Special Rapporteur and lead author) [Cobo]. By the late 1970s, Indigenous peoples' representatives began appearing before United Nations and other human rights bodies with increasing frequency, invoking the protection of universally applicable international human rights standards [McBeth, Nolan and Rice] and buoyed by a growing perception or belief that the international human rights system could effectively be utilized by the world's Indigenous peoples as a mechanism for law reform and policy-making at the domestic level. The United Nations, in turn, became increasingly accommodating of Indigenous concerns and aspirations [Davis], as evidenced by the creation in 1982 of the United Nations Working Group on Indigenous Populations.

The relevant international human rights normative framework can be traced back to 1965 when the United Nations adopted the *ICERD*, a multilateral treaty imposing binding legal obligations on States Parties. While not specifically or explicitly concerned with the rights of Indigenous peoples, the *ICERD* provisions encompass them. The Committee on the Elimination of Racial Discrimination (*ICERD* Committee), which monitors the compliance of States Parties with *ICERD*, has authoritatively declared that discrimination against Indigenous peoples falls within the scope of *ICERD*. As the peoples who were present when newly arrived settlers assumed a dominant position in society and who have retained distinct social, cultural and customary law systems, they *ipso facto* comprise a different 'race' for the purposes of *ICERD*. As such, the *ICERD* Committee has called on State Parties to include in their periodic reports full information on the situation of their Indigenous peoples and to recognize and respect Indigenous distinct culture, history, language and way of life [Committee for the Elimination of Racial Discrimination (1997)]. *ICERD* protects indigenous peoples from discrimination (Article 2), racial segregation (Article 3), and from being the subject of racial vilification or incitement to racial hatred (Article 4). *ICERD* guarantees Indigenous peoples the rights to equality before the law (Article 5(a)), public participation (Article 5(c)) and equality, without discrimination as to race, in the enjoyment of economic, social and cultural rights including the right to equal participation in cultural activities (Article 5(e)(iv)). The *ICERD* Committee has observed that the principle of equality upon which *ICERD* is based combines formal equality before the law with substantive or *de facto* equality in the enjoyment and exercise of human rights and that the discrimination proscribed includes both purposive or intentional direct discrimination and discrimination in effect (that is to say, indirect discrimination whereby a requirement, neutral on its face, disproportionately affects a group of people without a reasonable basis) [Committee for the Elimination of Racial Discrimination (1997)]. In undertaking its role in monitoring compliance by States Parties with its *ICERD* obligations, the *ICERD* Committee scrutinises their reports on the extent to which they have protected and enhanced the human rights of Indigenous peoples. It has been observed that the *ICERD* Committee now regularly applies the prevailing meaning of Indigenous peoples' rights as part of their process [Anaya and Williams].

One year after the *ICERD* was adopted, the United Nations General Assembly approved the *International Covenant on Civil and Political Rights* on 16 December 1966 (hereinafter referred to as the *ICCPR*). The two most significant substantive operative provisions in relation to Indigenous peoples include the right of all peoples to self-determination pursuant to which "they freely determine their political status and freely pursue their economic, social and cultural development" (Article 1(1)) and the right of members of ethnic, religious and linguistic minorities "to enjoy their own culture, to profess and practise their own religion, [and] to use their own language" (Article 27). Similar to *ICERD*, the *ICCPR* established a Human Rights Committee (Article 28) which is charged with the task of vetting periodic reports submitted to it by States Parties on the measures they have adopted to give effect in their domestic laws to the rights recognised in the *ICCPR* (Article 40). Like the *ICERD* Committee, the Human Rights Committee regularly applies the contemporary meanings of Indigenous peoples' rights when they monitor those portions of States Parties' reports which involve the human rights of Indigenous peoples [Anaya and Williams]. Later in this chapter, the degree of engagement between these two monitoring committees and the Australian Government will be assessed as well as the comments and recommendations they have made in relation to changes to Australian law and policy to better protect the human rights of Australian Indigenous peoples.

The Declaration on the Rights of Indigenous Peoples 2007

In 1982, the United Nations Sub-Commission on the Prevention of Discrimination and Protection of Minorities created a Working Group on Indigenous Populations (WGIP) comprising State representatives and Indigenous peoples' representatives to develop a *Draft Declaration on the Rights of Indigenous Peoples*. Some 25 years on, the UN General Assembly adopted the *Declaration on the Rights of Indigenous Peoples* on 13 September 2007. The *Declaration* contains 46 operative provisions as well as 24 preambular paragraphs and represents the most comprehensive UN instrument to date concerning the human rights of Indigenous peoples. The key principles upon which the *Declaration* is based include the right of Indigenous people to self-determination (Articles 3 and 20), the right to participate in decision-making (Articles 18 and 19), equality and non-discrimination (Article 2), and protection of culture (Article 11) and language (Article 13). The *Declaration* is the most authoritative statement today of how universally endorsed human rights norms apply in a specific or tailored manner to the particular circumstances of Indigenous peoples. As a *Declaration* adopted by UN General Assembly resolution, it does not impose under international law any legally binding obligations on UN Member States; however, the *Declaration* does contain widely accepted aspirational principles and statements of good policy which are intended to inform law-making and policy-making in the relevant areas. While not containing any new rights or standards, the *Declaration* does purport to interpret and elaborate upon how mainstream human rights obligations contained in international legal instruments such as the *ICERD* and the *ICCPR* apply specifically to Indigenous peoples.

The 25 years it took to achieve adoption of the *Declaration* is significant as the reasons for such delay may also negatively impact on the prospects of the provisions of the *Declaration* attaining legally binding status through their incorporation within a multilateral UN-sponsored treaty on the human rights of Indigenous persons. As one commentator has aptly observed, issues of concern to Indigenous peoples – including ancestral lands and natural resources – "strike at the very core of the Westphalian state system and state sovereignty" [Davis]. The most pressing obstacle of the adoption of the *Declaration* was recognition of the right to self-determination which, as noted previously in this chapter, has been explicitly recognised by Article 1(1) of the *ICCPR*. The right to self-determination explicitly recognised by Article 3 of the *Declaration* is one of its foundation principles for Indigenous peoples and is expressed in virtually identical terms to Article 1(1) of the *ICCPR* but for a specific reference to Indigenous peoples in the former instrument. The right to self-determination includes the right to "freely determine their political status and freely pursue their economic, social and cultural development." While the reference to self-determination in the *ICCPR* was contextualised in an era when its drafters were anticipating the post-colonial emergence of newly independent States, the concept of self-determination was perceived to constitute a more serious threat to State sovereignty and territorial integrity in the context of Indigenous peoples residing within established States. Such States were also wary of the potential financial implications posed by compensation as a form of redress. Nevertheless, most UN Member States considered that far from supporting secessionist movements, Article 3 of the *Declaration* facilitates the implementation of the Indigenous right to self-determination "within a democratic system without disrupting public institutions or the rule of law" [Davis]. The so-called "CANZUS" grouping comprising Canada, Australia, New

Zealand and the United States initially opposed recognition of Indigenous self-determination and thus voted against the UN General Assembly resolution which adopted the *Declaration*. However, all four CANZUS States have since reversed their position, with Australia (after a change of government) formally advising the UN of its support for the *Declaration* on 3 April 2009 [Macklin]. There may therefore be some grounds for optimism that, following the leads of the conversion of declarations protecting the human rights of women, children and persons with disabilities into legally binding conventions, the next logical step to codify the principles of the *Declaration* in a UN-sponsored and legally binding multilateral human rights treaty is not beyond the scope of negotiations. It may also be possible that in the fullness of time, the dual requirements of State practice and *opinio juris* may be satisfied such that the main principles of the *Declaration* can be said to have crystallised into Customary International Law. Apart from the right to self-determination, the rights to culture and practice of their spiritual traditions and customs contained respectively in Articles 11 and 12 of the *Declaration* are particularly important to Indigenous peoples. Apart from Article 27 of the *ICCPR* mentioned above, Article 27(1) of the *Universal Declaration of Human Rights* provides that "everyone has the right freely to participate in the cultural life of the community." Pursuant to Article 15(1)(a) of the *International Covenant on Economic, Social and Cultural Rights 1966* (hereinafter referred to as the *ICESCR*), the States Parties recognize the right of everyone to take part in cultural life. In its *General Comment No 21*, the United Nations Committee on Economic, Social and Cultural Rights (the *CESCR* Committee), set up to monitor States Parties' implementation of the *ICESCR*, observed that "culture, for the purpose of implementing article 15(1)(a), encompasses, inter alia, ways of life, language, oral and written literature, music and song, non-verbal communications, religion or belief systems, rites and ceremonies,…natural…environments, food, clothing and shelter and the arts, customs and traditions through which individuals, groups of individuals and communities express their humanity and the meaning they give to their existence, and build the world view" [United Nations Committee on Economic, Social and Cultural Rights]. Moreover, in relation to Indigenous peoples, the *CESCR* Committee has maintained that the "strong communal dimensions of indigenous peoples' cultural life is indispensable to their existence, well-being and full development, and includes the right to the lands, territories and resources which they have traditionally owned, occupied or otherwise used or acquired" [United Nations Committee on Economic, Social and Cultural Rights]. Further, the Committee observed that "Indigenous peoples' cultural values and rights associated with their ancestral lands and their relationship with nature should be regarded with respect and protected, in order to prevent the degradation of their particular way of life, including their means of subsistence, the loss of their natural resources and ultimately, their cultural identity" [United Nations Committee on Economic, Social and Cultural Rights]. The views of the *CESCR* Committee are highly persuasive for the *ICESCR* States Parties in relation to the interpretation and implementation of the relevant human rights within their own domestic legal systems.

The right of Indigenous peoples to practise their traditions and customs is also recognised under international human rights law, specifically by Article 27 of the *ICCPR* which obliges States Parties not to deny or interfere with the right of minorities "to enjoy their own culture, to profess and practise their own religion, or to use their own language." At the domestic level, Indigenous traditions and customs implicate both the private and public spheres in such matters as the custody of children and the imposition of punishment for criminal wrongdoing.

Customary Indigenous law is based on a collection of unwritten principles or guidelines on what constitutes socially acceptable behaviour and which are designed to restore harmony and maintain balance in the community. It is essentially based on the notion of restorative justice whereby the wrongdoer is obliged to compensate the victim for harm done to the latter as a condition precedent to his or her rehabilitation and re-integration within the community. There may be instances, however, when infliction of physical punishment under customary Indigenous law may violate both international human rights prohibitions against corporal punishment and domestic criminal law provisions. In these circumstances, a reconciliation and accommodation of the competing interests will be required through a balancing process and this may pose significant challenges [Australian Law Reform Commission].

RELEVANT UNITED NATIONS NORMS-DEVELOPMENT AND MONITORING MECHANISMS

The recent development of Indigenous human rights normative standards has been accompanied by the emergence of a variety of UN facilitative mechanisms designed not only to continue the process of standard-elaboration but also to develop a more systematic approach to standard-implementation. The UN Human Rights Council has appointed a Special Rapporteur on the Situation of Human Rights and Fundamental Freedoms of Indigenous People to document instances of alleged violations of the human rights of Indigenous peoples and make recommendations on how their human rights can be better protected [Preston, Vindig and Garcia-Alix]. The Special Rapporteur also conducts compliance inspections in those countries which consent thereto and those inspections are subsequently reported on to the Human Rights Council. The Special Rapporteur has visited and published country reports on countries with Indigenous populations covering North and South America, Africa, northern Europe, and Australasia (Australia and New Zealand), including a visit to Australia in 2009 [Anaya (2010)].

Another subsidiary body of the Human Rights Council is the Expert Mechanism on the Rights of Indigenous Peoples which superseded the Working Group on Indigenous Populations which had been created in 1982. The Expert Mechanism comprises independent experts and convenes annual sessions with Indigenous representatives, State representatives, NGOs, academics and inter-governmental organizations. Its prime task is to provide the Human Rights Council with thematic research and studies on the rights on Indigenous peoples; in 2009 and 2011 the Expert Mechanism respectively made recommendations on how the human rights of Indigenous peoples to education and to participate in decision-making might be more fully realised [United Nations Expert Mechanism (2009) and (2011)]. These recommendations are directed to UN Member States and are instrumental in assisting them to comply with their human rights treaty obligations and reporting requirements thereunder. This includes the new Universal Periodic Review (UPR) process undertaken by the UN Human Rights Council entailing review of the human rights performance of all 192 UN Member States once every four years [Office of the High Commissioner for Human Rights].

Transcending the mandates of the Special Rapporteur and the Expert Mechanism is that of the UN Permanent Forum of Indigenous Issues (hereinafter referred to as UNPFII) which advises the UN Economic and Social Council on a broad range of Indigenous issues relating to economic and social development, education, health, human rights, the environment and culture. UNPFII is comprised of 16 independent experts, half of which are nominated by States and the other half from prescribed regions which effectively include all continents. Australia has successfully nominated as expert members Professors Mick Dodson and Megan Davis. While meeting annually for rather modest 10-day sessions, UNPFII has addressed the following issues since its inaugural 2002 session:

- Indigenous children and youth
- Indigenous women
- poverty eradication
- universal primary education
- lands and natural resources
- climate change, bio-cultural diversity and livelihoods: the stewardship role of Indigenous peoples
- sustaining culture and identity
- study on constitutions and Indigenous peoples' human rights

In 2011, UNPFII called on States and their Indigenous populations to establish national programmes to implement in a timely manner the United Nations *Declaration on the Rights of Indigenous Peoples* and to report regularly to their national legislative bodies and to UNPFII on progress made, and shortcomings identified, in the implementation of the *Declaration* [United Nations Permanent Forum on Indigenous Issues (2011)].

Participation by Indigenous representatives and organizations in the work of the UN in the field of Indigenous rights has been significantly facilitated by the UN Voluntary Fund for Indigenous Populations set up by the UN General Assembly in 1985. It is funded by voluntary contributions from governments, non-governmental organizations and other public and private entities, designed to assist Indigenous community representatives and organizations to participate in the deliberations of relevant UN human rights bodies. Administered by the UN Secretary-General through the Office of the High Commissioner for Human Rights, the Fund has allocated over 1,100 grants to representatives of Indigenous communities and organizations to participate in the deliberations of the Work Group on Indigenous Populations, to observe sessions of the Permanent Forum on Indigenous Issues, and to participate in sessions of the Expert Mechanism on the Rights of Indigenous Peoples and the Human Rights Council [Office of the High Commissioner for Human Rights].

As a mark of the increasingly important place on the international human rights law agenda of Indigenous rights, the UN General Assembly declared the period 1995-2004 the International Decade of the World's Indigenous People (GA Res 52/108, A/RES/52/108) to strengthen international efforts to address issues relating to the health, education, environment, development and human rights of Indigenous peoples. In 2004, the UN General Assembly proclaimed a second International Decade of the World's Indigenous People to commence on 1 January 2005 (GA Res 59/174, A/RES/59/174) with five main objectives:

- non-discrimination and inclusion of Indigenous peoples in international, regional and national processes

- full and effective participation of Indigenous peoples in decisions that affect them
- ensuring development policies that are equitable and culturally appropriate
- setting concrete benchmarks for the development of Indigenous peoples, particularly women, children and youth
- strong monitoring and accountability mechanisms for international, regional and national legal, policy and operational frameworks

In 2010, the UN Secretary-General reported that although "substantive advances" had been achieved, a substantial gap remained between policy intentions and actual implementation of these five main objectives [United Nations Report of the Secretary-General]. Nevertheless, such an assessment is a common refrain in the development of soft law aspirational principles in any human rights field, at least until they have matured into hard law or binding treaty and/or customary law norms.

Australian Indigenous Peoples

It is widely recognized among anthropologists that Australian Aboriginal peoples possess the oldest surviving culture in the world today, with new scientific methods revealing that archaeological sites are much older than originally thought. Mitochondrial DNA indicates that Australian Aborigines arose 400,000 years ago from two distinct lineages, far earlier than any other racial group, and current estimates place their arrival in Australia some 68,000 years ago [Korff]. The various Australian colonies became a federal State in 1901 with the passage by the United Kingdom Parliament of the *Australian Constitution* contained in Clause 9 of the *Commonwealth of Australia Constitution Act 1900* (Imp). Despite their habitation of the Australian continent since time immemorial, the *Australian Constitution* was drafted "in the spirit of *terra nullius*" whereby "[l]and was divided, power was shared, structures were established, on the illusion of vacant land" [Gooda (2013)]. Aboriginal and Torres Strait Islander (ATSI) peoples were excluded from participating in the constitutional convention debates and drafting process based in part on the then prevailing belief that they were a "dying race" [Sawyer]. ATSI peoples were not counted in the "reckoning of the numbers of the people of the Commonwealth" pursuant to Section 127 of the *Australian Constitution* and therefore were not originally counted in the national census. Furthermore, the 'races' power contained in Section 51(xxvi) of the *Constitution* enabled the Australian Government to "make special laws for people of any race other than the aboriginal race." For much of the 20th century, and in significant part owing to the court-sanctioned legal fiction of *terra nullius*, ATSI peoples were subjected to a series of laws and policies that facilitated the forcible removal of ATSI children from their families in what has come to be known as "The Stolen Generation" [Gooda (2013); Australian Human Rights and Equal Opportunity Commission]. On 13 February 2008, Prime Minister Kevin Rudd expressed regret on behalf of the Australian nation for "The Stolen Generation" in the *National Apology to Australia's Indigenous Peoples* [Commonwealth of Australia]. It was not until 1992 that the High Court of Australia rejected *terra nullius* and recognized the concept of Indigenous native title in the landmark case of *Mabo v Queensland (No 2)* (1992) 175 CLR 1. One year later, and as a direct response to the High Court's decision, the Australian Government enacted the *Native*

Title Act 1993 (Cth) which set up a statutory scheme to recognise ATSI peoples' native title rights.

In 1967, constitutional reform redressed in part the omissions of the 1901 *Australian Constitution*. In that year, a successful referendum was held to address the systemic constitutional exclusion of ATSI peoples, resulting in the removal of Section 127 as well as the reference to the "aboriginal race" in Section 51(xxvi). For the very first time, ATSI peoples were counted in the national census and the Australian Government could make special laws for them. Such reform was remarkable in light of the fact that only eight of the 44 constitutional referenda have been successful since Federation in 1901, due largely to the demanding "double majority" requirement in Section 128 of the *Australian Constitution*. This required the majority of electors nation-wide to vote in favour of the referendum as well as the majority of electors in the majority of Australian states as a condition precedent to the referendum's success. Nevertheless, the 1967 constitutional changes did not recognize the unique and special position of ATSI peoples as the continent's first peoples. As one Australian Aboriginal lawyer and commentator shrewdly observed, the 1967 reforms provided a "neutral citizenship" for ATSI peoples but "[w]hat is still needed is a positive recognition of our status as the country's Indigenous peoples, and yet sharing a common citizenship with all other Australians" [Pearson]. The next logical step in constitutional reform in this field – that of recognition of ATSI peoples as the "first peoples" – will require another successful constitutional referendum with the same stringent double majority requirement. This will almost certainly require, at the federal or Commonwealth level, the bipartisan political support of the Liberal and Labor Parties.

As a result of the 1967 constitutional reforms which included the new power to enact laws for ATSI peoples, the Australian Labor Government under Prime Minister Gough Whitlam enacted the *Racial Discrimination Act 1975* (Cth) (hereinafter referred to as the *RDA*) which makes discrimination on the basis of race unlawful. This is one of the rare instances in which a United Nations human rights treaty – in this case the *International Convention on the Elimination of All Forms of Racial Discrimination 1965* (*ICERD*) – has been transformed into Australian domestic law, thereby enabling its substantive provisions to be directly legally enforceable by Australia courts and tribunals. Section 8(1) of the *RDA* established a specific exception to the operation of the Act for particular racial groups including ATSI peoples whereby "special measures" do not constitute racial discrimination, drawing upon Article 1(4) of *ICERD* which provides that special measures are to be undertaken for the sole purpose of securing adequate advancement of certain racial groups to ensure such groups have equal enjoyment of human rights and fundamental freedoms: *Gerhardy v Brown* (1985) 159 CLR 70.

THE CONSTITUTIONAL RECOGNITION OF AUSTRALIAN ABORIGINAL PEOPLES: FUTURE DIRECTIONS

In light of the current 'neutral' constitutional recognition of Australian Aboriginal Peoples, there have been both national and international calls for a more positive recognition of their Indigenous rights. Legislative recognition of such rights, in the absence of constitutional entrenchment, is subject to the whim of ephemeral governments and there has therefore been a long history of advocacy for their constitutional recognition as well as the status of Australian Aboriginal Peoples as the First Peoples of Australia [Pearson; Report of the Expert Panel]. In 2000, the Council for Aboriginal Reconciliation urged the federal Parliament to prepare legislation for a constitutional referendum, observing that constitutional reform was unfinished business in terms of the reconciliation agenda [Council for Aboriginal Reconciliation]. At the international level, UN special mechanisms have made similar calls. In his report on his mission to Australia, the Special Rapporteur on the Rights of Indigenous Peoples recommended that the federal and state governments "should pursue constitutional or other effective legal recognition and protection of the rights of Aboriginal and Torres Strait Islander peoples in a manner that would provide long-term security for these rights." [Anaya (2010)]. Both the Expert Mechanism on the Rights of Indigenous Peoples and the Permanent Forum on Indigenous Issues have noted the increasing international importance of the need for UN Member States to amend their constitutions to explicitly recognise the rights of Indigenous peoples and their "first peoples" status [United Nations Expert Mechanism (2011); United Nations Permanent Forum on Indigenous Issues (2012)]. The substantive content of positive constitutional recognition, whether in the preambular or operative portions of the constituent document, would almost certainly have to include reference to land custodianship/stewardship, ATSI peoples' "first peoples" status, their languages as part of the national heritage, and an entrenched equality/non-discrimination on the basis of race clause which is more tamper-proof than the *RDA*, an ordinary, as opposed to constitutionally entrenched, piece of legislation.

The Northern Territory Intervention: Well-Meaning but Misguided Paternalism

In early 2007, the Northern Territory Board of Inquiry released its report into the Protection of Aboriginal Children from Sexual Abuse, *Ampe Akelyernemane Meke Makarle "Little Children are Sacred"* [Northern Territory Board of Inquiry]. The *"Little Children are Sacred"* Report documented widespread sexual abuse of children in the Northern Territory, with its primary recommendation reading as follows:

> That Aboriginal child sexual abuse in the Northern Territory be designated as an issue of urgent national significance by both the Australian and Northern Territory Governments, and both governments immediately establish a collaborative partnership…It is critical that both governments commit to genuine consultation with Aboriginal people in designing initiatives for Aboriginal communities [Northern Territory Board of Inquiry *"Little Children are Sacred"* Report (2007)7].

Soon after the Report's release, and as a direct response thereto, the Australian Government announced in June, 2007 the Northern Territory Emergency Response (commonly referred to as the 'NTER' or the 'Northern Territory Intervention') "to protect Aboriginal children residing in the Northern Territory from physical and sexual abuse" [Minister for Families, Community Services and Indigenous Affairs, Media Release]. The main governmental measures included the following:

- introduction of compulsory health checks for Aboriginal children to identify and treat health problems and cases of substance abuse;
- introduction of widespread alcohol restrictions on Northern Territory Aboriginal land;
- increase of policing levels in prescribed communities;
- improvement of housing in prescribed communities;
- enforcement of school attendance through linkage of income support and family assistance payments to school attendance for all people residing on Aboriginal land;
- introduction of welfare reforms to decrease substance abuse and to ensure that funds earmarked for children's welfare are used for that very purpose.

These measures had a five-year life-span and targeted 73 Aboriginal communities located in the Northern Territory. They were deemed "special measures" under Section 8 of the *RDA* and the operation of Part II of the *RDA* in relation to the NTER legislation – *Northern Territory National Emergency Response Act 2007* (Cth); *Families, Community Services and Indigenous Affairs and Other Legislation Amendment (Northern Territory National Emergency Response and Other Measures) Act 2007* (Cth); *Social Security and Other Legislation Amendment (Welfare Payment Reform) Act 2007* (Cth) – was suspended. This resulted in the consequential suspension of protection from racial discrimination provided by the *RDA*.

These wide-ranging and targeted measures, perhaps unsurprisingly, raised concerns not only domestically but also internationally, including among the United Nations Committee on Economic, Social and Cultural Rights [Concluding Observations (2009)] and the Special Rapporteur on the Rights of Indigenous Peoples [Anaya (2010)]. In June, 2008, the Australian Government commissioned an independent review of the NTER and the NTER Review Board concluded that those who had been affected by the NTER measures believed that they had been discriminated against on the basis of their race which had engendered a "strong sense of injustice" [Report of the Northern Territory Emergency Response Review Board (2008)]. This, in turn, undermined the positive potential of the NTER measures. Moreover, the failure to effectively work with the Aboriginal communities affected by the measures made their effective implementation more difficult. As one Aboriginal commentator has observed, the "sad irony" of the NTER is that it was established as a response to the *"Little Children are Sacred"* Report but ignored its primary recommendations concerning the necessity for "genuine consultation" with Aboriginal communities in implementing the NTER measures [Gooda (2013)]. This also undermined the right of Aboriginal peoples to participate in decision-making and to be consulted in relation to matters affecting them. This constitutes a violation of Articles 18 and 19 of the United Nations *Declaration on the Rights of Indigenous Peoples* which respectively state in part that "Indigenous peoples have the right to participate in decision-making which would affect their rights" and "States shall consult and cooperate in good faith with … indigenous peoples." As Professor Gooda concluded, when governments take unilateral action, Indigenous communities are prevented from taking responsibility over serious issues which confront them, undermining their right to self-determination (as recognized in Articles 3 and 20 of the *UNDRIP*) and disempowering them [Gooda (2013)]. A more collaborative response to the child abuse problem which engaged Aboriginal communities in decision-making and implementation of the NTER measures was required by *UNDRIP* and would have resulted in more tailored and culturally acceptable solutions [Gooda (2013)]. In response to the NTER Review Board's *Report*, the Australian Government reinstated the *RDA* and redesigned the measures to ensure their application on a non-discriminatory basis, pursuant to the *Social Security and Other Legislation Amendment (Welfare Reform and Reinstatement of Racial Discrimination Act) Act 2010* (Cth). Among other things, income management measures were redesigned in such a way that they were not to be applied on a racially discriminatory basis and over-inclusive blanket alcohol bans were replaced by restrictions which were more tailored to individual community needs.

AUSTRALIA'S ENGAGEMENT WITH UNITED NATIONS HUMAN RIGHTS MONITORING MECHANISMS

For a long time, the Australian Government has ignored recommendations from United Nations human rights treaty-monitoring bodies concerning the improvement of the human rights situations of Australia's ATSI peoples. However, between 2007 and 2013 when the Rudd and Gillard Labor Governments were in power, Australia took a number of steps to more systematically engage with the UN in relation to recognizing and applying international human rights norms to its ATSI peoples, including:

- the formal endorsement of *UNDRIP* [Macklin]
- the constructive engagement in the Human Rights Council's Universal Periodic Review (UPR) process in 2011 [Office of the High Commissioner for Human Rights (2011)]
- the extension of an open invitation to all of the UN special procedures, which resulted in an official visit to Australia in 2009 of the Special Rapporteur on the Rights of Indigenous Peoples [United Nations Office of the High Commissioner for Human Rights – Standing Invitations].

The two UN human rights treaty-monitoring bodies which have most actively scrutinized the Australian Government have been the Committee on the Elimination of Racial Discrimination under the *International Convention on the Elimination of All Forms of Racial Discrimination 1965* and the Human Rights Committee under the *International Covenant on Civil and Political Rights 1966*. Both bodies have expressed concerns regarding the inability of ATSI peoples to enjoy their rights to ancestral lands and resources [Committee on the Elimination of Racial Discrimination (2005); Human Rights Committee (2009)]. Significantly, in the current Australian context of agitation for constitutional reform in this area and in light of the central place of equality and non-discrimination in *ICERD 1965* and *UNDRIP 2007*, the Committee on the Elimination of Racial Discrimination has expressed concern at the "absence of any entrenched protection against racial discrimination in the federal Constitution and that [certain provisions] of the Constitution in themselves raise issues of racial discrimination." [United Nations Committee on the Elimination of Racial Discrimination (2010)]. On some occasions, the views of the monitoring bodies have been inconclusive. For instance, Mr. Hagan, an Australian Aborigine, complained to the Committee on the Elimination of Racial Discrimination of the refusal by trustees of a sports ground to remove the term 'Nigger' from the E.S. 'Nigger' Brown Stand located at the ground. The Stand's name was based on the footballer Brown's nickname from the 1950s and 1960s. Although the Committee decided that "that use and maintenance of the offending term can at the present time be considered offensive and insulting, even if for an extended period it may not have necessarily been so regarded," it stopped short of concluding that there had been a breach of Articles 2 and 5 of the *International Convention on the Elimination of All Forms of Racial Discrimination 1965* CERD/C/62/D/26/2002, 14 April 2003. In commenting on its interpretative approach to the *Convention*, the Committee commented that the *Convention* is a "living instrument" which must be interpreted and applied by taking into account the circumstances of contemporary society. This decision was described as "curiously ambiguous" by one human rights commentator [Joseph]. In other instances, however, and despite what might be perceived as an unsuccessful human rights violation complaint, concrete Australian governmental remedial action has occurred. For example, the Human Rights Committee published its view in 1996 concerning a communication it had received from X, an Australian Aboriginal man who was a member of the Arrente people. X was a party in court proceedings with his former wife, a non-Aboriginal woman, concerning the division of matrimonial property and custody of the children. In order to protect the "best interests" of the children, the court excluded evidence of the children's Aboriginal heritage, the effect on Aboriginal peoples of their having been raised as 'whites' under Australia's assimilated policies, and the manner in which Australian Aboriginal children are raised and cared for in an extended family situation. X complained to the Human Rights Committee that the exclusion of this evidence violated his right to a fair hearing before the court which is guaranteed by Article 14(1) of the *International Covenant on Civil and Political Rights 1966*. X also complained that the court excluded evidence of his concerns to ensure that his children be educated in Aboriginal religious and moral customs, thereby denying him the right to manifest his beliefs which is protected by Article 18(1) of the *ICCPR 1966*. Finally, X complained that the court had insisted on a full explanation of his initiation ceremony, thereby making public sacred knowledge of the Arrente people which violated his right to enjoy his culture and practise his religion under Article 27 of the *ICCPR 1966*. As is frequently the case, the Human Rights Committee ruled X's communication inadmissible on the ground that he had not fully exhausted all Australian domestic remedies. Nonetheless, the concerns raised by X resulted in amendments to the Australian *Family Law Act 1975* (Cth) such that the Family Court is now required to consider the child's need to maintain a connection with Aboriginal lifestyle, culture and traditions when deciding the best interests of a child [McBeth, Nolan and Rice].

With the adoption in 2007 of the United Nations *Declaration on the Rights of Indigenous Peoples*, it is to be expected that UN Member States such as Australia will come under increasing scrutiny by UN monitoring bodies such as the Human Rights Committee and the Committee on the Elimination of Racial Discrimination. *UNDRIP* will effectively become a benchmark to measure how effectively Aboriginal peoples' human rights are being realized. This is envisaged in *UNDRIP* itself, Article 42 of which states that "[t]he United Nations, its bodies, including the Permanent Forum on Indigenous Issues, and specialised agencies, including at the country level, and States shall promote respect for and full application of the provisions of this Declaration and follow up the effectiveness of this Declaration." This has been reinforced by the Special Rapporteur on the Rights of Indigenous Peoples who recommended in his report on his mission to Australia that "[t]he Commonwealth and State governments should review all legislation, policies and programmes that affect Aboriginal and Torres Strait Islanders, in light of the Declaration" [Amaya (2010)].

CONCLUSION

As Professor Mick Dodson observes, "[t]he value of human rights is not in their existence; it is in their implementation" [Dodson]. Human rights have transformative qualities in the sense that they provide a minimum and objective benchmark or series of key performance indicators (KPIs) against which the performance of governments can be assessed. Human rights norms and standards can oversee the development of law reform, policy-making and programme implementation. As the Aboriginal and Torres Strait Islander Social Justice Commissioner of the Australian Human Rights Commission has eloquently remarked [Gooda (2011)]:

> [T]he [United Nations] Declaration [on the Rights of Indigenous Peoples] can be seen as a remedial instrument, designed to rectify a history of failings when it comes to protecting the rights of Indigenous peoples...The value of human rights is that they create a clear path to address disadvantage. The human rights standards contained in the Declaration offer practical guidance in developing responses to the challenges confronting Aboriginal and Torres Strait Islander peoples and communities in Australia.

Other instruments besides *UNDRIP* prescribe relevant and meaningful standards in this field; for instance, in the area of development, the United Nations Development Group (UNDG) has produced *Guidelines on Indigenous Peoples' Issues* to assist UN Member States in integrating issues relevant to Indigenous peoples into their policies and programmes [United Nations Development Group]. Implementing the *desiderata* of *UNDRIP* and the *Guidelines* will assist Indigenous peoples generally, and Aboriginal and Torres Strait Islander peoples in particular, in assuming greater control and self-determination in matters which are most important to them. Indigenous peoples' right to participate in decision-making and right to be consulted by government, as envisaged by Articles 18 and 19 of *UNDRIP*, can facilitate a partnership approach to law reform and programme and policy development and community control over Indigenous internal affairs which is an expression of self-determination [Anaya (2004)]. And more generally, to achieve formal and substantive equality, "the structures of society must be reorientated to account for and be guided by the voices, aspirations and choices of Aboriginal and Torres Strait Islander peoples." [Gooda (2011)].

If United Nations history repeats itself, in relation to the eventual transformation of aspirational declarations into legally binding international conventions in the fields of the human rights of children, women, persons with disabilities, and racial discrimination, the *Declaration on the Rights of Indigenous Persons* will eventually form the basis of a United Nations-sponsored multilateral treaty entailing *pacta sunt servanda* legal obligations: *Vienna Convention on the Law of Treaties 1969*, Article 26 of which states "Every treaty in force is binding upon the parties to it and must be performed by them in good faith." This will entail the full panoply of enforcement machinery, presumably through the creation of a Committee on the Rights of Indigenous Peoples. Until then, however, States will be guided by the aspirational *UNDRIP* principles and held accountable for their effective realization by the various UN monitoring mechanisms discussed in this chapter. For the time being, at least, ATSI peoples will have significant political and strategic leverage in the form of the *UNDRIP* in advocating their case for law and policy reforms within Australia to redress historical disadvantage.

REFERENCES

Anaya, J. (2004). *Indigenous Peoples in International Law* (2nd ed.) Chapter 3. Oxford: Oxford University Press.

Anaya, J. & Williams, R. A. (2001). The Protection of Indigenous Peoples' Rights over Lands and Natural Resources under the Inter-American Human Rights System. *Harvard Law Journal of Human Rights*, *14*, 33-86.

Anaya, J. *Report of the Special Rapporteur on the Situation of Human Rights and Fundamental Freedoms, Addendum: The Situation of Indigenous Peoples in Australia*, UN Doc A/HRC/15/37/Add.4 (2010) [74]-[75], Appendix B.

Australian Human Rights and Equal Opportunity Commission. (1997). Bringing them Home: Report of the National Inquiry into the Separation of Aboriginal and Torres Strait Islander Children from Their Families

Australian Law Reform Commission. (1986). The Recognition of Aboriginal Customary Laws, Report No 31 (Canberra: AGPS).

Carino, Joji. (2010). Poverty and Wellbeing. In Secretariat of the United Nations Permanent Forum on Indigenous Issues, *State of the World's Indigenous Peoples*, UN Doc ST/ESA/328, 13-51.

Cobo, José. & Martinez, R. Special Rapporteur of the Sub-Commission on Prevention of the Problem of Discrimination Against Indigenous Populations, *Study of the Problem of Discrimination Against Indigenous Populations*, Vols *1-5*, UN DOCs E/CN.4/Sub.2/1986/7, E/CN.4/Sub.2/1986/7/add1, E/CN.4/Sub.2/1986/7/add2, E/CN.4/ Sub.2/-1986/7/add3, E/CN.4/Sub.2/1986/7/add4, (1981-1983 reprinted in 1986) (The Cobo Study).

Commonwealth of Australia, *Parliamentary Debates*, House of Representatives (13 February 2008) 171 (The Hon Kevin Rudd, MP, Prime Minister).

Council for Aboriginal Reconciliation, Recommendation, (2000). *Reconciliation: Australia's Challenge* 3. Retrieved from <http://www.austlii.edu.au/au/other/IndigLRes/car/2000/ 16/text10.htm>.

Davis, M. (2008). Indigenous Struggles in Standard-Setting: The United Nations Declaration on the Rights of Indigenous Peoples. *Melbourne Journal of International Law*, *9*(2), 439-471.

Dodson, M. (2010). Foreword. In Amnesty International Australia, *United Nations Declaration on the Rights of Indigenous Peoples*, GA Resolution 61/295 (Annex), UN Doc A/RES/61/295.

Gooda, M. (2011). Aboriginal and Torres Strait Islander Social Justice Commissioner, *Social Justice Report 2011*, Australian Human Rights Commission, 113-114.

Gooda, M. (2013). Human Rights and Australia's Indigenous Peoples. In Gerber, P., and Castan, M., (eds) *Contemporary Perspectives on Human Rights Law in Australia*, 300-331. Thomson Reuters.

International Law Association. (2010). Rights of Indigenous Peoples Committee. *The Rights of Indigenous Peoples*: Interim Report, Report to the Hague Conference, 7-8.

Joseph, S. (2003). UN Human Rights Treaty Bodies: Recent Decisions. *Human Rights Law Review*, *3*(2), 291-300.

Korff, J. (2015). *Australian Aboriginal history timeline*. Retrieved 6 November 2015, from <http://www.creativespirits.info/aboriginalculture/-history/Australian-aboriginal-history-timeline#axzz3m4JoFwiA>.

Macklin, J. (2009). Federal Government Formally Endorses the Declaration on the Rights of Indigenous Peoples. *Indigenous Law Bulletin*, *7*(11), 6-8.

McBeth, A., Nolan, J. & Rice, S. (2011). *The International Law of Human Rights*, 451-472. Oxford: Oxford University Press.

Minister for Families, Community Services and Indigenous Affairs, *National Emergency Response to Protect Children in the NT*, Media Release (21 June 2007) (The Hon Mal Brough MP).

Northern Territory Board of Inquiry into the Protection of Aboriginal Children from Sexual Abuse, (2007). Ampe Akelyernemane Meke Makarle "Little Children are Sacred" Report. Retrieved from <http://www.inquirysaac.nt.- gov.au/pdf/bipacsa_final_report.pdf>.

Northern Territory Emergency Response Review Board, Attorney-General's Department, (2008). *Report of the Northern Territory Review Board, 9*. Retrieved from <http://www.nterreview.gov.au/docs/report_nter_-review/default.htm>.

Office of the High Commissioner for Human Rights. (2010). *Practical Implications of a Change in the Mandate of the Voluntary Fund for Indigenous Populations*, 15th sess, Human Rights Council, A/HRC/15/38.

Office of the High Commissioner for Human Rights, (2011). *Universal Periodic Review – Australia*. Retrieved from <http://www.ohchr.org/EN/HRBodies/UPR/Pages/AUSession10.aspx>.

Office of the High Commissioner for Human Rights, *Standing Invitations*. Retrieved from <http://www.ohchr.org/EN/HRBodies/SP/Pages/Invita-tions.aspx>.

Office of the High Commissioner for Human Rights, *Universal Periodic Review*. Retrieved from <http://www.ohchr.org/en/hrbodies/upr/pages/-uprmain.aspx>.

Pearson, N. (2012). Aboriginal Referendum a Test of National Maturity. Cited in Report of the Expert Panel. *Recognising Aboriginal and Torres Strait Islander Peoples in the Constitution* (January).

Preston, J., Vinding, D. & Garcia-Alix, L. (2007). The UN Special Rapporteur: Indigenous Peoples' Rights: Experiences and Challenges (Copenhagen: International Working Group for Indigenous Affairs).

Report of the Expert Panel. *Recognising Aboriginal and Torres Strait Islander Peoples in the Constitution* (January 2012) Chapter 1.

Sawyer, G. (1966). The Australian Constitution and the Australian Aboriginal. *Federal Law Review*, *2*, 17-36.

United Nations, Committee for the Elimination of Racial Discrimination, *General Recommendation No 23: Indigenous Peoples*, 51st sess, UN Doc A/52/18 (18 August 1997) annex V.

United Nations, Committee for the Elimination of Racial Discrimination, (2009). *General Recommendation No 32: The meaning and scope of special measures in the International Convention on the Elimination of Racial Discrimination*, CERD/C/GC/32 (24 September 2009).

United Nations, Committee on Economic, Social and Cultural Rights, *Concluding Observations of the Committee on Economic, Social and Cultural Rights: Australia*, UN Doc E/C.12/AUS/CO/4 (2009) [15].

United Nations, Committee on Economic, Social and Cultural Rights, *General Comment No 21: Right of Everyone to Take Part in Cultural Life*, E/C.12/GC/21 (21 December 2009) paras 13, 36.

United Nations, Committee on the Elimination of Racial Discrimination, *Concluding Observations of the Committee on the Elimination of Racial Discrimination: Australia*, UN Doc CERD/C/AUS/CO/15-17 (2010) [10].

United Nations, Committee on the Elimination of Racial Discrimination, *Concluding Observations of the Committee on the Elimination of Racial Discrimination*, UN Doc CERD/C/AUS/CO/14 (2005) [16].

United Nations, Committee on the Elimination of Racial Discrimination, *General Recommendation No 8: Identification with a Particular Racial or Ethnic Group*, UN Doc A/45/18 (22 August 1990).

United Nations, *Convention on Biological Diversity*, 5 June 1992 (entered into force 29 December 1993), 1760 UNTS 79.

United Nations, *Declaration on the Rights of Indigenous Peoples*, GA Res 61/295, UN GAOR, 61st sess, 107th plen mtg, UN Doc A/RES/61/295 (13 September 2007).

United Nations, Development Group, *Guidelines on Indigenous Peoples' Issues*, February, 2008. Retrieved from <http://www.2.ohcr.org/english/-issues/indigenous/docs/guidelines.pdf>.

United Nations, Expert Mechanism Advice No 1. (2009). on the Right of Indigenous Peoples to Education. Annexed to the *Study on Lessons Learned and Challenges to Achieve the Implementation of the Right of Indigenous Peoples to Education*, UN Doc A/HRC/12/33 (2009).

United Nations, Expert Mechanism on the Rights on Indigenous Peoples, *Final Report of the Study on Indigenous Peoples and the Right to Participate in Decision-making*, UN Doc A/HRC/18/42 (2011) [20]-[21], [28], Annex [31].

United Nations, General Assembly, *International Covenant on Economic, Social and Cultural Rights 1966*, 993 UNTS 3 (16 December 1966).

United Nations, Human Rights Committee, *Concluding Observations of the Human Rights Committee: Australia*, UN Doc CERD/C/AUS/CO/15-17 (2009).

United Nations, *International Convention on the Elimination of All Forms of Racial Discrimination* 660 UNTS 195 Adopted and opened for signature by UN General Assembly resolution 2106 A(XX) of 21 of December 1965 (entry into force 4 January 1969).

United Nations, *International Covenant on Civil and Political Rights*, opened for signature 16 December 1966, 999 UNTS 171 (entered into force 23 March 1976).

United Nations, Permanent Forum on Indigenous Issues, (2011). *Report on the tenth session*, UN Doc E/C.19/2011/14 [47].

United Nations, Permanent Forum on Indigenous Issues, (2012). *Proposed Organization of Work*, 11th session, UN Doc E/C.19/2012/L.1.

United Nations, Permanent Forum on Indigenous Issues. (2006). *Factsheet: Who are Indigenous Peoples?*. Retrieved from: <http://www.un.org/esa/-socdev/unpfii/documents/5session_factsheet1.pdf>.

United Nations, Report of the Secretary-General: *Mid-Term Assessment of the Progress made in the Achievement of the Goal and Objectives of the Second International Decade of the World's Indigenous People*, UN Doc A/65/166 (23 July 2010).

United Nations, *Universal Declaration of Human Rights 1948*, UN General Assembly, 10 December 1948, 217A(111).

In: International Human Rights and Justice
Editor: Doug Hodgson

ISBN: 978-1-63484-709-4

Chapter 5

Quality of Interpretation in Interrogations of Detained Persons during the Pre-Trial Stage of Criminal Investigations as a Concern under Article 5(2) of the European Convention on Human Rights

Stefan Kirchner [*]
University Lecturer for Fundamental and Human Rights,
University of Lapland, Faculty of Law, Rovaniemi, Finland;
Senior Researcher, Vytautas Magnus University, Faculty of Law,
Kaunas, Lithuania

Abstract

Interpreting plays a key role in criminal proceedings involving defendants who do not speak or understand the language used by the authorities as well as for the realization of procedural human rights, which are protected, for example, under Articles 5 and 6 of the *European Convention on Human Rights* (ECHR). Often, though, the pool of effectively available interpreters is limited. While often confused by outsiders, translation and interpretation are very different professions. This chapter is only concerned with the work of interpreters. In this chapter, the minimum requirements imposed by Article 5(2) ECHR on interpreters in the pre-court stage of criminal cases will be outlined with special regard to the rights of persons who have already been detained. This norm provides a person who has been arrested with the right to be informed about the reasons of the arrest and of any charges. This has to be done in a way which enables that person to understand his or her situation.

Keywords: language, detention, interpretation, criminal law, European Convention on Human Rights, police, crime

---

[*] Corresponding author: stefan.kirchner@crosslegal.com.

1. Equality of Arms in Criminal Proceedings

The idea of an "equality of arms"[18] [Janis, Kay & Bradley p. 792; Leach pp. 256 *et seq.*] between the parties to a legal dispute in court is an essential element of a fair trial and thus it is also an important aspect of the right to a fair trial under Article 6 of the *European Convention on Human Rights*[19] (ECHR). It has been said that "the nature of legal proceedings precludes a perfect equality between the parties." [Janis, Kay & Bradley p. 792] This is especially true when it comes to criminal law, although some commentators already consider the presumption of innocence to amount to "a significant disadvantage" [Janis, Kay & Bradley p. 792] for the state. This harsh assessment seems to go too far as the use of presumptions in private law is fundamentally different from the use of presumptions in criminal law. Private law can afford to start from a neutral position but in criminal proceedings, in particular in cases in which the defendant has been arrested and is in the physical power of the state prior to a judgment, there is no neutrality. The defendant, by virtue of being held by the state, is already in a disadvantaged position. Legal guarantees, such as the right to a lawyer[20] or the presumption of innocence[21] only serve to provide some compensation for the defendant in light of his or her already disadvantaged position vis-à-vis the state. The use of presumptions does not have to lead to a violation of the right to a fair trial[22] [Janis, Kay & Bradley p. 792] but the presumption of innocence in criminal proceedings has a fundamentally different function than the use of presumptions in civil cases because the relationship between plaintiff and defendant in private law cases can hardly be seen as on *par* with the relationship between the state and the defendant in a criminal case.

To determine whether a trial has been sufficiently fair to pass the test of Article 6 ECHR, it is necessary to look at the proceedings as a whole and the same also applies to the question of the equality of arms, which is an element of the fairness of a trial. According to Janis, Kay and Bradley, who refer to the case of *Bernard v. France*,[23] "[t]he [ECtHR]]'s examination of the presence or absence of equality of arms is not to be directed at a particular feature of procedure in isolation." [Janis, Kay & Bradley p. 798] But while the overall situation in the proceedings has to be understood properly, this should not be extended so far as to have the effect that a single aspect, which can have an overwhelming effect on the procedure as a whole, would be ignored only because it is the only issue raised by the applicant (keeping in mind that in practice the Court will hardly have the time to investigate on its own but will have to work with the parties' respective submissions).

---

[18] See European Court of Human Rights, *Dombo Beheer B.V. v. Netherlands*, Application No. 14448/88, Judgment of 27 October 1993, para. 33.

[19] *Convention for the Protection of Human Rights and Fundamental Freedoms 1950* [*European Convention on Human Rights* (ECHR)], European Treaty Series No. 5, available online at http://www.echr.coe.int/Documents/Convention_ENG.pdf.

[20] Article 6 (3) (c) ECHR.

[21] Article 6 (2) ECHR.

[22] See European Court of Human Rights, *Salabiaku v. France*, Application No. 10519/83, Judgment of 7 October 1988, para.28.

[23] European Court of Human Rights, *Bernard v. France*, Application No. 159/1996/778/979, Judgment of 23 April 1998.

2. Competencies and Interests of Interpreters

The term 'interpreter' is used very widely here and includes everybody who might engage in some sort of interpretation, i.e., certified and non-certified interpreters; the former including specifically trained and certified interpreters and legal interpreters, i.e., certified interpreters who also have some law-related training and work experience; the latter referring to everybody who provides interpretations but has no formal documentation to certify his or her skill level when it comes to language skills (for the purposes of this chapter, the term 'certified' refers to any form of formal recognition of interpretation skills). The latter group might also include law graduates, regardless of the profession they exercise, who have some relevant foreign language skills. This can include the suspect's attorney. Often, non-certified translators might have gained many years of experience but might have entered the system without much formal training. They can further be categorized based on their relationship to the authority in question. They might act on an ad hoc basis or it may be that they are already known to the court or other authority in question or that they might be freelancers working for the relevant authorities within a framework contract or even as employees of the authority.

The small number of certified interpreters poses a particularly severe problem if the language in question is not widely spoken. This problem is felt now in many parts of Europe as the number of, for example, Arabic-speaking people who recently migrated to Europe but who do not speak local languages has increased sharply in the course of the year 2015. Often, persons who act as interpreters in such situations are not trained translators but simply happen to speak the local official language and the language of the person concerned. It is to be hoped that they are known to the court or the local authorities so that those who have to make decisions based on their translation are able to assess if not their language skills then at least their reliability and trustworthiness. In the absence of professional legal translators, the right to a fair trial raises a number of questions. It has to be asked whether a state can actually fulfill its obligations under Article 5(2) ECHR by relying on persons who act as interpreters who are not certified or trained as interpreters, let alone legal interpreters.

Also, it has to be understood that the interpreter might have particular interests which follow from the association with the person who is appearing in court through the shared language. These interests of the interpreter can have their origins also in relationships or conflicts in a shared country of origin. This can lead to different interests, which can work in favor of, but also be detrimental to, the person who is charged with a crime.

Both judicial and executive authorities rely on non-professional translating agents who might be lacking not only formal legal training but also formal language training and who might have undisclosed interests which potentially undermine the fairness of the trial. As the lack of certified interpreters is likely to remain a substantial issue in many jurisdictions and because training new interpreters takes time, practical considerations will make it difficult for police, courts and other authorities in many places to access a sufficiently large pool of certified interpreters. European Union (EU) member states are under a legal obligation to ensure that interpreters are trained adequately. [Directive 2010/64/EU] In states which have ratified the ECHR but are not members of the EU, but also in EU member states which have not yet fully realized this obligation, this raises the question under which conditions the use of non-certified interpreters in the pre-trial stage of criminal proceedings can be compatible with the *European Convention on Human Rights*. At the pre-trial stage of criminal proceedings, this refers specifically to the obligations under Article 5(2) ECHR, according to which the state has to inform persons who have been arrested about the reasons for the arrest.

3. ARTICLE 5(2) ECHR

3.1. Fairness in Investigations

Indeed, the problem of fairness becomes relevant long before the defendant first sets foot into the courtroom. While the right to a fair trial under Article 6 ECHR has received a lot of attention from both the European Court of Human Rights and academic writers, the right protected by Article 5(2) ECHR appears to have been less interesting for academic writers so far. This poses a problem because such a (at least relative) lack of interest on the part of academic writers can directly affect the perception of legal practitioners. The right protected by Article 5(2) ECHR, though, protects a detained person at a very early stage. How he or she behaves, specifically, which information the detained person provides to the police or other authorities, can be decisive for future proceedings. But the norm is relevant also outside the context of any potential impact on future criminal proceedings: the right to personal freedom, which is protected by Article 5 ECHR, is one of the most fundamental human rights, not just in Europe but around the world. When physically holding a person, the state exercises power in the most direct way possible (with the exception of the death penalty). Knowing the reasons why somebody is being held and understanding any potential charges is an essential aspect of the right to physical freedom.

In protecting all detained persons, Article 5(2) ECHR also protects persons who have not (yet) been formally arrested [Reid p. 510] by the police but who have been detained otherwise, [Leach pp. 221 *et seq.*] e.g., in house arrest[24] or in the case of asylum seekers in transit areas.[25] Rather than referring only to criminal law approaches, the European Court of Human Rights has used the concept of autonomous interpretation [Letsas pp. 279-305] also with regard to the concept of 'arrest' within the specific meaning of Article 5(2) ECHR.[26] It has to be noted, though, that "[t]he degree of information [which the state is obliged to provide to the detained person] will also depend on the kind of arrest or detention." [Reid p. 511]

3.2. Wording of the Norm

The question this chapter seeks to answer is how the quality of translation services can affect the enjoyment of this right. That language matters in criminal law cases already follows from the wording of Article 5(2) ECHR, according to which "Everyone who is arrested shall be informed promptly, *in a language which he understands*, of the reasons for his arrest and

---

[24] See European Court of Human Rights, *Lavents v. Latvia*, Application No. 58442/00, Judgment of 28 November 2002.

[25] See European Court of Human Rights, *Amuur v France*, Application No. 19776/92, Judgment of 25 June 1996.

[26] European Court of Human Rights, *van der Leer v. Netherlands*, Application No. 11509/85, Judgment of 21 February 1990, paras. 27 *et seq.*

of any charge against him."[27] The term "any charge" also shows that there can be detentions which are compatible with the ECHR but which do not require any suspicion. [Reid p. 511]

3.3. Detainee's Capacity to Understand Charges Brought against One

Indeed, the interpretation of the obligation of states under Article 5(2) ECHR has been extended by the court to mean not only that "*a* language"[28] [Reid p. 511] understood by the arrestee is used but also that the terms used are actually understood by the suspect as a legal layman or –woman.[29] [Leach pp. 231 *et seq.*] In a case of, for example, a Russian-speaking suspect who is detained and interrogated in Germany, it is therefore not enough to provide an interpretation from German to Russian; the terminology used also has to take into account the capability of the suspect to understand the charges. The interpreter therefore not only has to understand both languages, including the legal terminology, but also has to assess the suspect's level of understanding not only of the destination language but also has to be able to use terminology which is legally and linguistically correct and is understood by the receiver. The person who has been deprived of his or her personal liberty has to be "told, in simple, non-technical language that he can understand, the essential legal and factual ground"[30] which led to the detention.

3.4. No Undue Delay

It was held by the European Court of Human Rights in *Fox, Campbell and Hartley v. United Kingdom* that this does not have to happen at the exact moment of the arrest,[31] [Leach p. 234; van Dijk, van Hoof & van Rijn p. 486] nor by the arresting police officer,[32] Already decided some years earlier, it had been held that a delay of less than 90 minutes between the arrest and the beginning of question did not amount to a violation of the *European Convention on Human Rights*.[33] [Reid p. 512] In any case, "no more than a few hours should elapse [between detention and information] save in exceptional circumstances such as the serious incapacity of the arrested person to comprehend the reasons that might have been given," although in the European Court's decision in *Lowry* a delay of 48 hours had been accepted as well.[34] Also, the potential "incapacity" [Reid p. 512] cannot include an inability to understand the language in question since it refers to "the reasons that […] have been given," [Reid p. 512] which refers to the information provided by the authorities, which in

[27] Article 5(2) ECHR, emphasis added.

[28] Emphasis added. This is also the view held by Christoph Grabenwarter, *Europäische Menschenrechtskonvention*, 3rd ed., C.H. Beck, Munich, 2008, p. 172.

[29] European Court of Human Rights, *Fox, Campbell and Hartley v. United Kingdom*, Applications Nos. 12244/86, 12245/86 and 12383/86, Judgment of 30 August 1990, para. 40; European Court of Human Rights, *HB v. Switzerland*, Application No. 26899/95, Judgment of 5 April 2001, para. 47.

[30] European Court of Human Rights, *Fox, Campbell and Hartley v. United Kingdom*, *supra* note 13, para. 40.

[31] *Ibid.*

[32] *Ibid.*

[33] European Court of Human Rights, *Murray v. United Kingdom*, Application No. 14310/88, Judgment of 28 October 1994, paras. 78 *et seq.*

[34] European Court of Human Rights, *Lowry v. Portugal*, Application No. 42296/98, Decision of 6 July 1999 (no paragraph numbering).

turn at least have to be in a language understood by the detained person. Even beyond that, the reference to "incapacity" [Reid p. 512] is questionable, as it places persons who might lack the mental capacity to understand the information at a distinct disadvantage. As the right to personal freedom, which is protected by Article 5(2) ECHR, is of a most fundamental and personal nature, such an interpretation risks opening the door to a discriminatory interpretation of the norm, which would be incompatible with the equal treatment clause contained in Article 14 ECHR.

Today's expectations – a quarter of a century after *Fox, Campbell and Hartley v. United Kingdom* was decided — can be different. While the arresting police officer, who is not required to give all [van Dijk, van Hoof & van Rijn p. 486] but at least some information, [van Dijk, van Hoof & van Rijn p. 486] cannot reasonably expected to speak every possible language (although it might not be too much to ask that he or she should be able to communicate sufficiently in English, local minority languages and, at least in areas, in the languages of neighboring countries – none of which can be taken for granted in many parts of Europe) and translating agents regardless of qualification might be used as long as the suspect understands what he or she is accused of,[35] the use of the word "promptly"[36] as referred to in Article 5(2) ECHR shows that the information in question indeed has to be provided "at the very moment of arrest or during interrogation within a few hours of the arrest." [Grabenwarter (2014) p. 86]

Peters observes that in practice this information is often only provided at the police station [Peters p. 97] and only requires the information to be provided prior to the first interrogation [Peters p. 97] as it would not be possible to define "promptly" *in abstracto.* [Peters p. 97] The case law of the European Court of Human Rights has been very generous to the police forces. [van Dijk, van Hoff & van Rijn p. 486] This development is questionable as it seems hardly compatible with the ordinary meaning of the word "promptly." In the interpretation of international treaties, as is also evidenced by Article 3(1) of the *Vienna Convention on the Law of Treaties 1969*,[37] the "ordinary meaning"[38] of words has to be given precedence. If "promptly"[39] is understood to mean 'without undue delay,' then the detaining authority has to make use of all means at its disposal. That will usually mean having to ensure the presence of an interpreter at short notice. The information which has to be provided to comply with the obligation under Article 5(2) ECHR does not have to be complete but only "in general terms," [Rainey, Wicks & Ovey p. 240] although "a bare indication of the legal basis for an arrest could not, on its own, be sufficient." [Rainey, Wicks & Ovey p. 241] Nor does the information required under Article 5(2) ECHR have to be in writing [Harris, O'Boyle, Bates & Buckley p. 334] as authorities can make use of texts and translations rather than interpretations, as well.

---

[35] It has to be kept in mind that many legal systems in states which are parties to the *European Convention on Human Rights* will require the presence of an attorney, or at least the possibility of the presence of an attorney, at the interrogation. This, too, however, cannot be taken for granted and suspects' perception of their rights under domestic law might often be more influenced by mass media perceptions than by the *lex lata*. The ECHR, though, at times falls short of standards with which even a casual viewer of US television shows will be familiar with, such as the *Miranda* rule.

[36] Article 5(2) ECHR.

[37] *Vienna Convention on the Law of Treaties 1969* (VCLT), 1155 United Nations Treaty Series I 18232, available online at https://treaties.

[38] Article 31 (1) VCLT.

[39] Article 5(2) ECHR.

The use of online services, such as *Google Translate*, is, however, problematic with regard to data protection rules as everything which is entered into the search field is sent to *Google*'s server. If a local police force were to use *Google Translate* to write the charge into the search field and display to the suspect the translation provided by *Google*, the information would have been made available to *Google*. While the ubiquity of services such as *Google Translate*, e.g., on mobile phones, would make this approach practical, police officers would risk running afoul of privacy rights and data protection laws if they were to enter too much information. Translating simple terms such as "involuntary manslaughter" might be permissible in many legal systems; however, entering the facts of a case might hardly be compatible with data protection laws and privacy rights in many jurisdictions.

3.5 Ensuring Understanding

As already said, Article 5(2) ECHR refers not only to a language understood by the detainee but indeed requires the relevant authorities to use "simple, non technical language that can be easily understood."[40] This means that the authorities have to use a language which is understandable. It also means that any interpreter will have to do the same - to remain on a level of language usage which does not provide undue obstacles for the detained person. Especially when specific legal terms are used, it is crucial to ensure that the language used towards the detained person is not only easy to understand but also that it is accurate from a legal perspective. The latter aspect can be particularly challenging when legal concepts or phrases simply do not exist in the other legal system. As the interpreter has to take into account the receiver's ability to understand, legal interpretation at the pre-trial stage can require a set of skills which goes far beyond learning two or more languages.

4. Limited Demands of Article 5(2) ECHR

The demands imposed on the standard of interpretation at the pre-trial stage, though, are limited. The person who is being questioned has to understand the reasons for the detention, which essentially means that the events related to the detention and their connection to the fact of detention have to be clarified. The focus on the ability to understand also explains why the interpretation does not have to be to the mother tongue or first language of the detained person. Rather, any language understood by the detained person is sufficient.[41] If the detained person is represented by a third person, such as an attorney, the detaining state does not violate its obligations under Article 5(2) ECHR if the information is provided to that third person.[42]

[40] European Court of Human Rights, *Musaev v. Turkey*, Application No. 72754/11, Judgment of 21 October 2014, para. 34.

[41] European Court of Human Rights, *Parlanti v Germany*, Application No. 45097/04, Decision of 26 May 2005, Part "The Law," para. 2.

[42] K. Reid *A Practitioner's Guide to the European Convention on Human Rights* (3rd ed.). Sweet & Maxwell, London, p. 511, with reference to European Court of Human Rights, *Saadi v. United Kingdom*, Application No. 13229/03, Judgment of 29 January 2008, para. 53, but also highlighting that the ECtHR seems to have been less clear about this in para. 55 of the same judgment.

This opens the door to interpretation services by non-certified interpreters. Indeed, the relatively low standard imposed by Article 5(2) ECHR makes it relatively - when compared to the requirements under Article 6 ECHR - easy to comply with the *European Convention on Human Rights* also in the absence of certified interpreters.

At this early stage of the proceedings, when a suspect has already been detained but not yet formally charged, the interpreter does not have to explain legal concepts in much detail and the detained person's mother tongue does not have to be used (which in many European states will mean that only a translation to English will be necessary, if the detained person understands this language). Often compliance with Article 5(2) ECHR can be achieved through the presence of an attorney. If the attorney is capable of communicating with his or her client, it seems likely that the attorney will be able to transmit the required information. In cases where the detained person is so represented, the state's obligation only extends to transmitting the relevant information to the attorney. To this extent, the obligation under Article 5(2) ECHR should, at least in theory, be easy to comply with for the state.[43]

The situation becomes more problematic in the case of immigrants who have not yet mastered the language of the host country but who are accompanied by children who have already done so. While the state can rely on an attorney to transmit such information correctly, the state cannot necessarily rely on minors who speak the national language as a foreign language in order to free itself from its legal obligations under the *European Convention on Human Rights*. While Article 5(2) ECHR does not provide for a right to have an attorney present, [Reid p. 512] and while access to medical staff and to relatives seems to be protected under Article 5, [Reid p. 513] the term "representative" [Reid p. 511] should therefore be interpreted narrowly to a person freely chosen by the detained person. This freedom of choice is not realized if there is only, for example, a member of the detainee's own family who might be able to interpret.

Conclusion

Involving non-certified interpreters is therefore not *per se* incompatible with the obligations of states under Article 5(2) ECHR. Upholding minimum standards of informing persons who have been detained about the reasons for the detention will, however, require effective interpretation. The question whether Article 5(2) ECHR has been complied with therefore cannot be answered *in abstracto* but only based on the concrete circumstances of every specific case. Article 5(2) ECHR is notable — and challenging — because it requires the state to understand the capability of the detained person to understand the explanation provided to him or her and to act accordingly. The ability of the state to make use of third persons who are either neutral, closer to the authorities, or are working for, or are potentially even related, to the detained person only adds another layer of complexity. The obligation of the state is to "ensure"[44] the rights of the detained person. Article 5(2) ECHR requires less from the state than Article 6 (3) (a) ECHR [Grabenwarter (2014) p. 85] and the former norm provides the authorities with a significant level of flexibility but the use of this flexibility also

[43] As the suspect has to raise a potential violation of Article 5(2) ECHR already in domestic proceedings (European Court of Human Rights, *Parlanti v. Germany*, *supra* note 48, Part "The Law," para. 2), the state is fairly well protected against claims under Article 5(2) ECHR also in procedural terms.

[44] Article 1 ECHR.

forces the state to engage in a sufficient level of supervision. Non-certified interpreters are a permissible option under Article 5(2) ECHR but the state carries the risk of any shortcomings of the interpretation. Any interpretation has to be "meticul[ous] and precis[e]." [Harris, O'Boyle, Bates & Buckley p. 335]

Case Law

European Court of Human Rights, *Amuur v France*, Application No. 19776/92, Judgment of 25 June 1996.

European Court of Human Rights, *Bernard v. France*, Application No. 159/1996/778/979, Judgment of 23 April 1998.

European Court of Human Rights, *Dombo Beheer B.V. v. Netherlands*, Application No. 14448/88, Judgment of 27 October 1993.

European Court of Human Rights, *Fox, Campbell and Hartley v. United Kingdom*, Applications Nos. 12244/86, 12245/86 and 12383/86, Judgment of 30 August 1990.

European Court of Human Rights, *HB v. Switzerland*, Application No. 26899/95, Judgment of 5 April 2001.

European Court of Human Rights, *Lavents v. Latvia*, Application No. 58442/00, Judgment of 28 November 2002.

European Court of Human Rights, *Lowry v. Portugal*, Application No. 42296/98, Decision of 6 July 1999.

European Court of Human Rights, *Murray v. United Kingdom*, Application No. 14310/88, Judgment of 28 October 1994.

European Court of Human Rights, *Musaev v. Turkey*, Application No. 72754/11, Judgment of 21 October 2014.

European Court of Human Rights, *Parlanti v Germany*, Application No. 45097/04, Decision of 26 May 2005.

European Court of Human Rights, *Saadi v. United Kingdom*, Application No. 13229/03, Judgment of 29 January 2008.

European Court of Human Rights, *Salabiaku v. France*, Application No. 10519/83, Judgment of 7 October 1988.

European Court of Human Rights, *van der Leer v. Netherlands*, Application No. 11509/85, Judgment of 21 February 1990.

Other Texts

Convention for the Protection of Human Rights and Fundamental Freedoms 1950 [European Convention on Human Rights (ECHR)], European Treaty Series No. 5, available online at http://www.echr.coe.int/-Documents/Convention_ENG.pdf.

Directive 2010/64/EU of the European Parliament and the Council of 20 October 2010 on the right to interpretation and translation in criminal proceedings, Official Journal 2010 L 280/1, available online at http://eur-lex.europa.eu/LexUriServ/LexUriServ.do?uri=OJ:L:2010:280:0001:0007:en:PDF.

Vienna Convention on the Law of Treaties 1969 (VCLT), 1155 United Nations Treaty Series I 18232, available online at https://treaties.

REFERENCES

Grabenwarter, C. (2008). *Europäische Menschenrechtskonvention* (3rd ed.). C.H. Beck, Munich.

Grabenwarter, C. (2014). *European Convention on Human Rights, Commentary* (1st ed.). C.H. Beck, Munich.

Harris, D. J., O'Boyle, M., Bates, E. P. & Buckley, C. M. (2014). *Law of the European Convention on Human Rights* (3rd ed.). Oxford University Press, Oxford.

Janis, M. W., Kay, R. S. & Bradley, A. W. (2008). *European Human Rights Law – Text and Materials* (3rd ed.). Oxford University Press, Oxford.

Leach, P. (2005). *Taking a Case to the European Court of Human Rights* (2nd ed.). Oxford University Press, Oxford.

Letsas, G. (2004). The Truth in Autonomous Concepts: How to Interpret the ECHR. *European Journal of International Law, 15*, 279-305, available online at http://www.ejil.org/pdfs/15/2/351.pdf.

Peters, A. (2003). *Einführung in die Europäische Menschenrechtskonvention* (1st ed.). C.H. Beck, Munich.

Rainey, B., Wicks, E. & Ovey, C. (2014). *The European Convention on Human Rights* (6th ed.). Oxford University Press, Oxford.

Reid, K. (2008). *A Practitioner's Guide to the European Convention on Human Rights* (3rd ed.). Sweet & Maxwell, London.

van Dijk, P., van Hoof, F., van Rijn, A. & Zwaak, L. (2006). *Theory and Practice of the European Convention on Human Rights* (4th ed.). Intersentia, Antwerp.

In: International Human Rights and Justice
Editor: Doug Hodgson

ISBN: 978-1-63484-709-4

Chapter 6

The Reindeer Herding Right in Norway and Sweden as a Protected Right under the European Convention on Human Rights

Stefan Kirchner *

Rechtsanwalt (Attorney, admitted to the bar in Germany), CrossLegal, Antrifttal, Germany,
University Lecturer for Fundamental and Human Rights, with Special Focus on Indigenous Rights, University of Lapland, Rovaniemi, Finland,
Senior Researcher for Minorities,
Migration and Cultural Rights in the Nordic and Baltic States,
Vytautas Magnus University, Kaunas, Lithuania

Abstract

Reindeer herding is an important source of indigenous livelihood across the global North and in particular among the indigenous Sámi people. Sápmi, the homeland of the Sámi people, is currently administered by Norway, Sweden, Finland and Russia. In Norway and Sweden, the right to herd reindeer is limited to indigenous persons. The legal nature of this right is still the object of debate from multiple perspectives. While the European Court of Human Rights in Strasbourg has only rarely had the opportunity to deal with questions concerning the human rights of indigenous peoples, the right to herd reindeer is protected under the European Convention on Human Rights. In this chapter, it is shown, using case law from different international human rights bodies, how indigenous peoples have used international human rights litigation to defend and define their rights. While the European Court of Human Rights has played a relatively minor role in the development of indigenous rights in international law, especially when compared to the Human Rights Committee or the Inter-American human rights bodies, it does indeed have a role in protecting the indigenous right to reindeer herding in Sápmi.

---

* Corresponding author: Email: stefan.kirchner@crosslegal.com.

Keywords: reindeer herding, property rights, indigenous rights, European Convention on Human Rights, European Court of Human Rights

Reindeer herding is an important source of indigenous livelihood across the global North and in particular among the indigenous Sámi people. Today the Sámi homeland is administered by Norway, Sweden, Finland and Russia. In Norway and Sweden, the right to herd reindeer is limited to indigenous persons. The legal nature of this right is still the object of debate from multiple perspectives. In this short commentary the question will be addressed if the reindeer herding right in Norway and Sweden is protected as a property right under the *European Convention on Human Rights* (ECHR).[45]

In the *Skattefjäll* case[46] it was held as early as 1981 that the reindeer herding right is a property right. Up to this date, the European Court of Human Rights did not have the opportunity to deal with the same issue in the context of Article 1 of *Protocol 1 to the European Convention on Human Rights*.[47] Article 1 protects the peaceful enjoyment of possessions:

> *"Every natural or legal person is entitled to the peaceful enjoyment of his possessions. No one shall be deprived of his possessions except in the public interest and subject to the conditions provided for by law and by the general principles of international law. The preceding provisions shall not, however, in any way impair the right of a State to enforce such laws as it deems necessary to control the use of property in accordance with the general interest or to secure the payment of taxes or other contributions or penalties."*

Therefore the norm is not restricted to property, although it is widely accepted that property is protected under the norm. The material scope of Article 1 of *Protocol 1* is fairly wide and protects a whole range of (but not all) economic and business interests. Protection under that norm, however, does not mean that the holder of the right has property rights.

While there have been some cases before the European Court of Human Rights related to indigenous rights[48] and despite the fact that indigenous Sámi litigants have been trailblazers when it comes to using international human rights law to protect indigenous rights (for example in cases such as *Kitok v. Sweden*,[49] *I. Länsman and others v. Finland*[50] and *J. E.*

[45] Convention for the Protection of Human Rights and Fundamental Freedoms [European Convention on Human Rights], 4 November 1950, European Treaty Series No. 5, <http://conventions.coe.int/treaty/en/Treaties/Html/005.htm> (last visited 15 June 2015).

[46] Högstä domstolen [Supreme Court of Sweden], Skattefjällsmålet (1981), Nytt juridiskt arkiv 108, 1.

[47] Protocol I to the Convention for the Protection of Human Rights and Fundamental Freedoms, 20 March 1952, European Treaty Series No. 9, <http://conventions.coe.int/treaty/en/Treaties/Html/009.htm> (last visited 15 June 2015).

[48] For an overview of the case law of the European Court of Human Rights with regard to indigenous rights see T. Koivurova (2011), Jurisprudence of the European Court of Human Rights Regarding Indigenous Peoples: Retrospect and Prospects, International Journal on Minority and Group Rights, 18, 1-37.

[49] Human Rights Committee, Ivan Kitok v. Sweden, Communication No. 197/1985, CCPR/C/33/D/197/1985 (1988), 27 July 1988, <http://www1.umn.edu/humanrts/undocs/197-1985. html> (last visited 15 June 2015).

[50] Human Rights Committee, Ilmari Länsman et al. v. Finland, Communication No. 511/1992, U.N. Doc. CCPR/C/52/D/511/1992 (1994), 8 November 1994, <http://www1.umn.edu/humanrts/undocs/html/vws511.htm> (last visited 15 June 2015).

Länsman and others v. Finland[51]), the same cannot necessarily be said about litigation before the European Court of Human Rights, although there have been some cases.

But for example in *Handölsdalen Saami Village and others v. Sweden*[52] the applicants emphasized the right to a fair trial under Article 6 (1) *ECHR*,[53] which reads as follows:

> *"In the determination of his civil rights and obligations or of any criminal charge against him, everyone is entitled to a fair and public hearing within a reasonable time by an independent and impartial tribunal established by law. Judgment shall be pronounced publicly but the press and public may be excluded from all or part of the trial in the interests of morals, public order or national security in a democratic society, where the interests of juveniles or the protection of the private life of the parties so require, or to the extent strictly necessary in the opinion of the court in special circumstances where publicity would prejudice the interests of justice."*

In the case of *G. and E. v. Norway* reindeer herding was seen through the lens of Article 8 (1) *ECHR*,[54]

> *"Everyone has the right to respect for his private and family life, his home and his correspondence."*

This approach essentially treats indigenous ways of life just like any other lifestyle choice, in light of the international legal developments in the years since the latter case has been decided, such as the adoption of the *Indigenous and Tribal Peoples Convention*, commonly referred to as the *International Labour Organization Convention No. 169*[55] and of the *United Nations Declaration on the Rights of Indigenous Peoples*[56] (UNDRIP).

The reindeer herding right is a land use right which is neither identical to, nor dependent on having, property. But Article 1 of *Protocol 1 to the ECHR* does not only protect property but the "peaceful enjoyment of possessions."

In *G. and E. v. Norway,* the applicants' claim based on Article 1 of *Protocol 1 to the ECHR* was rejected as the applicants had failed to "substantiate[…] that they have any property rights or claims."[57] Notably, the Commission did not say that the applicants did not have rights, only that the applicants had not substantiated their claims, thereby leaving the door open to future applicants. Given the legal situation both under international law and under domestic laws of the Nordic countries, today it should be no problem to find reindeer

[51] Human Rights Committee, Jouni E. Länsman et al. v. Finland, Communication No. 671/1995, U.N. Doc. CCPR/C/58/D/671/1995 (1996), 14 March 1996, <http://www1.umn.edu/humanrts/undocs/html/VWS67158.htm> (last visited 15 June 2015).

[52] European Court of Human Rights, Handölsdalen Sami Village and others v. Sweden, Application No. 39013/04, Judgment of 30 March 2010, <http://hudoc.echr.coe.int/sites/eng/pages/search.aspx?i=001-97993> (last visited 15 June 2015).

[53] Ibid., paras. 48 et seq.

[54] European Commission of Human Rights, G. and E. v. Norway, Joined Applications No. 9278/81 and 9415/81, Decision of 3 October 1983, <http://hudoc.echr.coe.int/webservices/content/pdf/001-74157> (last visited 15 June 2015), p. 36.

[55] Indigenous and Tribal Peoples Convention, 27 June 1989, <http://www.ilo.org/dyn/normlex/en/f?p=NORMLEXPUB:12100:0::NO::P12100_ILO_CODE:C169> (last visited 15 June 2015).

[56] United Nations Declaration on the Rights of Indigenous Peoples, 13 September 2007, <http://www.un.org/esa/socdev/unpfii/documents/DRIPS_en.pdf> (last visited 15 June 2015).

[57] European Commission of Human Rights, G. and E. v. Norway, Joined Applications No. 9278/81 and 9415/81, Decision of 3 October 1983, <http://hudoc.echr.coe.int/webservices/content/pdf/001-74157> (last visited 15 June 2015), p. 36.

herding rights within the material scope of Article 1 of *Protocol 1 to the ECHR*. Indeed, from the perspective of human rights litigation it would be beneficial to do so because the right to a fair trial under Article 6 of the *ECHR* only applies to civil and criminal law, not to administrative law. For example on the domestic level, a legal fight against a permit issued to a mining company will remain within the realm of administrative law and thus exclude claims under Article 6 of the *ECHR*, but if reindeer herding is claimed and regarded as a right under either Article 8 of the *ECHR* or Article 1 of *Protocol 1 to the ECHR*, this opens the door to the possibility of later claims under Article 6 of the *ECHR* as well.

Over the last decades indigenous peoples around the world have used international law to their benefit and they have played an important role in the development of international law in this regard, in particular in the context of the adoption of the *United Nations Declaration on the Rights of Indigenous Peoples*. But there is an important difference between human rights activism, even for the creation of new norms in international law, and human rights litigation on the international level. The difference is that the former can be seen as an extension of politics while the latter is a distinct legal task. International human rights lawyers can play an important role in making sure that rights exist not only on paper but that these obligations are also understood and implemented effectively.

In: International Human Rights and Justice
Editor: Doug Hodgson

ISBN: 978-1-63484-709-4

Chapter 7

PROTOCOLS NO. 14 AND NO. 15: UNDERMINING THE PROTECTIVE MECHANISM OF THE EUROPEAN CONVENTION ON HUMAN RIGHTS

Gino J. Naldi[1,*] and Konstantinos D. Magliveras[2]
[1]Researcher in International Law and Human Rights.
[2]Department of Mediterranean Studies, University of the Aegean, Rhodes, Greece

ABSTRACT

For many years now the European Court of Human Rights has undergone various reforms in order to enable it to cope more efficiently and briskly with the large numbers of complaints. Protocols 14 and 15 to the *European Convention on Human Rights* amend certain procedures of that judicial body. However, aspects of these changes raise concerns that the protective machinery of the *European Convention on Human Rights* could be undermined. *Protocol 14* introduced, *inter alia*, a new, more exacting, admissibility requirement for individual applications which *Protocol 15*, not yet in force, seeks to make even stricter. *Protocol 15* further provides, *inter alia*, for greater prominence to be given to the principles of subsidiarity and the margin of appreciation and for a reduction in the time-limit within which an application must be made to the European Court of Human Rights. On balance these measures may result in a denial of justice. They have the potential to tilt the balance in favour of the respondent State and weaken the rights of applicants.

Keywords: European Convention on Human Rights, Protocol No. 14, Protocol No. 15, significant disadvantage, margin of appreciation, subsidiarity, time-limits

[*] Corresponding author: ginonaldi57@yahoo.co.uk.

INTRODUCTION

The European Court of Human Rights may be said to have become a victim of its own success (O'Boyle, 2008, pp. 1-4). The end of the Cold War, the collapse of the Soviet Union, and the democratisation of post-communist Eastern and Central Europe led to the expansion in the membership of the Council of Europe [CoE] from twenty-two Member States in 1989 to its current membership of forty-seven States (Sands & Klein, 2009, p. 163). In accordance with the terms of the *Vienna Declaration* adopted by the CoE on 9 October 1993 membership of the CoE was made contingent on accession to the *European Convention on Human Rights 1950* [ECHR or Convention] (ETS No. 5) and its Protocols, and acceptance of the jurisdiction of the control mechanisms, the European Commission of Human Rights and European Court of Human Rights, [Court] and the procedure of individual petition. The legacy of decades of Communist rule, with its arbitrary laws and pervasive abuses of human rights, and the systemic and structural flaws in these national legal systems, led to an exponential growth in the number of applications to the European protective organs which placed the monitoring machinery under severe pressure. In an attempt to deal with the ever-increasing workload of the control machinery, the CoE adopted *Protocol No. 11* [*Protocol 11*] in 1994 which radically transformed the then existing system (*Protocol No. 11 to the Convention for the Protection of Human Rights and Fundamental Freedoms*, restructuring the control machinery established thereby, ETS No. 155). The main changes effected by *Protocol 11* were the creation of a single court, doing away with the European Commission of Human Rights, and making the right of individual petition mandatory (Merrills & Robertson, 2001, pp. 297-302). Thus contracting parties to the ECHR no longer had the discretion whether to accept the right of individual petition, as is still the case with other regional human rights courts (Shaw, 2008, pp. 387, 394-395). However, *Protocol 11*, which entered into force only on 1 November 1998, did not have the desired effect and the number of applications continued to grow (Keller, Fischer & Kühne, 2010, pp. 1027-1029). But what was particularly troubling was the fact that a vast number of these cases were clearly repetitive or "unmeritorious" (Keller et al., 2010, p. 1026). Consequently it was decided that further reform of the supervisory machinery was called for in order for the Court to manage its case-load more efficiently, leading eventually to the adoption of *Protocol No. 14* in 2004 (*Protocol No. 14 to the Convention for the Protection of Human Rights and Fundamental Freedoms*, amending the control system of the Convention, CETS No. 194). Among the useful reforms introduced by *Protocol No. 14* [*Protocol 14*] is the Single Judge Formation, so that a single judge, as opposed to three previously, can declare applications inadmissible, and the Three Judge Committees, so that such Committees can rule on admissibility and on the merits in repetitive cases falling within well-established case law (Harris, O'Boyle & Warbrick, 2009, pp. 864-865; Mowbray, 2004, pp. 331-333). Due to Russia's belated accession to *Protocol 14* it did not enter into force until 1 June 2010, by which time the Court's workload had continued to grow relentlessly as did the ensuing backlog of cases. In fact, in an attempt to bypass Russian intransigence *Protocol 14bis*was adopted in May 2009 allowing the Court to apply these procedures to those States that had ratified *Protocol 14* pending its entry into force (*Protocol No. 14 bis to the Convention for the Protection of Human Rights and Fundamental Freedoms*, CETS No. 204). Nonetheless, by the end of 2010 nearly 140,000 applications were pending before a judicial formation (Annual Report 2010, p. 145). The debate on further reforms to the system therefore continued and at three high-level conferences, Interlaken, Izmir and Brighton, a road-map to that end was agreed (Council of Europe, *Reforming the European Convention on Human Rights*, 2014). On 24 June 2013 the CoE adopted another Protocol to the ECHR amending, *inter alia*, certain procedures of the protective machinery, *Protocol No. 15* [*Protocol 15*] (*Protocol No. 15 amending the Convention for the Protection of Human Rights and Fundamental Freedoms*, CETS No. 213). According to Article 7 of *Protocol 15* the Protocol must be ratified by all forty-seven States parties to the ECHR in order for it to enter into force. As of October 2015 the Protocol had received twenty-two ratifications. But both Protocols contain contentious elements that have given rise to concerns that the protective mechanism of the ECHR is being insidiously undermined. In particular, *Protocol 14* brought in a new admissibility requirement for individual applications raising the threshold of disadvantage a victim must have suffered (Harris et al., 2009, p. 865; Mowbray, 2004, pp. 333-335). Whereas *Protocol 15* provides for references to the principles of subsidiarity and margin of appreciation to be inserted in the Preamble to the ECHR and seeks to shorten the time-limit within which an application must be made to the Court from a period of six months to four months. These controversial changes form the focus of this Chapter.

But it is important to bear in mind that these changes are not being driven forward simply by a desire to streamline and improve the effectiveness of the Court's procedures. There is another agenda, pursued by those of a statist (Donnelly, 1997, p. 28) or Grotian (Cassese, 2005, p. 21) outlook, as well as conservative and Europhobic circles nostalgic for Diceyan parliamentary sovereignty, or more accurately executive sovereignty (Chakrabarti, 2015, p. xxiv), which aim to shake off the strictures imposed by judicial accountability and international legal obligations (Policy Exchange, 2011; Lambrecht, 2014, pp. 412, 431). British Conservative politicians in particular have baulked at a series of adverse rulings of the Court in cases such as *Hirst v. United Kingdom (No. 2)*(2006) 42 EHRR 41 GC, on the right of prisoners to vote, and *Othman (Abu Qatada) v. United Kingdom* (2012) 55 EHRR 1, on the lawful deportation of terrorist suspects (Vogiatzis, 2015, pp. 135-136). Objections, frequently ill-informed or exaggerated, mendacious even, often based on a misunderstanding of the Court's role, are raised at the Court's perceived judicial activism, at the way the ECHR is being interpreted by the Court to broaden the scope of human rights and thus to impose obligations upon States that were not initially assumed (Harris et al., 2009, pp. 5-8). But these criticisms, which are by no means new (van Dijk & van Hoof, 1990, pp. 617-618), are not always without substance. One writer has commented that "the Court has modified, or even reversed, its jurisprudence in a number of...cases, all directed to enhance, more than in the past, the protection of human rights" (Cassese, 2005, p. 397). A leading example of this approach is provided by the case of *Selmouni v. France* (1999) 29 EHRR 403, para. 101, where the Court stated that "the increasingly high standard being required in the area of the protection of human rights...correspondingly and inevitably requires greater firmness in assessing breaches of fundamental values of democratic societies. "The Court is additionally attracting negative comment for meddling with national decision-making and imposing uniformity. Unelected judges override the democratic will of Parliament and consequently subvert democracy (Raab, 2012). In short, the Court lacks democratic legitimacy (Bellamy, 2014). It is not our purpose to address directly these criticisms which lie beyond the scope of this essay, and which have been responded to eloquently elsewhere (Chakrabarti, 2015; Hale, 2012; Spano, 2014). But they are broached because they provide a context to the ECHR reforms, which are not motivated simply by a desire to address the flood of applications. The

Brighton Declaration, adopted in April 2012, with the British Government chairing the Committee of Ministers of the CoE, must also be seen from this perspective (Vogiatzis, 2015, pp. 130, 133-136). The *Brighton Declaration* called, *inter alia*, for greater prominence to be given to the principles of subsidiarity and margin of appreciation, that in the interests of legal certainty, foreseeability and equality before the law, the Court should not depart without sound reason from precedent, and that the Court focus its efforts on serious or widespread violations, systemic and structural problems, and important questions of interpretation and application of the ECHR (Council of Europe, *Reforming the European Convention on Human Rights*, 2014, p. 89). Implicit in these terms are demands for the Court to exercise greater restraint and to defer to national authorities (Rozenberg, 2013). This could be considered as attempts at partial repatriation to States Parties of sovereign rights transferred to the Court, or at the very least, a reminder to the Court that it should not exceed the boundaries of the powers granted it. Indeed, the British Government had placed on the record its understanding of *Protocol 15* that one of its purposes was to "define the boundaries of the Court's role" and to "give a clear statement of the proper role of the Court" (Cm. 8951).

The Lack of 'Significant Disadvantage' as a Ground for Declaring Individual Applications Inadmissible

The rules pertaining to any court of justice, be it domestic or transnational, stipulate the circumstances in which any application lodged may be declared inadmissible. This follows from the general rule of procedural law that courts are not obligated to entertain any and all cases brought before them but have the right to determine which cases they can decline hearing. At the same time, these instances must be clearly laid down and apply equally to all applicants. Thus, it is not permissible to accept a specific application but then to refuse to examine an identical complaint. This would otherwise amount to unequivocal discrimination by showing preference to one applicant over another. The very legitimacy of courts (an attribute which is broader than the democratic legitimacy of the Court referred to above) is intricately related to the principle of equal treatment as the right to equality before the law and the right to equal protection before the law (Bingham, 2010, pp. 55-59).

All courts have in place admissibility criteria, effectively grounds for refusing to hear a case. The stricter the admissibility criteria are, the fewer cases a court will hear. Principally, the admissibility criteria allow courts to concentrate on the more important cases and avoid spending valuable resources in frivolous applications or applications having no real substance to adjudicate. However, if the admissibility criteria are made too harsh, the legitimacy of courts could be called into question. Therefore, a balance is required between not hindering access to the courts but, at the same time, protecting them from dealing with applications of obvious insignificance. Especially for transnational courts as the European Court of Human Rights, where decisions on inadmissibility cannot be appealed against, this balance must become a fine equilibrium.

In the ECHR the admissibility criteria are laid down in Article 35. The first paragraph of Article 35 applies to both inter-state applications and individual applications while the second and third paragraphs thereof only apply to individual applications. To that extent, States could be considered as privileged applicants compared to private persons. Moreover, according to

Article 35(4), if at any stage of the proceedings the Court considers that an application is inadmissible for one or more of the reasons laid down in the previous paragraphs, the Court is obliged to reject it. It follows that the Court does not have the discretion to decide that an inadmissible application should proceed even if its merits would have warranted it.

The *Brighton Declaration* views the admissibility criteria as 'practical tools' allowing the Court to deal only with those cases where the alleged violation is significant or where the underlying principle or the alleged breach would justify its consideration. Therefore the *Brighton Declaration* considers that the Court's purpose and goal are not to consider each and every alleged violation of the ECHR by contracting parties. The rigour of the system created by the ECHR demands that the Court applies the admissibility criteria strictly and consistently, while it is the Court itself which must ensure that its workload is not unduly onerous (*Brighton Declaration*, 2012, point 14). Notwithstanding the concern emanating from the text of the *Brighton Declaration* that the Court should not be thrown into disarray on account of its ever-increasing workload, it should be noted that the *raison d'être* of establishing it has never been changed in its many years of operation. Thus, as laid down in Article 19 ECHR, the Court plays a supervisory role in ensuring "the observance of the engagements undertaken by the High Contracting Parties in the Convention and the Protocols thereto." While contracting parties had the opportunity to revise the Court's role in May 1994 when they adopted *Protocol 11* which overhauled the ECHR's institutional system, they chose to leave the wording of Article 19 unchanged, exactly as originally agreed in 1950. It follows that, even though it is inherent in the Court's functioning to rule on whether respondent States have, or have not, violated the protected rights in specific instances, its principal role remains similar to that of any intergovernmental organisation's judicial organ, namely to record infractions, which *in casu* means if contracting parties have failed to honour their commitments. To the extent that the Court's primary responsibility has never been altered, it is perhaps of no relevance if an application concerns significant violations of the ECHR or not. And this is because the Court is mandated to record all contracting parties' infringements, whether important or unimportant.

However, it could be argued that, in an indirect fashion, the function of the Court has been revised. This brings the discussion to Article 12 of *Protocol 14*, which augmented the scope of the admissibility criteria by adding the notion of 'significant disadvantage' as a further ground for refusing to hear individual applications. In particular, *Protocol 14* inserted a new indent (b) to Article 35(3), which reads as follows:

> Article 35 Admissibility criteria
>
> 1. …
>
> 2. …
>
> 3. The Court shall declare inadmissible any individual application submitted under Article 34 if it considers that:
>
> a. … or
>
> b. the applicant has not suffered a significant disadvantage, unless respect for human rights as defined in the Convention and the Protocols thereto requires an examination of the application on the merits and provided that no case may be rejected on this ground which has not been duly considered by a domestic tribunal."

The Explanatory Report to *Protocol 14* emphasized that the new requirement should not be construed as restricting the right of individuals to apply to the Court or negating the principle that all individual applications shall be examined as regards their admissibility (Explanatory Report, para. 39). Thus the dilemma was either to introduce this new criterion or to let the Court become totally paralyzed and unable to fulfil its central mission, namely to "offer legal protection of human rights at the European level" (Explanatory Report, para. 78). The Report makes no attempt to delineate the parameters of 'significant disadvantage.' It just states that a definition of the term will eventually be developed through the Court's consistent case law, a process which it admits will take considerable time (Explanatory Report, paras. 67, 84).

It is submitted that the other admissibility criteria enumerated in Article 35, namely that domestic remedies must have been exhausted, that the application must neither be anonymous nor substantially the same case as previously examined by the Court, nor be *sub judice* before another competent international organ or body, while it must be compatible with the provisions of the ECHR, have an objective character and their satisfaction can be ascertained in a relatively straightforward manner. To the contrary, the new criterion is clearly of a subjective nature. Moreover, the wording of Article 35(3)(b) does not answer the question whether the Court bears the onus of showing that the applicant has not suffered a significant disadvantage or whether it is reversed and, consequently, it is the applicant who should demonstrate to the Court's satisfaction that substantial harm was endured through the action or inaction of the respondent State. However, given that at present Rule of Court 47(1)(f) initially places the burden of proof on the applicant, it seems reasonable to expect that this is also the case with the new requirement.

The legal basis of the 'significant disadvantage' criterion is the so-called *de minimis* rule, which is based on the Latin axiom "de minimis non curat praetor" (Ruedin, 2008). From a procedural point of view, it means that the Court is permitted to refuse to hear cases which are considered as 'minor' (*Practical Guide on Admissibility Criteria*, 2014, pp. 88 *et seq.*). In *Korolev v. Russia*, App. no. 25551/05, ECtHR, Judgment of 1 July 2010, p. 4, the Court stated that "a minimum level of severity" had to be attained to merit examination. The *de minimis* rule is a well-known concept in international law, and has been applied by the Court of Justice of the European Union [EU] specifically in the area of competition law and could be regarded as a general principle of EU law (Case 5/69 *Völk v. Vervaecke* [1969] ECR 275; Craig & de Búrca, 2008, p. 976). Moreover, as a general principle of procedural law, it should be deemed to exist in all legal systems, even if it is not expressly envisaged in the relevant rules. Equally, a court should be entitled to invoke it if it is satisfied that justice would be better served by dismissing a case (or a group of cases) on account of its (their) apparent insignificance or because the impact will not be appreciable, the 'unmeritorious' cases. In such instances, while the applications ought to have been examined and the court have issued judgments, the fact that their content was regarded as unworthy would justify the court's refusal to exercise its duties.

In its judgment in *Korolev v. Russia*, which was rendered exactly one month after *Protocol 14* had entered into force, the Court confirmed that the new criterion was 'inspired' by the *de minimis* rule. In the present case, the applicant had complained that the Russian authorities had failed to pay him the amount of 22.50 roubles (around €0.50). The Court had no hesitation in applying the 'significant disadvantage' criterion and refused to examine the application on its merits. Pursuant to a good number of decisions invoking the new admissibility criterion, the content of 'significant disadvantage' will invariably be whether the applicant was significantly disadvantaged from a *financial* point of view (emphasis added).

Thus in *Ionescu v. Romania*, the first case where the new criterion was applied, the Court was not impressed that the applicant's alleged loss was €90 because the amount involved had no bearing on his personal life (*Ionescu v. Romania* (2010) 51 EHRR 527). Similar cases include *Vasilchenko v. Russia* (App. no. 34784/02, ECtHR, Judgment of 23 September 2010; *Rinck v. France* (Application no. 18774/09, ECtHR, Judgment of 19 October 2010); and *Gaftoniuc v. Romania* (App. no. 30934/05, ECtHR, Judgment of 22 February 2011). But more important than the actual sums in question is the effect on the applicant (Buyse, 2013, p. 8). However, in those cases where applicants have claimed some other disadvantage, such as where an applicant alleges a violation of his/her personal identity, the Court ought to devise objective rules in order to quantify the component of substantial detriment in order better to decide whether to reject the application or to examine it. To carry this argument further, there may be cases which appear trivial or where the applicant has not suffered significant harm but which nevertheless give rise to important points of law or principle. To offer an example: on account of the severe budgetary, economic and banking crisis which has plagued Greece during the last six years, unprecedented measures have been promulgated, including restrictions on bank deposits and the free circulation of capital, through the imposition of so-called 'capital controls.' If, for the sake of argument, the applicant, who has complained before the Court that these measures violate the ECHR including its *First Protocol*, has a bank balance of only €100, would his/her application be dismissed for lack of significant disadvantage? It has been suggested that even minor breaches of the core values of the Convention, such as non-derogable rights, would never be insignificant (Buyse, 2013, p. 8). Consequently, the fact that the applicant lost her job as a result of a conviction for petty theft was deemed not to be insignificant (*Luchaninovava. Ukraine*, App. no. 16347/02, ECtHR, Judgment of 9 June 2011). In *Giusti v. Italy* (App. no. 13175/03, ECtHR, Judgment of 18 October 2011, para. 34) the Court therefore proceeded to list three criteria to this end: the nature of the right allegedly violated; the gravity of the alleged violation; and their effect on the personal situation of the applicant.

Before returning to this question, it is submitted that the Court need not have rejected the aforementioned cases relying on 'no significant disadvantage' but by invoking the admissibility criterion of abusing the right of application, which is laid down in Article 35(3)(a) ECHR (Harris et al., 2009, pp. 785-786). Indeed, had the judgment on *Korolev* and the other cases been rendered *before* the entry into force of *Protocol 14*, this would have been the ground for rejection. This submission is based on the fact that one of the categories of cases declared by the Court as abusing the right of application are cases manifestly vexatious or devoid of any real purpose (*Practical Guide on Admissibility Criteria*, 2014, p. 37). Thus, in *Bock v. Germany*, where the applicant had complained of the non-reimbursement of €7.99 by a public authority, the Court employed Article 35(3)(a) to declare his application inadmissible. And this despite the fact that the Court concluded that the domestic court proceedings were excessively long and reiterated Germany's obligation to adopt an effective remedy against this violation of Article 6(1) (*Bock v. Germany*, App. no. 22053/07, ECtHR, Judgment of 19 January 2010).

According to the *Practical Guide on Admissibility Criteria* (2014, p. 39), following the entry into force of *Protocol 14*, applications of this kind are "more readily dealt with" under Article 35(3)(b). This is not a very convincing statement and possibly is even incompatible with the principle of legal certainty. As has been argued above, the Court is mandated to examine all the applications lodged with it and meeting the admissibility criteria of Article

35(1) and (2). The admissibility criteria of Article 35(3) are effectively additional restrictions to the right to application which, however, have been legitimized on account of the need to secure the Court's sound and seamless functioning. It follows that the latter criteria should be employed sparingly. The fact that there is considerable overlap between the 'abuse of the right of application' and the 'no significant disadvantage' criteria should have been addressed in legal terms and perhaps the Court could have resolved it by regarding the former as *lex generalis* and the latter as *lex specialis*.

However, there is an important difference between these two criteria. In particular, the rejection of applications under Article 35(3)(b) is not automatic in the sense that the Court is mandated to examine whether two specific caveats apply, while a similar provision is not envisaged in Article 35(3)(a). These caveats are safeguard clauses ensuring that, despite their apparent insignificance, certain applications should be examined on their merits (Buyse, 2013, p. 5). The content of these caveats is self-evident. It is inconceivable for a judicial mechanism protecting human rights to operate without them. But the fact that they were expressly included could be explained by the introduction of another admissibility criterion restricting further the right of application. According to the first caveat, even if an individual application cannot pass the test of 'significant disadvantage' suffered by the applicant, the Court has the discretion to examine its merits, provided that the respect for human rights, as defined in the ECHR and its Protocols, requires it to do so. To return to our question posed earlier regarding the applicant having €100 in his/her bank account, it follows that the Court will have the discretion to examine the merits, while, if the applicant's bank balance was one million Euro, the provision of Article 35(3)(b) would not have come into play at all. This is clearly an unsatisfactory situation.

According to the second caveat (and effectively a limitation to the Court's privilege to reject applications), no application may be dismissed if the case has not previously received due consideration by the respondent state's courts. It is designed to avoid denials of justice (Buyse, 2013, p. 10). Presumably these will be instances where the criterion of prior exhaustion of domestic remedies does not apply, for example, if there was no point in accessing the competent domestic courts. As has been argued, the usefulness of the new admissibility criterion presupposes that the judiciaries on the national level function properly (Keller et al., 2010, p. 1039). As anyone can ascertain by looking at the Court's jurisprudence, especially on Article 6(1) of the ECHR, for many a contracting party this is far from reality.

There is no doubt that the introduction of the 'significant disadvantage' criterion offers to the Court a large measure of flexibility in how to handle its workload. It allows the Court to focus on (what it itself regards as) applications raising key issues in safeguarding human rights and fundamental freedoms. And there is no indication that the Court will attempt to misuse its powers. However, the following question invariably arises: which body is going to deal with all the other less important violations and which body will see to it that the victim's rights are finally redressed? After all, regardless of the magnitude of the violation, when an individual's human rights and freedoms have been breached, he/she becomes a victim and all victims deserve protection and assistance. Conceivably, a situation could occur where an alleged violation escapes scrutiny by a judicial body (Joint NGO Statement, 2013, para. C). A further consideration is that a violation may be trivial as regards a specific individual on his/her own but if the same trifling violation concerns a whole group of individuals then it can no longer be treated as such (Reiss, 2009, pp. 303-304).

Notwithstanding the fact that the protection should be commensurate to the violation, arguably there is a minimum standard of protection, especially if the victim had to endure long and arduous domestic proceedings. As argued by a number of NGOs and the Law Society of Scotland before the House of Lords and House of Commons' Joint Committee on Human Rights deliberating the ratification of *Protocol 15* by the United Kingdom, even if a case is deemed to be minor, no denial of justice can be allowed (Joint Committee on Human Rights, 2014, p. 22; Joint NGO Statement, 2013, para. C). These questions should forcefully be put to Court itself and the CoE's Member States.

These considerations are perhaps even more relevant when the changes to Article 35(3)(b), which are envisaged in *Protocol 15*, come into force. In particular, Article 5 thereof stipulates that the second caveat, namely that no case will be rejected if it has not been duly considered by a domestic tribunal, shall be repealed. *Protocol 15* was drafted in the closing months of 2012 (it was finally adopted in June 2013), at a time when evidently it was too early for the Court to have concluded its interpretation of the 'significant disadvantage' criterion, including the question of how the two safeguard clauses are to be applied. Thus during the period July 2010 – July 2012 it was applied to only 26 complaints and considered but rejected in a further 16 complaints (*The new admissibility criterion under Article 35 § 3 (b) of the Convention*, 2012, para. 32). The decision to delete the second caveat had already been taken by contracting parties more than a year earlier at the Brighton High Level Conference, which, interestingly enough, had imposed the end of 2013 as the deadline for having the amending instrument adopted (*Brighton Declaration*, 2012, point 15(c)).

It follows that the decision to reduce drastically the safeguard clauses of Article 35 was the express wish of contracting parties and, therefore, clearly a political decision. One commentator writing in 2011 has argued that "the time has come for political leadership in the field of human rights" (Christoffersen, 2011, 181). Even if one were to agree with this submission, one should also ask the following question: where does political expediency end and where does judicial independence commence? Moreover, the justification given in the Explanatory Report, namely that the amendment is intended to give greater effect to the *de minimis* rule, is not at all convincing (Explanatory Report to Protocol 15, para. 23). And this because, in the absence of any detailed written tenets on how this rule is to be enforced, it is up to the Court to determine it. The Court should be left free to settle on a restrictive or an expansive application, provided that it is always consistent. Finally, equally problematic is the assertion in the Opinion on draft *Protocol 15*, which was adopted by the Parliamentary Assembly, the CoE's organ representing national legislatures, that the proposed changes are "principally of a technical and uncontroversial nature" (Council of Europe, Parliamentary Assembly, Opinion No. 283 (2013)).

The paramount aim of this safeguard clause is to prevent instances where there would be a denial of justice, one of the fundamental principles of the rule of law and the one which is most characteristic of the legitimacy of courts. The effect of deleting it is none other than the risk of having cases alleging violations of the ECHR not heard by domestic courts or the Court. Thus, in the name of maintaining the Court's ability to manage its workload, the CoE's Member States accept that there are bound to be instances where applicants with rightful grievances (although perhaps not of considerable significance) will not be examined and any infraction by contracting parties will not be recorded. Given that Article 6 ECHR guarantees to everyone his/her entitlement to a fair and public hearing within a reasonable time by an independent and impartial domestic tribunal, it is not unrealistic to ask whether everyone is entitled, provided that the procedural rules are observed, to have his/her application heard by the Court.

At a domestic level, to avoid frivolous applications, certain Member States have imposed the payment of court fees as a further condition before applications are regarded as admissible. If the domestic court examines the merits of the case and finds in favour of the applicant, the fee is returned, otherwise it is forfeited. This court fee is not a payment to have an application heard by the competent court, in other words applicants are not required to pay to have their case adjudicated (as happens, for example, with arbitral tribunals). On the contrary, its purpose is to avoid what in English law is referred to as 'vexatious litigation' (in German law it is known as 'schikanöse Klagen' and in French law as 'poursuites vexatoires'), a term which for all intents and purposes corresponds to the abuse of the right to petition as envisaged in Article 35(3)(a) of the ECHR. Thus it would not be unreasonable to suggest that Member States consider measures to improve the Court's work load along these lines and not interfere with the substantial issue of unhindered access to the Court.

One final observation concerns Article 5, which shall apply from the *Protocol 15*'s entry into force. As previously mentioned, at the time of writing *Protocol 15* has received twenty-two ratifications. It cannot be predicted when, or if, it will become operative. Nevertheless, on the assumption that it does, after that date the Court will not have to consider whether cases which were determined not to be of significant disadvantage to applicants were duly considered by a domestic tribunal. But up to the very day prior to its entry into force, the Court will be obliged to examine this fact as well. Given the very large number of cases considered by the Court, it may be that this arrangement does not promote legal certainty because similar applications may be rejected or examined on their merits depending solely on when the Protocol comes into effect. Arguably legal certainty points towards applying the new Article 35(3)(c) to those applications which will be lodged *after* the Protocol's entry into force, although it may have to be accepted as one of those facts of life that such random circumstances create winners and losers.

The Principles of the Margin of Appreciation and Subsidiarity

Article1of *Protocol 15* makes provision for references to the principles of subsidiarity and margin of appreciation to be added to the Preamble to the ECHR. The new recital reads:

> Affirming that the High Contracting Parties, in accordance with the principle of subsidiarity, have the primary responsibility to secure the rights and freedoms defined in this Convention and the Protocols thereto, and that in doing so they enjoy a margin of appreciation, subject to the supervisory jurisdiction of the European Court of Human Rights established by this Convention.

According to Cassese (2015) it would appear that the new recital views the margin of appreciation and subsidiarity as "two different principles, as if they had different content. "This observation corresponds to our understanding of the principles, that despite similarities and overlap they address different situations. However, it is possible to view the margin of appreciation as a sub-principle to that of subsidiarity, "according to which the national authorities, who are in direct and continuous contact with the vital forces of their countries, are best placed to assess the multitude of factors surrounding each particular situation" (*Interlaken Follow-Up: Principle of Subsidiarity*, 2010, para. 45). Indeed, it is possible to detect in the Court's recent jurisprudence a convergence of the two principles which stripped to the essentials pronounces the Convention remedy to be of a subsidiary nature. Be that as it may, they do share one thing in common, and that is that their incorporation into the ECHR is intended by some to "define the boundaries of the Court's role" (*Explanatory Memorandum on Protocol 15*, 2014). From this perspective, it constitutes a warning to the Court to reign in its maximalist inclinations. However, others are of the view that the new recital does not in fact impose many constraints on the Court and is thus an acceptable compromise between politicians and European judges (Vogiatzis, 2015, pp. 136, 143).

The margin of appreciation is a doctrine of judicial self-restraint developed by the Court which balances the supervisory control exercised by it with the discretion of States Parties (Grant & Barker, 2009, p. 361; *Handyside v. United Kingdom* (1979-80) 1 EHRR 737, paras. 48-50). This is because the Court has been alive to "the tension between the preferences of national decision-makers and the requirements" of the ECHR (Helfer & Slaughter, 1997, p. 316). The Court therefore allows States a leeway, or latitude of action, with regard to how they protect fundamental rights subject to its ultimate control and supervision. According to the Explanatory Report on Protocol 15:

> The jurisprudence of the Court makes clear that the States Parties enjoy a margin of appreciation in how they apply and implement the Convention, depending on the circumstances of the case and the rights and freedoms engaged. This reflects…that national authorities are in principle better placed than an international court to evaluate local needs and conditions. The margin of appreciation goes hand in hand with supervision under the Convention system. In this respect, the role of the Court is to review whether decisions taken by national authorities are compatible with the Convention, having due regard to the State's margin of appreciation.

Thus the margin of appreciation is said to recognize the "political sovereignty of…states while legitimizing its own decisions against them" (Helfer & Slaughter, 1997, p. 317).

But the margin of appreciation can apply in different contexts. It extends both to domestic legislatures and judicial bodies(*Handyside v. United Kingdom*, para. 48). Hence regarding domestic legislation the Court "will respect the legislature's judgment…unless that judgment was manifestly without reasonable foundation" (*Lithgow and Others v. United Kingdom* (1986) 8 EHRR 329, para. 122). With regard to qualified rights "the Contracting States enjoy a certain but not unlimited margin of appreciation in the matter of the imposition of restrictions, but it is for the Court to give the final ruling on whether they are compatible with the Convention" (*Silver v. United Kingdom* (1983) 5 EHRR 347, para. 97).

The difficulty that then exists with the margin of appreciation doctrine is that by its very flexible nature (Merrills & Robertson, 2001, pp. 222-223) its content and application have eluded precise definition (van Dijk & van Hoof, 1990, p. 588; Hutchinson, 1999, p. 641). It has been described as a "tool to define relations between the domestic authorities and the Court" (*A and Others v. United Kingdom* (2009) 49 EHRR 29, para. 184). It varies depending upon the content of the rights in question, wider with regard to sensitive issues such as national security, for example, or where a Europe-wide consensus is lacking, but narrower with regard to freedom of expression (Harris et al., 2009, p. 13; Merrills & Robertson, 2001, pp. 222-28). Nevertheless, the margin of appreciation doctrine as such has become a well-established feature of the Court's jurisprudence (Hutchinson, 1999, p. 638; Sweeney, 2005, p. 459). Indeed, it could be described as a cornerstone of European human rights law. It has also been adopted by other regional human rights bodies, such as the Inter-American Court of Human Rights (*Proposed Amendments to the Naturalization Provisions of the Constitution of Costa Rica*, Advisory Opinion OC-4/84, Series A No. 4, (19 January 1984), paras. 58, 62-63), the African Commission on Human and Peoples' Rights [African Commission] (*Garreth Anver Prince v. South Africa*, Communication No. 255/2002, 18th Activity Report 2002–2003, paras. 51–52), and the UN Human Rights Committee (Conte & Burchill, 2009, pp. 42-44). But it is a judge-made doctrine and, until *Protocol 15*, finds no explicit mention in the ECHR. What *Protocol 15* therefore does is that it embeds in the treaty text a reference to a judicially developed principle without, probably sensibly, any attempt at a definition.

Fears that certain States would take the opportunity during the negotiating process on *Protocol 15* to water down the doctrine, either by arrogating to themselves the right to interpret it, or by inserting a treaty definition inimical with its accepted meaning, were resisted and did not materialise. In fact, the Explanatory Report states that the intention of the amended Preamble is to ensure consistency with the doctrine of the margin of appreciation as developed by the Court in its case law. This was to address the fears of certain States that the balance between deference to national sovereignty and judicial supervision had swung too far in the latter's direction and had to be rectified. Nevertheless, this formulation, chiefly that the margin of appreciation is subject to the supervision of the Court, appears to be interpreted as confirming the *status quo* rather than effecting radical change (Joint NGO Statement, 2013, para. A; Vogiatzis, 2015, pp. 138, 144-146). But the principle of the margin of appreciation has not remained static and has been subject to a process of evolution over the years (Sweeney, 2005, p. 467) so that by this stage it was already possible to detect a deferential shift in the Court's approach to the margin of appreciation. In *Von Hannover v. Germany (No. 2)* (2012) 55 EHRR 15 GC the Court found that the German courts had struck a fair balance between protection of privacy and freedom of expression in conformity with the Court's case-law, and that it would therefore require strong reasons to substitute its view for that of the national courts. It seems that the Court was keen to stress that it would intervene only for compelling reasons. It may be that the Court was conscious of the strong views expressed by certain States at the high-level conferences on the ongoing reforms to the ECHR that the role of the Court is to review whether decisions taken by national authorities are compatible with the ECHR, having due regard to the State's margin of appreciation, and calling upon the Court to give greater prominence to this principle in its case law. The doctrine of the margin of appreciation has now undergone a modification in its meaning so that it "now means that if the independent and impartial national courts have analysed in a comprehensive and convincing manner the contested legal measure on the basis of the relevant human rights standards, the…Court will need strong reasons to substitute its own, different analysis for that of the national judges" (Mahoney, 2014, p. 9). This interpretative approach is predicated upon the national authorities getting it right and should not be considered as an abdication of responsibility by the Court (Mahoney, 2014, p. 10). Given its entrenched status in European human rights law, it seems unlikely that the reference to the margin of appreciation doctrine in the Preamble will lead to any substantive changes in the law. Indeed, the Court itself has expressed the view that "there clearly was no common intention of the High Contracting Parties to alter either the substance of the Convention or its system of international, collective enforcement" (*Opinion of the Court on Draft Protocol No. 15* [*Opinion of the Court*]). This approach evidently refuses to question the motives and integrity of certain States. But, as previously indicated, there are already disturbing discernible indications that the Court is adopting a more deferential attitude towards States and *Protocol 15* may have the effect of accelerating this approach in the practice of the Court. Ultimately, however, the upshot must be that "the doctrine of the margin of appreciation should not in any circumstances exempt the Court from the duty…to ensure the observance of the engagements undertaken" by the States (*Lautsi and Others v. Italy* (2012) 54 EHRR 3, Dissenting Opinion of Judge Malinverni joined by Judge Kalaydjieva, para. 1).

The reference to subsidiarity raises other, and possibly more polemical, issues. Subsidiarity has been described by the Court as being "at the very basis of the Convention" (*Austin and Others v. United Kingdom* (2012) 55 EHRR 14, para. 61 GC) but it invites comment that a principle apparently considered foundational has eluded detailed examination for so long. Again *Protocol 15* aims to provide a legislative foundation for this principle but eschews any attempt at a definition. This appears to have been desired by the Court which did not wish to be dictated to by politicians (Vogiatzis, 2015, pp. 143-144). The principle of subsidiarity is capable of many different meanings (Cassese, 2015, p. 8) but in modern international law it is principally associated with EU law (Schilling, 1994). Simply put, it provides that outside of its areas of exclusive competence, the EU should act only where that would be more effective than at national level. It is a form of devolved authority. Introduced by the *Treaty on European Union* in 1992, better known as the *Maastricht Treaty*, ([1992] OJ C 191; Cass, 1992, p. 1107) it now finds expression in Article 5(3) *Treaty on European Union 2007* ([2010] OJ C 83/13). In the context of EU law, it has been argued that "a certain degree of subsidiarity is implicitly reflected in the existing fundamental rights law" of the EU (Carozza, 2003, 56). Subsequently, it has found explicit expression in the Preamble and Article 51(1) EU *Charter of Fundamental Rights 2000* ([2010] OJ C 83/02; Carozza, 2003, pp. 53-56). But the principle's distinct nature in European human rights law from that in EU law has been stressed, pointing to the ECHR's internationalist make-up as opposed to the EU's supranational and integrationist set-up (*Interlaken Follow-Up: Principle of Subsidiarity*, 2010, para. 3). Because of its identification with EU law, it might have been preferable to have steered clear of its use and chosen a different term. Nevertheless, subsidiarity's overt manifestation as a discrete principle in European human rights law is relatively recent, emerging with the reform process undertaken at Interlaken. Less explicitly, the Court has in fact relied on it since its early days (*Belgian Linguistics Case* (1979-80) 1 EHRR 252, para. 10; *Handyside v. United Kingdom*, para. 48). But absent much in the way of explanation what exactly does subsidiarity mean in the context of *Protocol 15*, and in what situations could it apply? Viewed from one perspective, analogous to its role in EU law, subsidiarity may be considered an element of judicial review, its purpose being "to check the uniformity of the application of supranational principles and rules in national contexts" (Cassese, 2015, pp. 7-8, 12). Or in other words, to curb the Court's judicial activism and restrict it only to the most egregious violations. Reflecting the Grotian model of international law, the Contracting States have taken the opportunity to put forward claims for a decentralized structure of human rights, reiterating that the ECHR was concluded on the basis of the sovereign equality of States (*Interlaken Follow-Up: Principle of Subsidiarity*, 2010, para. 9; *Brighton Declaration*, 2012, point 3) and, based on the doctrine of attributed powers, that other international actors, such as the Court, must act strictly within the scope of the powers conferred upon them

(*Jurisdiction of the European Commission of the Danube between Galatz and Braila*, Advisory Opinion, 1927 PCIJ Rep. Series B No. 14, 64; Klabbers, 2009, pp. 55-58). But calls that States be given *carte blanche* to override the Court have been rightly resisted by European judges (Bratza, 2014, p. 82; Costa, 2003, p. 460) since the ECHR would then serve little purpose. Official explanations of subsidiarity therefore point in a different direction. According to the Explanatory Report on Protocol 15, reflecting dicta by the Court (*Austin v. United Kingdom*, para. 61; *Varnava v. Turkey* (2010) 50 EHRR 467, para. 164 GC), the ECHR is subsidiary to the safeguarding of human rights at the national level. In this framework, it means that:

> the task of ensuring respect for the rights enshrined in the Convention lies first and foremost with the authorities in the Contracting States rather than with the Court. The Court can and should intervene only where the domestic authorities fail in that task (*Interlaken Follow-Up: Principle of Subsidiarity*, 2010).

Subsidiarity is thus referred to as 'complementary,' in that "the Court's powers of intervention are confined to those cases where the domestic institutions are incapable of ensuring effective protection of the rights guaranteed by the Convention" (*Interlaken Follow-Up: Principle of Subsidiarity*, 2010). It therefore necessitates a 'shared responsibility' between the Court and States Parties (*Interlaken Declaration*, 2010, para. 3; *Brighton Declaration*, 2012, point 3). It constitutes an international separation of powers (Sweeney, 2005, p. 472). Understood in this context it can safely be asserted that subsidiarity does not introduce any new concepts into European human rights law but is merely an expedient shorthand term that encapsulates the relationship between European human rights law, indeed international human rights law, and national law.

It needs to be recalled that one of the defining characteristics of the human rights construct is that it imposes an element of international scrutiny (Buergenthal, 2000, pp. 13-20). But the international system plays a secondary and supplementary role to the national order and access to international organs by complainants is a last resort, rather than the first port of call (*A, B and C v. Ireland* (2011) 53 EHRR 13, para. 142 GC; *Anuak Justice Council v. Ethiopia*, Communication No. 299/05, 20th Activity Report 2005–2006, para. 48). This association was indeed acknowledged in the early days of the ECHR (*Belgian Linguistics Case*, para. 10) and as a judge of the Court put it, "subsidiarity applies insofar as the Court has always considered its role as subsidiary" (Costa, 2003, p. 456). And it is why all major human rights instruments, reflecting a general principle of international law (*Interhandel Case* (Preliminary Objections) [1959] ICJ Rep 6, p. 27; Amerasinghe, 2004), insist on the prior exhaustion of existing effective local remedies, allowing the State the initial opportunity to right any wrongdoing (Article 35(1) ECHR; Article 46(1)(a) *American Convention on Human Rights 1969*, 1144 UNTS 123 [ACHR]; Articles 2 and 5(2)(b) *Optional Protocol to the International Covenant on Civil and Political Rights 1966*, 999 UNTS 171; Article 56(5) *African Charter on Human and Peoples' Rights 1981*, 1520 UNTS 217 [*African Charter*]; Harris et al., 2009, pp. 764-76; Spano, 2014, p. 500; Vogiatzis, 2015, p. 139; Pasqualucci, 2003, pp. 129-35; Conte & Burchill, 2009, pp. 33-34; Magliveras & Naldi, 2014, pp. 267-73). In the European context the point has been made that the Court is not a court of fourth instance, an appeal court revisiting questions of fact or law decided by domestic courts (*Austin v. United Kingdom*, para. 61; *Er and Others v. Turkey*, App. No. 23016/04, ECtHR,

31 July 2012, para. 57; Harris et al., 2009, pp. 14-15; *Interlaken Follow-Up: Principle of Subsidiarity*, 2010, paras. 27-39; *Izmir Declaration*, 2011, para. F(2)(c)). The primary responsibility for guaranteeing human rights lies with the States Parties; under Article 1 ECHR States Parties must 'secure' the rights and freedoms contained therein to persons within their jurisdiction, and to provide an effective remedy before a national authority for everyone whose rights are violated(Robertson & Merrills, 1996, pp. 124, 202; Steiner & Alston, 2000, p. 797) and States have traditionally had choices as to how this is achieved (Fawcett, 1987, p. 4). All constitute expressions of subsidiarity (Vogiatzis, 2015, p. 142). But for subsidiarity to function appropriately, it is clear that the ECHR must be properly and effectively implemented at the national level (Bratza, 2014, p. 82; Costa, 2003, p. 460; Helfer, 2008). This essential point was accepted by the *Brighton Declaration* which affirmed that States Parties must effectively resolve violations at the national level (*Brighton Declaration*, 2012, point 3). But subsidiarity also finds practical expression in other ways. One such method is the procedure known as pilot judgments which empower the Court to indicate remedial measures which the respondent State must take domestically where structural and systematic problems exist (Rule of Court 61; *Burdov v. Russia (No. 2)*) (2009) 49 EHRR 2, paras. 126-128; O'Boyle, 2008, pp. 7-8).

The principal understanding of subsidiarity that has been espoused by the Court is that:

> the object and purpose underlying the Convention, as set out in Article 1, is that the rights and freedoms should be secured by the Contracting State within its jurisdiction. It is fundamental to the machinery of protection established by the Convention that the national systems themselves provide redress for breaches of its provisions, the Court exerting its supervisory role subject to the principle of subsidiarity. In that context, Article 13, which requires an effective remedy in respect of violations of the Convention, takes on a crucial function (*Z and Others v. United Kingdom* (2002) 34 EHRR 97, para. 103; *Scordino v. Italy (No. 1)* (2007) 45 EHRR 7, para. 140; *Varnava v. Turkey*, para. 164).

For these reasons, subsidiarity "implies careful application by the domestic authorities of the relevant Convention standard" and avoids undue "over-dependence on the European Court" (Spielmann, 2013). If the national authorities and the Court continued on this path there would be little basis for alarm. It constitutes an eminently sensible way of sheltering the Court from avoidable applications. If States take their responsibilities seriously and secure fundamental rights domestically then it is plain that fewer complaints will be lodged in Strasbourg. But disappointingly there has already been a troubling admission by a judge of the Court that in its recent case law it is reinterpreting the concept of subsidiarity in a more deferential manner towards States as a result of the *Brighton Declaration* and *Protocol 15* (Spano, 2014, pp. 497-499). This deferential approach is conditional on the safeguard that the challenged domestic measure is subjected to careful and rigorous scrutiny by the national authorities (Spano, 2014, p. 498) but it nonetheless introduces an element of deep concern. *Austin v. United Kingdom* is a case in point which has caused profound dismay because the Court did not seem to confine itself to applying the principle of subsidiarity to findings of fact only, but to the interpretation of substantive rights as well (Oreb, 2013).

According to some observers, the fact that the principles of margin of appreciation and subsidiarity have now been codified could have important outcomes. On the one hand, the new preamble could give the Court greater leave to take account of these principles in its jurisprudence (Vogiatzis, 2015, p. 143). The fact that reference to them has been restricted to the preamble has been welcomed because if they had been inserted into the operative text of the ECHR, States would have been given licence to invoke them as a means of attempting to constrain the scope of the rights and thereby limit international supervision (Vogiatzis, 2015, p. 142). Nevertheless, it seems likely that it will only be a matter of time before States rely upon these principles in litigation (Cassese, 2015, p. 6; Vogiatzis, 2015, pp. 144-146). Whether the Court would pronounce on the actual legal validity of the preamble other than to confirm that it enjoys the right to supervise whether Contracting Parties have exceeded the margin of appreciation in a given case or whether it would feel the need to expand on these principles is a matter of speculation. This may well arise once *Protocol 15* enters into force but it would be well to bear in mind that a treaty preamble has in itself no binding force (*Right of US Nationals in Morocco Case* [1952] ICJ Rep 176) although it may be taken into account in the treaty's interpretation as part of the context of that treaty (Article 31(2) *Vienna Convention on the Law of Treaties 1969*, 1155 UNTS 331). However, it is important to note that the Court has frequently had recourse to the ECHR's Preamble to determine the object and purpose of the provision under consideration (*Golder v. United Kingdom* (1979-80) 1 EHRR 524, para. 34; Vogiatzis, 2015, pp. 141-142).

The Four-Month Time-Limit

Probably the most significant change introduced by Article 4 of *Protocol 15* is the reduction in the time-limit under Article 35(1) ECHR from a period of six months to four months following the date of the final domestic decision within which an application must be submitted to the Court. This time-limit, which is a mandatory rule which the Court can apply of its own motion(*Assanidze v. Georgia* (2004) 39 EHRR 32, para. 160 GC), applies both to individual applications and inter-state cases (*Cyprus v. Turkey* (2002) 35 EHRR 731). The six-month rule is "a public policy rule" (*Sabri Güneş v. Turkey*, App. no. 27396/06, EctHR, Judgment of 24 May 2011, para. 33) in its narrow sense of being "declaratory of standards of *ordre public* common to all the contracting States" (Fawcett, 1987, p. 330). Additionally, it is "an autonomous rule which has to be interpreted and applied in such a manner as to ensure to any applicant claiming to be a victim of a violation...the effective exercise of the right of individual petition" (*Sabri Güneş v. Turkey* (2013) 56 EHRR34, para. 41 GC). As originally set out in former Article 26(1) ECHR, the rule provides for legal certainty in that it prevents the State measure or inaction being challenged while at the same time providing the complainant a reasonable period of time within which to submit an application. In the words of the Court, the primary purpose of the rule is to maintain:

> legal certainty by ensuring that cases...are examined within a reasonable time, and to prevent the authorities and other persons concerned from being kept in a state of uncertainty for a long period of time. It also affords the prospective applicant time to consider whether to lodge an application and, if so, to decide on the specific complaints and arguments to be raised and facilitates the establishment of facts in a case, since with the passage of time, any fair examination of the issues raised is rendered problematic (*Practical Guide on Admissibility Criteria*, 2014, para. 87; *Alzery v. Sweden* ECtHR 2004-IV, p. 7; *Sabri Güneş v. Turkey*, 2013, para. 39).

The Court has stressed that legal certainty is "a binding requirement which ensures the equality of litigants before the law…and constitutes one of the fundamental elements of the rule of law" (*Sabri Güneş v. Turkey*, 2013, para. 42). Furthermore, it:

> marks out the temporal limit of the supervision exercised by the Court and signals, both to individuals and State authorities, the period beyond which supervision is no longer possible. It reflects the wish of the High Contracting Parties to prevent past judgments being constantly called into question and constitutes a legitimate concern for order, stability and peace (*Practical Guide on Admissibility Criteria*, 2014, para. 88; *Sabri Güneş v. Turkey*, 2013, para. 40).

The wish for closure has been stressed (Harris et al., 2009, p. 776). These rationalizations have been approved by other regional human rights bodies. According to the Inter-American Commission on Human Rights the "rule exists to allow for juridical certainty while still providing sufficient time for a potential petitioner to consider her position" (Pasqualucci, 2003, p. 126). The African Commission considers the purpose of the time-limit is to ensure that the complainant is "vigilant and to discourage tardiness" (*Darfur Relief and Communication Centre v. Sudan*, Communication No. 310/2005, 27th Activity Report 2009, para. 78).

In calculating time-limits the Court applies its own criteria which are distinct from national rules, thereby ensuring "legal certainty, proper administration of justice, and…the practical and effective functioning of the Convention mechanism" (*Practical Guide on Admissibility Criteria*, 2014, para. 106; *Sabri Güneş v. Turkey*, 2013, para. 56), and which may therefore differ from the time-limits identified by the respondent State (*Practical Guide on Admissibility Criteria*, 2014, para. 108). While national rules and practices are important, they are not decisive in determining the starting point of the six-month rule (*Sabri Güneş v. Turkey*, 2013, paras. 49, 52 and 56). It is interesting to note, however, that the Court has observed that taking account of such domestic laws constitutes a practical example of the principle of subsidiarity in action (*Sabri Güneş v. Turkey*, 2011, para. 43). It is important to note that there is flexibility built into the six-month rule dependent on circumstances. At present the time-limit starts to run on the day following the date on which the final domestic decision was pronounced in public or from the date of the applicant's notice thereof (*Practical Guide on Admissibility Criteria*, 2014, para. 105) ending the process of exhaustion of domestic remedies (*Assanidze v. Georgia*, para. 159). In cases where domestic remedies are unavailable, ineffective or non-existent, the time-limit in general runs from the date of the act complained of. Cases of disappearances also call for a less rigid approach (*Varnava v. Turkey*, paras. 162-164). The date an application is deemed to have been submitted to the Court is that of the date of the first letter (*Alzery v. Sweden*, p. 6) as evidenced by the postmark on the letter (Rule of Court 47(6)(a); *Practical Guide on Admissibility Criteria*, 2014, para. 112; Harris et al., 2009, pp. 777-81). Presumably, the new shorter time frame will apply, *mutatis mutandis*, to these different circumstances in the future.

The initiative for effecting this change appears to have originated with the Court which took the view that in the digital age and the consequent development of swifter communications technology, a reduction in the time-limit was feasible (*Preliminary opinion of the Court in preparation for the Brighton Conference*, 2012, para. 37). According to the Explanatory Report on Protocol 15, this was a persuasive factor in taking this change forward.

In the absence of any explicit indication to that end, either in *Protocol 15* itself or the Explanatory Report, it is unclear whether this signals an intention to require the completion and submission of application forms online to the exclusion of other forms of communication. It would suggest so. There is certainly an evident trend these days in government departments to adopt the paperless office. But the present Rules of Court require the initiation of individual applications to be in writing and to be submitted via post (Rules of Court 45(1) and 47(6)(a)). Consequently, the adoption of the paperless office would necessitate the amendment of the Rules of Court. Nevertheless, the given reason in the Explanatory Report seems a disingenuous argument. It must be borne in mind that, as a number of NGOs have observed, not everybody is connected to the internet or has access, or reliable access, to it (Joint NGO Statement, 2013, para. B). It may be that, like electricity, at some time in the future the overwhelming majority of people will be connected to the internet but that time has not yet arrived. And many people are still unfamiliar with computers. Such people may therefore find themselves marginalised from mainstream society. Of course, it could be argued that there is an expectation that in this day and age, every lawyer's office will have internet connection, but such an assumption cannot be made. In fact, not all complainants are represented by lawyers. But it is vital to remember that under the present system, the crucial date for the submission of applications is the postmark date on the letter of application, not the date of receipt by the Registry. If done online it can be assumed that the crucial date will be the day the application is submitted. Whether the form-filling is done online or on paper, the time required to do so will be essentially the same; there is no logical reason why a two-month reduction is called for simply because it is done online. But if submission of applications via post is still permitted once *Protocol 15* enters into force, and the postmark date on the letter of application remains the crucial date, it means that complainants will still have lost two months for no apparent reason. The invocation of swifter communications technology seems an irrelevance, a sleight of hand designed to mask the actuality of tightening access to the Court. Neither should administrative convenience become the determining consideration. The observation must therefore be made that the reduction of two months seems disproportionate in the circumstances. In our view no compelling reasons exist necessitating amending the six-month rule. Account should also be taken of the fact that in directed, or controlled, 'democracies,' such as Russia or some other former Soviet republics, reduced time-limits may provide the authorities with a further opportunity to impede access to the Court notwithstanding Article 34 ECHR which states that States parties must not "hinder in any way the effective exercise of this right" (*Practical Guide on Admissibility Criteria*, 2014, paras. 46-49; *Sabri Güneş v. Turkey*, 2013, para. 57; Harris et al., 2009, pp. 820-21).

Another reason given for this move in the Explanatory Report is that the ECHR would be brought into line with similar time-limits extant in the Member States. However, such a condescending approach fails to take appropriate account of the possibility that national lawyers may lack expertise in European human rights law or, indeed, that the seriousness of the alleged violation and of the possible complexities of a case may be underestimated (Joint NGO Statement, 2013, para. B). Moreover, the justification given for this change is at odds with the fact that, as mentioned above, the Court applies its own distinct criteria in calculating time-limits quite independent of national rules. However, according to the Explanatory Report, national, shorter, rules have now assumed a compelling importance. Further weight is therefore given to misgivings that States are seeking to loosen the sometimes stringent legal restraints imposed by human rights obligations. It must be observed that the imposition of procedural conditions such as time-limits are not in themselves unfair but such time-limits must be consistent with the proper administration of justice and the imposition of over-restrictive time-limits that objectively fail to allow the applicant sufficient time to prepare their case adequately could be deemed unreasonable and amount to a denial of justice (Harris et al., 2009, pp. 309-310). In light of the fact that the Court has previously commented that the six-month time-limit is a sufficient period of time to enable potential applicants to consider whether to make a complaint (*Sabri Güneş v. Turkey*, 2013, para. 57), it is disappointing that a short time afterwards the Court was recommending a reduction in the time-limit, and doubly so that such a move should have been initiated from the Court.

Another negative aspect associated with this change is that the ECHR will move out of step with the other regional human rights systems. The ACHR thus incorporates the six-month rule (Article 46(1)(b) ACHR). And while the African Charter does not stipulate a specific time-limit, stating only that the communication must be submitted within a reasonable period, (Article 56(6) of the *African Charter*) the African Commission regards the six-month rule applied by the European and American systems as a useful guide(*Darfur Relief and Communication Centre v. Sudan*, paras. 75–77; *Majuru v. Zimbabwe*, Communication No. 308/2005, 25th Activity Report 2008, para. 109; Magliveras & Naldi, 2014, p. 273).

While, as has been stated, the time-limit applies both to individual applications and inter-state cases, it is evident that the actual reduction in the time period is purposely directed at the former. States, with the resources at their disposal, will hardly be incommoded by this move, although it could potentially have an adverse effect on any diplomatic negotiations aimed at settling the dispute in question, whereas it could have a considerable damaging impact on individuals. Tightening this particular admissibility requirement appears to be designed to set a higher threshold for individuals and to trip up the unwary. As the Court has observed, applicants must be alert so as to comply with procedural rules (*Sabri Güneş v. Turkey*, 2013, para. 57). Six months amounts to a reasonable period of time but it is our considered opinion that four months constitutes an imbalanced period of time unwarranted by circumstances and which is likely to prejudice individuals. While getting to grips with the crisis of applications is a laudable aim, it should not be done at the expense of justice for individuals.

CONCLUSION

The enormous buildup in applications to the Court has been the impetus driving forward reform of the European system for many years. Sensible reforms are deserving of praise and should be supported. *Protocol 14* introduced a number. One of these is the creation of Single-judge formations and committees. Another is the pilot judgments procedure. Or giving the Court a greater role in supervising the execution of its judgments under Article 46(5) ECHR. But this Chapter has drawn attention to a number of changes which are questionable because they appear capable of eroding the protective mantle of human rights in Europe. The concept of no significant disadvantage is replete with difficulty. The fact that *Protocol 15* intends to repeal the safeguard that no case will be rejected if it has not been duly considered by a domestic tribunal appears to us deeply troubling. The reduction in the time-limit proposed by *Protocol 15* seems ill-advised and the justification for it, improved communications, is unconvincing. The proposed references to the principles of subsidiarity and margin of appreciation in the preamble to the ECHR may be unwise. They certainly seem unnecessary in light of their accepted nature in European human rights law.

But the integrity of the reform process is open to doubt because it has been partially hijacked by forces with reactionary instincts. These elements wish to subvert the special nature of the ECHR system which is "an instrument of European public order (ordre public) for the protection of individual human beings" (*Loizidou v. Turkey* (Preliminary Objections) (1995) 20 EHRR 99, para. 93; *Wemhoff v. Germany* (1979-80) 1 EHRR 55, para. 8; *Ireland v. United Kingdom* (1979-80) 2 EHRR 25, para. 154; *Soering v. United Kingdom* (1989) 11 EHRR 439, para. 87), an approach sustained in other jurisdictions(*Effect of Reservations on the Entry into Force of the American Convention on Human Rights (Arts. 74 and 75)*, Advisory Opinion OC-2/82, Series A No 2 (24 September 1982)); Human Rights Committee, 1997, para. 8), into a statist model based on an exchange of mutual obligations between States the sovereignty of which can be constrained only with their clear consent (*Ireland v. United Kingdom* (1979-80) 2 EHRR 25, Separate Opinion of Judge Fitzmaurice, para. 239; *Golder v. United Kingdom* (1979-80) 1 EHRR 524, Separate Opinion of Judge Fitzmaurice, para. 37). They also favour a textual, literal approach to the interpretation of the ECHR, as if it were a mere statute. These objectives we believe are ultimately doomed to failure because the Court's assumption of a neo-constitutional role is deep (Warbrick, 1989, pp. 711, 714) and the whole ECHR *acquis* is unlikely to be reversed. But in the meantime it has the capacity to inflict damage on the ECHR. The reform process has given the appearance at times of seeking to influence the Court, subtly sometimes, more forcefully others, to adopt a mindset more sympathetic to respondent States as they battle the myriad problems of contemporary society. But taken too far such suasion can have the effect of calling into question the independence of the judges, one of the foundations of a democratic society (Bingham, 2010, p. 91). Indeed, a former President of the Court felt the need to make this point (Bratza, 2014, pp. 80-81). If the perception were to take hold with the public that the Court's independence was somehow compromised the whole system would lose credibility. This would indeed be a crisis for Europe.

References

Amerasinghe, C.F. (2004). *Local Remedies in International Law* (2nd ed.). Cambridge: Cambridge University Press.

Bellamy, R. (2014). The Democratic Legitimacy of International Human Rights Conventions: Political Constitutionalism and the European Convention on Human Rights. *European Journal of International Law*, *25*, 1019.

Bingham, T. (2010). *The Rule of Law*. London: Allen Lane.

Bratza, Sir Nicolas. (2014). Opening Addresses. In Council of Europe. *Reforming the European Convention on Human Rights: Interlaken, Izmir, Brighton and Beyond* (pp. 80-83). Strasbourg: Council of Europe.

Buergenthal, T. (2000). International Human Rights in an Historical Perspective. In J. Symonides (Ed.), *Human Rights: Concept and Standards*, (pp. 3-30). Aldershot: Ashgate & UNESCO.

Buyse, A. (2013). Significantly Insignificant? The Life in The Margins of the Admissibility Criterion in Article 35 § 3 (b) ECHR. In B. McGonigle Leyh, Y. Haeck, C. Burbano Herrera, D. Contreras Garduno (Eds.), *Liber Amicorum of Leo Zwaak*. Antwerp: Intersentia. Retrieved from http://ssm.com/abstract=2244283.

Carozza, P.G. (2003). Subsidiarity as a Structural Principle of International Human Rights Law. *American Journal of International Law*, *97*, 38.

Cass, D. (1992). The Word that Saves Maastricht? The Principle of Subsidiarity and the Division of Powers Within the European Community. *Common Market Law Review*, *29*, 1107.

Cassese, A. (2005). *International Law* (2nd ed.). Oxford: Oxford University Press.

Cassese, S. (2015, January). *Ruling Indirectly: Judicial Subsidiarity in the ECtHR*. Paper presented at the seminar held to mark the official opening of the judicial year of the European Court of Human Rights, Strasbourg.

Chakrabarti, S. (2015). *On Liberty*. London: Penguin.

Christoffersen, J. (2011). Individual and Constitutional Justice: Can the Power Balance of Adjudication be Reversed? In J. Christoffersen & M. Rask Madsen (Eds.), *The European Court of Justice between Law and Politics*, (pp. 181-203). Oxford: Oxford University Press.

Conte, A. & Burchill, R. (2009). *Defining Civil and Political Rights: The Jurisprudence of the United Nations Human Rights Committee* (2nded.). Farnham: Ashgate.

Costa, J. P. (2003). The European Court of Human Rights and Its Recent Case Law. *Texas International Law Journal*, *38*, 455.

Craig, P. & de Búrca, G. (2008). *EU Law: Text, Cases & Materials* (4th ed.). Oxford: Oxford University Press.

Council of Europe. (2013). *Explanatory Report on Protocol No. 15 amending the Convention for the Protection of Human Rights and Fundamental Freedoms*.

Council of Europe. (2014). *Reforming the European Convention on Human Rights: Interlaken, Izmir, Brighton and Beyond.* Strasbourg: Council of Europe.

Council of Europe. (2014). *Explanatory Report on Protocol 15*. Strasbourg: Council of Europe. Retrieved from http://www.echr.coe.int/-Documents/Protocol_15_explanatory_report_ ENG.pdf.

Council of Europe, Parliamentary Assembly. (2013). Opinion No. 283 (2013).

Donnelly, J. (1997). *International Human Rights*. (2nd ed.). Boulder: Westview.

European Court of Human Rights. (2010). *Interlaken Follow-Up: Principle of Subsidiarity*. Strasbourg: Registry of the European Court of Human Rights.

European Court of Human Rights. (2011). *Annual Report 2010*. Strasbourg: Registry of the European Court of Human Rights.

European Court of Human Rights. (2012). *The new admissibility criterion under Article 35 § 3 (b) of the Convention: case-law principles two years on*. Strasbourg: Council of Europe.

European Court of Human Rights. (2012). *Preliminary opinion of the Court in preparation for the Brighton Conference*. Retrieved from http://www.coe.int/t/brighton-conference/ Documents/Court-Preliminary-opinion_en. pdf.

European Court of Human Rights. (2013). *Opinion of the Court on Draft Protocol No. 15 to the European Convention on Human Rights.*

European Court of Human Rights. (2014). *Practical Guide on Admissibility Criteria*. Strasbourg: Registry of the European Court of Human Rights. Retrieved from http://www.echr.coe.int.

European Court of Human Rights. (2014). *Rules of Court*. Retrieved from http://www.echr.coe.int.

Fawcett, J.E.S. (1987). *The Application of the European Convention on Human Rights*. (2nd ed.). Oxford: Clarendon Press.

Grant, J.P. & Barker, J.C. (2009). *Parry & Grant Encyclopaedic Dictionary of International Law* (3rd ed.). New York: Oxford University Press.

Hale, B. (2012). *Argentoratum Locutum*: Is Strasbourg or the Supreme Court Supreme? *Human Rights Law Review* 12, 1.

Harris, D.J., O'Boyle, M. & Warbrick, C. (2009). *Law of the European Convention on Human Rights* (2nd ed.). London: Sweet & Maxwell.

Helfer, L. (2008). Redesigning the European Court of Human Rights: Embeddedness as a Deep Structural Principle of the European Court of Human Rights. *European Journal of International Law*, *19*, 125.

Helfer, L. & Slaughter, A.M. (1997). Toward a Theory of Effective Supranational Litigation. *Yale Law Journal*, *107*, 273.

Hutchinson, M.R. (1999). The Margin of Appreciation Doctrine in the European Court of Human Rights. *International & Comparative Law Quarterly*, *48*, 638.

Joint Committee on Human Rights. *Protocol 15 to the European Convention on Human Rights*. Fourth Report of Session 2014–15, HL 71 /HC 837.

Joint NGO Statement. (2013). *Protocol 15 to the European Convention on Human Rights must not result in a weakening of human rights protection*. Retrieved from http://www.interights.org/document/278/index.html.

Keller, H., Fischer, A. & Kühne, D. (2010). Debating the Future of the European Court of Human Rights after the Interlaken Conference: Two Innovative Proposals. *European Journal of International Law*, *21*, 1025.

Klabbers, J. (2009). *An Introduction to International Institutional Law*. (2nd ed.). Cambridge: Cambridge University Press.

Lambrecht, S. (2014). Bringing Rights *More* Home: Can a Home-Grown UK Bill of Rights Lessen the Influence of the European Court of Human Rights? *German Law Journal*, *15*, 407.

Magliveras, K. D. & Naldi, G.J. (2014). *The African Union: Institutions and Activities*. Alphen aan den Rijn: Kluwer Law International.

Mahoney, P. (2014). The Changing Face of the European Court of Human Rights: Its Face in 2015? *Queen Mary Human Rights Law Review* 1, 4.

Merrills, J.G. & Robertson, A.H. (2001). *Human Rights in Europe* (4th ed.). Manchester: Manchester University Press.

Ministry of Justice. (2014). *Explanatory Memorandum on Protocol 15 amending the Convention for the Protection of Human Rights and Fundamental Freedoms*. (Cm. 8951). London: TSO.

Mowbray, A. (2004). Protocol 14 to the European Convention on Human Rights and Recent Strasbourg Cases. *Human Rights Law Review*, *4*, 331.

O'Boyle, M. (2008). On Reforming the Operation of the European Court of Human Rights. *European Human Rights Law Review*, *1*.

Oreb, N. (2013). The Legality of Kettling after Austin. *Modern Law Review*, *76*, 735.

Pasqualucci, J.M. (2003). *The Practice and Procedure of the Inter-American Court of Human Rights.* Cambridge: Cambridge University Press.

Policy Exchange. (2011). *UK 'should cut links to European Court of Human Rights.'* Retrieved January 18, 2012, from http://www.bbc.co.uk/news/uk-politics.

Raab, D. (2012, January 24). The Strasbourg Court is still a cranks' paradise. *Daily Telegraph.* Retrieved from http://www.telegraph.co.uk/news-/worldnews/europe/9035934/The-Strasbourg-Court-is-still-a-cranks-paradise.html.

Reiss, J.W. (2009). Protocol No. 14 ECHR and Russian Non-Ratification: The Current State of Affairs. *Harvard Human Rights Journal*, *22*, 293.

Robertson, A.H. & Merrills, J.G. (1996). *Human Rights in the World*, (4th ed.). Manchester: Manchester University Press.

Rozenberg, J. (2013, June 3). Protocol 15 gives Tories what they want on European court of human rights - so why leave? *The Guardian.* Retrieved from http://www.theguardian.com/law/2013/jun/03/european-humanrights -protocol-15.

Ruedin, X. B. (2008). De minimis non curat the European Court of Human Rights: the introduction of a new admissibility criterion (Article 12 of Protocol 14). *European Human Rights Law Review, 180.*

Sands, P. & Klein, P. (2009). *Bowett's Law of International Institutions* (6th ed.). London: Sweet & Maxwell.

Schilling, T. (1994). A New Dimension of Subsidiarity: Subsidiarity as a Rule and a Principle. *Yearbook of European Law*, *14*, 203.

Shaw, M. (2008). *International Law* (6th ed.). Cambridge: Cambridge University Press.

Spano, R. (2014). Universality or Diversity of Human Rights: Strasbourg in the Age of Subsidiarity. *Human Rights Law Review*, *14*, 487.

Spielmann, D. (2013, September). *Judgments of the European Court of Human Rights: Effects and Implementation.* Keynote speech at the Conference at the Paulinerkirke Göttinggen, Georg-August-University, Göttinggen.

Steiner, H. J. & Alston, P. (2000). *International Human Rights in Context: Law, Politics, Morals* (2nd ed.). Oxford: Oxford University Press.

Sweeney, J.A. (2005). Margins of Appreciation: Cultural Relativity and the European Court of Human Rights in the Post-Cold War Era. *International & Comparative Law Quarterly*, *54*, 459.

United Nations Human Rights Committee. (1997). General Comment 24. *Compilation of General Comments and General Recommendations adopted by Human Rights Treaty Bodies*. HRI/GEN/1/Rev.3.

van Dijk, P. & van Hoof, G.J.H. (1990). *Theory and Practice of the European Convention on Human Rights* (2nd ed.) Deventer: Kluwer.

Vogiatzis, N. (2015). When 'reform' meets 'judicial restraint': Protocol 15 amending the European Convention on Human Rights. *Northern Ireland Legal Quarterly*, *66*, 127.

Warbrick, C. (1989). "Federal" Aspects of the European Convention on Human Rights. *Michigan Journal of International Law*, *10*, 698.

In: International Human Rights and Justice
Editor: Doug Hodgson
ISBN: 978-1-63484-709-4

Chapter 8

CULTURAL PROPERTY AS A CASUALTY OF ARMED CONFLICT: A COMMENT ON THE LESSONS FROM IRAQ AND SYRIA

Lara Pratt*

School of Law, The University of Notre Dame Australia
(Fremantle Campus)

"You can wipe out an entire generation, you can burn their homes to the ground and somehow they'll still find their way back. But if you destroy their history, you destroy their achievements and it's as if they never existed. That's what Hitler wants and that's exactly what we are fighting for."

George Clooney as Frank Stokes in *The Monuments Men* (2014)

ABSTRACT

Cultural property has long been a casualty of war. Buildings and artefacts of cultural property are vulnerable to direct attack, theft and incidental damage as a result of nearby fighting. International humanitarian law (IHL) has sought to protect cultural property during armed conflict – imposing on States both positive obligations to protect and negative obligations to refrain from targeting. This brief commentary will explain the principled basis of the protection of cultural property and discuss the significance of particular incidents of cultural property destruction in the recent conflicts in Iraq and Syria.

BACKGROUND

From its beginnings in the late 19th Century, modern international humanitarian law (IHL) has had an emphasis on physical safety. Although lacking a universal definition, the principle of humanity underlies the specific rules of IHL found in treaty and customary

* Corresponding author: Email: lara.pratt@nd.edu.au.

international law (Fast, 2015; Coupland, 2001) and guides participants in conflict to minimize the cruelties (both deliberate and consequential) of war (see, for example, Preamble of *St Petersburg Declaration 1868*).

After the Second World War, IHL began to expand beyond obligations with regard to treatment of enemy soldiers (and associated personnel) and introduced rules which minimized (so far as is possible) the impact of war on civilian populations (in particular *Geneva Convention IV 1949; Additional Protocol I 1977*). The rules of IHL relevant to the protection of cultural property are those focused on the prohibition of targeting (and prohibition on use for military purposes) of civilians and civilian objects (see especially Articles 48 and 53 of *Additional Protocol I*, 1977). The combination of customary and treaty rules has the interrelated purposes of minimizing civilian casualties and minimizing the overall effect that conflict has on the civilian population while recognizing the realities of military necessity (Solf, 1986). IHL recognizes the distinct identity of the civilian populations and maintains an (albeit limited) form of the right to self-determination even in the context of armed conflict when that population is under the temporary control of an occupying (foreign/enemy) power, retaining an (admittedly limited) degree of autonomy and entitlement to the protections of IHL (Article 44, *Geneva Convention IV 1949*).

Cultural property[58] as defined in Article 1(a) of the *Hague Convention on the Protection of Cultural Property in the Event of Armed Conflict 1954 (Hague Convention)* is a broad term which encompasses tangible artefacts "of great importance to the cultural heritage of every people such as monuments of architecture, art or history, whether religious or secular; archaeological sites; groups of buildings which, as a whole, are of historical or artistic interest; works of art; manuscripts, books and other objects of artistic, historical or archaeological interest; as well as scientific collections and important collections of books or archives." Article 1(b) of the *Hague Convention* extends the legal protections to modern buildings such as museums and libraries which house and shelter collections of cultural property.

The protection of cultural property may initially appear at best a peripheral consequence of IHL and at worst a distraction from the core purpose (Paroff, 2004). Rather than protecting the present safety and future continuance of civilian communities, the IHL rules protecting cultural property seek to protect the evidence of the past. However, in another sense, the specific protection offered by IHL to cultural property is entirely compatible with the core purposes of IHL and reflects both the common humanity which is at the basis of IHL and the right of a community to a self-identity that serves as a basis for post-war reconstructive efforts and reassertion of self-determination (Freeman, 1998; Kasymov, 2011). It has even been suggested that the destruction of cultural property during armed conflict can impact on the levels of violence during the post-conflict reconstruction period and hinder the re-establishment of society (Isakhan, 2013).

Global outrage at deliberate actions such as the bombing of the historic town of Dubrovnik during the Yugoslav conflict,[59] the 2001 destruction of the Buddhas of Bamiyan in

---

[58] The term "cultural property" is not wholly uncontroversial. There is debate about the appropriateness of terms such as "cultural heritage" which similarly recognizes the intangible. However, it is the terminology used in IHL and is thus adopted in this commentary. (See Frigo, 2004).

[59] The Old Town of Dubrovnik is a walled city in Croatia with architecture dating from around the 15th – 16th Century. The siege of Dubrovnik is discussed in Balcells (2015) including analysis as to how the Balkans

Afghanistan (albeit not strictly within the context of armed conflict)[60] and more recently the Islamic State (also known as ISIS, ISIL or Daesh) deliberate razing of the 2000-year-old temple of Bel at Palmyra in Syria (UNITAR, 2015)[61] suggests cultural property is not just a concern for the territorial residents in which it is found. The loss of these sites resonated not merely out of sympathy for the Croatians, Afghanis and Syrians who had lost places of historic significance but because they are, as Bokova (2012) put it, "a loss to all humanity."

Protection of Cultural Property in Human Rights and International Humanitarian Law

Outside the context of armed conflict, the right to cultural property has limited express recognition in human rights law.[62] For example, Article 27 of the *Universal Declaration of Human Rights 1948 (UDHR)* does not specifically mention cultural property; instead, it recognizes a "right to freely to participate in the cultural life of the community" and references sharing in art and scientific advancement. The equivalent Article 15(1) (a) and (b) of the *International Covenant on Economic, Social and Cultural Rights 1966* recognizes the right to take part in culture and Article 15(2) obliges States Parties to take steps to conserve culture – presumably including cultural property.

The right to cultural property is largely derived from the right to self-determination and reflects the acknowledged relationship between culture and both individual and community identity (Freeman, 1998; Kasymov, 2011). Under Article 22 of the *UDHR*, cultural rights are recognized to be 'indispensable' to personal development. Cultural heritage is intrinsically linked to community and national identity (Freeman, 1998). To this end, Article 11 of the United Nations *Declaration on the Rights of Indigenous Peoples 2007* gives specific recognition of the importance of cultural property to the identity of Indigenous Persons (Alderman, 2011). In these various ways, human rights law recognizes culture and cultural property in a way that is intrinsically tied to effective self-identity and self-determination (Alderman, 2011). It follows, therefore, that it ought to be given special protection in humanitarian law which is concerned with the survival of communities post-conflict.

IHL has taken a slightly different approach to cultural property. While IHL acknowledges that cultural property primarily belongs to the people from whose history, territory or religion the particular property derives, the efficacy of the protection is dependent on a recognition that "damage to cultural property belonging to any people whatsoever means damage to the cultural heritage of all mankind, since each people makes its contribution to the culture of the world" (See the second preambular paragraph of the *Hague Convention 1954*; Ishwara Bhat, 2001).

conflicts and subsequent criminal tribunal proceedings contributed to policies and changing attitudes towards the protection of cultural property in armed conflict.

[60] The Bamiyan Buddhas were 55-metre-high statues carved into the cliffs in Bamiyan. For a brief overview of the destruction see 'Nothing remains' of Bamiyan Buddhas. (2002). Consideration of the cultural significance of the region can be found at: Cultural Landscape and Archaeological Remains of the Bamiyan Valley (undated).

[61] Discussion of the significance of the Palmyra and pre-2015 damage to the site can be found in a report produced by UNITAR (2014). See also: ISIL blows up Arch of Triumph in Syria's Palmyra. (2015).

[62] A more detailed overview of cultural property as a human right can be found in Alderman (2011).

There are both general and specific protections offered to cultural property in IHL. Cultural property undeniably falls within the category of "civilian objects" which are not to be the subject of specific attack (see, for example, Article 27 of the *Hague Regulations 1907*). Buildings dedicated to special (cultural) purposes such as religion, science and art as well as "historic monuments" are especially identified as not being legitimate subjects of attack and should not be made so by use for military purposes (ICRC, 2015).[63] These prohibitions are widely accepted as having the status of customary international law (ICRC, 2015; Toman, 2005).

While some attempts had been made to codify the special protection of cultural property prior to the Second World War, it was the combination of the deliberate destruction of historic buildings, monuments and towns (for example, as part of aerial bombardments) combined with the widespread theft and destruction of artworks during the war that led to the *Hague Convention* (Schipper & Frank, 2013). The *Hague Convention* imposes specific obligations on States Parties to both refrain from targeting and to actively protect places and artefacts of universal historic significance (Article 4 *Hague Convention 1954*; Article 5 *Second Protocol 1999*). Article 8 requires States Parties to proactively identify sites of cultural significance in peacetime and, for moveable cultural property, allows for the creation of refuges which are given "special protection," identified by a blue shield symbol. As Ishwara Bhat (2001) has pointed out, this "special protection" is still severely limited by Article 11 which allows that the protection can be lost where commanders in the field make a calculation of military necessity.

The availability of military necessity as a legitimate 'exception' to both the general prohibition on targeting cultural property and the protections offered by the *Hague Convention* has, in part, been addressed by the *Second Protocol to the Hague Convention 1999 (Second Protocol)* (Ishwara Bhat, 2001). Under Article 6 of the *Second Protocol*, the military necessity exception still exists, but the cultural property must already have been used for military purposes (by the opposing side) to become a legitimate military target *and* there must be no other "feasible alternative" to ending the military use of the cultural property.

Enhanced protection is also available for sites identified by the International Committee for Protection of Cultural Property (ICPCP). While military necessity may temporarily make an ICPCP-identified site the target of an attack, the protection remains until formally removed by the ICPCP (Ishwara Bhat, 2001; Articles 10, 13 and 14 of the *Second Protocol 1999*). Further, the decision to make an "enhanced protection" site a target on the basis of military necessity must be made by someone no less senior than a battalion commander and only after the opposing forces are given "reasonable time" to remove whatever they have done to make the site an object of military use (Article 13 of the *Second Protocol 1999*; Ishwara Bhat, 2001).

Parallel to the obligation not to target, the *Hague Convention* requires States Parties to actively protect. Under Article 3 of the *Hague Convention 1954*, States Parties are required to take action in peacetime to make preparations to safeguard cultural property that is likely to be at risk in the event of armed conflict. In addition, taking cultural property as loot is to be prohibited and under Article 4(3) of the *Hague Convention 1954*, States Parties are obliged to "put a stop to any form of theft, pillage or misappropriation of, and any acts of vandalism

[63] Rule 38 of the International Committee of the Red Cross's Customary IHL Database provides a concise explanation of the rule requiring respect for cultural property in armed conflict (ICRC, 2015).

directed against, cultural property." This goes beyond the customary international law obligations and requires that action be taken – both in war and peacetime – to secure cultural property. Where theft and looting have occurred, the *Convention on the Means of Prohibiting and Preventing the Illicit Import, Export and Transfer of Ownership of Cultural property 1970* requires States Parties to take action to prevent the trade in stolen cultural artefacts.

Where a military force fails to comply with the IHL protection of cultural property, those responsible may be criminally liable. Deliberate targeting, theft and wanton destruction of cultural property was identified in the *London Charter 1945* for the Nuremburg trials and the *Statute of the International Criminal Tribunal for the former Yugoslavia 1993*. Articles 8(2)(b)(ix) (international conflicts) and 8(2)(e)(iv) (non-international conflicts) of the *Rome Statute of the International Criminal Court 1998* criminalize intentional "attacks against buildings dedicated to religion, education, art, science or charitable purposes, historic monuments . . . provided they are not military objectives." Admittedly there are both practical and jurisdictional challenges to achieving prosecution, but such concerns are beyond the scope of this brief comment.[64]

PROTECTION OF CULTURAL PROPERTY IN CONTEMPORARY CONFLICTS

The practice of deliberately targeting cultural property is not a modern invention – destruction, looting and plundering were a common feature (and even an objective) of ancient wars (Merryman, 2005; Tomen, 2005). The looting of conquered territory was historically viewed as a privilege of the victor (Polybius of Athens in Merryman, 2005). While the above-mentioned modern laws of IHL have removed the perceived 'right' of destruction and theft, cultural property remains particularly vulnerable in armed conflict.

The 21st Century conflicts in Iraq and Syria have brought to light two types of challenges facing the practical realization of protection of cultural property in armed conflicts. The first challenge is the lack of priority given to the protection of cultural property, placing it at risk of damage, destruction and looting – not only as a consequence of battle, but because the lack of protection and value of the artefacts make them attractive targets for looters and thieves (Bogdanos discussed in Paroff, 2004). The second challenge is the proliferation of conflicts in which (at least) one party is not a signatory to the relevant conventions, rejects customary international law and has an ideological commitment to the destruction cultural history.

In 2003, as US and Coalition troops entered Baghdad, the Iraqi National Museum was left unprotected (Phuong, 2004; Stone, 2012). The US was, at the time, not a party to the *Hague Convention*[65] and thus its legal obligations with regard to the Museum were limited to the *Geneva Convention IV* and customary international law obligations. Once they became an occupying power, there existed a general obligation to take efforts to maintain law and order (for example, Article 43 of the *Hague Regulations 1907*). Although, as Phuong (2004) points out, maintaining law and order conceivably includes the prevention of looting, it is unlikely

[64] More detailed commentaries on the historical development of cultural property protections in IHL can be found, for example, in Drazewska (2015); Schipper & Frank (2013); Van der Auwera (2013).

[65] The USA has subsequently ratified the Hague Convention. A complete list of signatories can be found at: State Parties Convention for the Protection of Cultural Property in the Event of Armed Conflict with Regulations for the Execution of the Convention (undated).

that, at the time of the looting, the Coalition forces were exercising sufficient control over the area to cross from 'invading' to 'occupying' power (Paroff, 2004). The consequence was, as experts had predicted, that the Museum was looted and irreplaceable artefacts destroyed and stolen (Paroff, 2004; Stone, 2012).

While the looting was not undertaken by Coalition troops, commentary as to responsibility appeared focused on the US troops who had been warned of the vulnerability of the Museum and were in the best position to protect the Museum at the time (see, for example, O'Rourke, 2003; Thurlow, 2005; Stone, 2012). The reasons for the US failure to protect the Museum are complex – it does not appear to have been attributable to the non-ratification of the *Hague Convention*, as both the UK and US indicated a commitment to work within the "spirit of the Convention" (Stone, 2012). There is some evidence that Coalition forces had given some consideration to cultural property, but when viewed in the context of the larger conflict, where significant damage occurred to a range of sites, it is clear that protection of cultural property did not appear to be a significant priority to senior Coalition officials when planning military action in Iraq (Isakhan, 2013; Stone, 2012). "[F]rom a cultural property perspective, the whole Iraq conflict can only be regarded as a complete catastrophe" (Stone, 2012).

Whatever the actual sentiment of the forces in Iraq, the public response to the failure to protect was overwhelmingly negative and contributed to the wariness of the local Iraqi population to the incoming Coalition troops (Stone, 2012; Thurlow, 2005). The impact of the images of the curators sitting amongst the ruins of antiquities do appear to have had some positive outcomes. At the very least, the USA –the most visible participant in the conflict – has subsequently ratified the *Hague Convention* and is therefore now bound by the more specific obligations.[66]

There has been a renewed US (and global) commitment to retrieving stolen artefacts and supporting the establishment of pre-emptive protections in Iraq (Thurlow, 2005). In early 2015 the Iraqi National Museum reopened – including in its collections many artefacts that had been looted in 2003 and, as the result of a global effort, had been identified and recovered (Romney, 2015). In addition, the ease with which the looting had occurred in 2003 highlighted the deficiencies in Iraq's preparatory measures (Paroff, 2004). With the return of artefacts and the re-opened Museum, efforts have been taken to create secure vaults – presumably within the context of Article 8 of the *Hague Convention 1954* places of security (refuge) - where moveable items of cultural property may be stored and protected against the very real threat that Baghdad will once again be the site of armed conflict (Romney, 2015).

Although not wholly attributed to the Iraqi example,[67] the mainstream awareness of the risks to cultural property in armed conflict has had a wider impact. For example, the United Nations Multidimensional Integrated Stabilization Mission in Mali (MINUSMA) – the peacekeeping mission in Mali – expressly includes the protection and restoration of cultural property in its mandate (Cultural Heritage, undated; *UNSC Resolution 2100*, 2013). UN

[66] At the time of writing, the UK has not ratified the Hague Convention but has indicated an intention to do so. See, for example, Helm, (2015).

[67] Balcells (2015) provides an excellent analysis as to how the Balkans conflicts and subsequent criminal tribunal proceedings contributed to policies and changing attitudes towards the protection of cultural property in armed conflict. Balcells, M. (2015). Left Behind? Cultural Destruction, the Role of the International Criminal Tribunal for the Former Yugoslavia in Deterring it and Cultural Heritage Prevention Policies in the Aftermath of the Balkan Wars. *European Journal on Criminal Policy and Research,* 21(1), 1-13. doi: 10.1007/s10610-013-9220-8.

peacekeeping missions are limited to their mandate. If, for example, the mandate only permits the protection of life, peacekeepers would not be authorized to step in should they become aware of threats to property. Without express mention of cultural property as part of the mandate of peacekeepers, they are unlikely to be able to respond to threats to cultural property (Van Der Auwera, 2010). At best, the legal status of peacekeeper intervention to protect cultural property is ambiguous (Van Der Auwera, 2010). This express inclusion in MINUSMA's mandate is indicative of a wider awareness of the fragility of archaeological sites during times of conflict and a recognition that protecting cultural property can have a valuable role in attaining peace (Bokova, 2013). It also reflects a move towards clarifying the relationship between post-conflict peacekeepers and cultural property and giving peacekeepers a defined role in the protection of cultural property (Culture stands on the front-line, 2015; UN peacekeepers to protect world heritage sites, 2015). More broadly, there is some indication that military forces are open to measures which would better enable them to protect cultural property during conflict (see, for example, Jachec-Neale, 2015; Stone, 2012).

The threat facing Baghdad in 2015 is ISIS gaining access and control over more locations of cultural significance. Whereas the experience of 2003 highlighted the lack of priority given to protection of cultural property, the ISIS threat shows a different problem. The deliberate destruction of cultural property by ISIS has been well documented (Curry, 2015; UNITAR, 2014).[68] When ISIS forces took control of the 2000-year-old UNESCO World Heritage-listed Temple of Bel at Palmyra in early 2015, they captured Khaled al-Asaad, the head curator, and ultimately executed him when he refused to give up the location of the movable items of cultural property (Shaheen & Black, 2015). Although there was an initial promise not to harm the historic site, within a couple of months images were released of fighters carrying barrels of explosives into the Temple of Bel followed by images of the explosion (Curry, 2015). The temple was completely destroyed (Curry, 2015; UNITAR, 2015).

Where a belligerent party has little or no respect for IHL, cultural property can be a desirable target. ISIS is not a State and is therefore not party to the *Hague Convention* and not bound by the obligations it contains. Arguably, as a non-state/non-party, ISIS is similarly not bound by the *Geneva Conventions*. However, that becomes somewhat irrelevant inasmuch as the relevant obligations with regard to non-destruction of cultural property are of a customary international law nature and thus binding on non-parties and non-state-actors such as armed groups (Howe, 2012).[69] This individual responsibility for the war crime of wanton destruction and looting of cultural property under international law has been confirmed in the *Rosenberg Judgement* (1946) at Nuremburg and the *Strugar* (2005) decision of the International Criminal Tribunal for the Former Yugoslavia. Further, a case of a situation quite similar to the ideological destruction undertaken by ISIS is currently before the International Criminal Court. Ahmad Al Mahdi Al Faqi, a member of a militant group known as 'Al Qaeda in the Islamic Maghreb,' has been surrendered to the ICC to face prosecution at the ICC for destruction of various mausoleums in Timbuktu, including at least one UNESCO-listed World Heritage Site (Situation in Mali, 2015).

Perhaps the biggest practical challenge facing the protection of cultural property is that it requires a commitment from both or all belligerents in a conflict. As a part of their "cultural

[68] The focus of this discussion will be on ISIS in Syria. However, the damage is not confined to Syria. See, for example, the discussion of Iraq's experience in Neely & Simpson (2015).

[69] For a more complete discussion of the applicability of IHL laws with regard to the protection of cultural property by non-state actors, see Howe (2012).

cleansing" of the areas of Syria and Iraq over which they have control, ISIS has made clear an intention to destroy artefacts and property identified as contrary to their religious perspectives (Bokova, 2013). The immediate demoralizing effect of seeing the enemy destruction of artefacts is often believed to be tied to national pride and national identity (Bokova, 2013; Van Der Auwera, 2010). The destruction of cultural property is symbolic of destruction of the people and their history (Pessendorfer, 2013; Van Der Auwera, 2010). Further, where the fighters[70] refuse to recognize cultural items as having universal value, there can be a strategic benefit in destroying evidence of an enemy's historical achievements - forcibly asserting the superiority of one's own culture's historical achievements and diminishing the evidence of alternative historical narratives (Abtahi, 2001; Bugnion, 2004; Van Der Auwera, 2010). This would appear to be a core purpose of ISIS's actions (ISIL blows up Arch of Triumph, 2015).

Against the backdrop of the other atrocities (allegedly) committed by ISIS – "crimes of unspeakable cruelty have been reported, such as mass executions, sexual slavery, rape and other forms of sexual and gender-based violence, torture, mutilation, enlistment and forced recruitment of children and the persecution of ethnic and religious minorities" – prevention and, ultimately, the prosecution of the "wanton destruction of cultural property" may appear to be a secondary concern – an "also mentioned" crime among those crimes which more immediately impact on life and limb (Statement of The Prosecutor of the ICC, 2015).

However, the person vs property framework is a false dichotomy. The destruction of cultural property is causing harm to the community as a whole and reflects the broader ideological warfare being undertaken by ISIS. As Bokova (2013) has explained: "[s]uch acts of destruction cannot be decoupled from the killing of people, as violent extremists attack anything that can sustain diversity, critical thinking and freedom of opinion—schools, teachers, journalists, cultural minorities, and monuments. In this context, the protection of heritage is more than a cultural issue: it is a security necessity." (Bokova, 2013).

In addition, the United Nations Security Council, in Resolution 2199 (2015), has recognized the intrinsic link between the illegal trade of moveable items of cultural property and the funding of terrorism. Although the specific treaties obliging States Parties to take action to bring an end to the illegal trade in moveable cultural property has not been the focus of this paper, it is clear that ISIS's ideological objection to cultural property does not appear to extend to the destruction of artefacts stolen from the destroyed museums and sites that are being sold and used to fund their activities (Watson, 2015). Although Iraq led to a greater awareness of the risks of looting of cultural property and there has been significant action taken with regard to already-stolen items, Brodie (2015) points to the ineffectiveness of various *ad hoc* policies which respond to particular emergencies. The lessons of Iraq did not result in sufficient global measures to place a significant hurdle to ISIS's looting, and thus the international response is once again to respond rather than prevent (Brodie, 2015). Whether ISIS intends to destroy or appropriate the property from any particular site is unknown (and potentially dependent on the ease of transport of particular items found at larger sites). Consequently, protecting cultural property additionally serves to limit unlawful use of that property to fund ISIS activities.

[70] In light of the legal implications of the term 'combatants,' it is not used in this context.

Conclusion

Cultural property has intrinsic value both to local communities and to the wider global community. Just as destruction of cultural property is used as a weapon of war and a way of undermining community identity, cultural property has a significant role to play in post-war re-establishment of community in post-conflict regions. As Jachec-Neale (2015) has stated: "Cultural heritage has a crucial role to play in reconciliation and unification of the nation in the aftermath of conflict, and in the emotional survival of people during it – and it's the world's responsibility to preserve it." The post-WWII era brought recognition of the value of cultural property both for specific communities and humanity as a whole. However, conflicts at the end of 20th Century and early 21st Century once again saw armed conflict which took place with little apparent concern for the protection of cultural property. It has taken recent incidents, including the destruction and looting of the Iraqi National Museum in Baghdad and the levelling of the Temple of Bel at Palmyra, to once again remind the world of the collective value – indeed the collective responsibility – to protect this irreplaceable cultural property.

While there remain many challenges to the effective protection of cultural property, it is clear that the experiences of the early 21st Century have highlighted the vulnerability of cultural property and encouraged a renewed, if moderate, commitment to its protection in times of armed conflict.

Legal Sources

Agreement for the Prosecution and Punishment of the Major War Criminals of the European Axis, and Charter of the International Military Tribunal. (1945). Retrieved from: https://www.icrc.org/ihl/INTRO/350? OpenDocument. (*London Charter*).

Declaration Renouncing the Use, in Time of War, of Explosive Projectiles Under 400 Grammes Weight. (1868, December 11). Retrieved from: https://www.icrc.org/applic/ihl/ihl.nsf/52d68d14de6160e0c12563da005fdb1b/dbe0afb2065e0d7ec125641e0031f38c?OpenDocument. (*St Petersburg Declaration*).

Declaration on the Rights of Indigenous Peoples 2007. United Nations GA Res 61/295, UN GAOR, 61st sess, UN Doc A/RES/47/1. Retrieved from: www.un.org/esa/socdev/unpfii/documents/DRIPS_en.pdf.

Convention on the Means of Prohibiting and Preventing the Illicit Import, Export and Transfer of Ownership of Cultural Property 1970, opened for signature 14 November 1970, 823 UNTS 231 (entered into force 24 April 1972). Retrieved from http://portal.unesco.org/en/ev.php-URL_ID=13039&URL_DO=DO_TOPIC&URL_SECTION=201.html.

Convention (IV) respecting the Laws and Customs of War on Land and its annex Hague Regulations Respecting the Laws and Customs of War on Land 1907 opened for signature 18 October 1907 (entered into force 26 January 1908), Article 27. Retrieved from https://www.icrc.org/ihl/INTRO/195. (*Hague Regulations*).

Geneva Convention (IV) relative to the Protection of Civilian Persons in Time of War, opened for signature 12 August 1949, 75 UNTS 287 (entered into force 21 October 1950). Retrieved from: https://www.icrc.org/ihl/INTRO/380. (*Geneva Convention IV*).

Hague Convention on the Protection of Cultural Property in the Event of Armed Conflict 1954, opened for signature 9 May 1954, in force 7 August 1956, 249 UNTS 240. Retrieved from: http://portal.unesco.-org/en/ev.php-URL_ID=13637&URL_DO=DO_TOPIC&URL_-SECTION=201.html. (*Hague Convention*).

International Covenant on Economic, Social and Cultural Rights 1966, opened for signature 16 December 1966, 993 UNTS 3 (entered into force 3 January 1976). Retrieved from: http://www.ohchr.org/-EN/ProfessionalInterest/Pages/CESCR.aspx. (*ICESCR*).

Prosecutor v Strugar (2005, January 31) International Criminal Tribunal for the Former Yugoslavia, Trial Chamber II, Case No. IT-01-42-T). Retrieved from www.icty.org/x/cases/strugar/tjug/en/str-tj050131e.pdf.

Protocol Additional to the Geneva Conventions of 12 August 1949, and relating to the Protection of Victims of International Armed Conflicts, opened for signature 8 June 1977, 1125 UNTS 3 (entered into force 7 December 1979). Retrieved from: https://www.icrc.org/ihl/INTRO/470. (*Additional Protocol I*).

UNSC Resolution 2100 (2013), UN SCOR, 6952nd mtg, 68th sess, S/RES/2100(2013) (25 April 2013). Retrieved from: http://www.un.org/en/peacekeeping/missions/minusma/documents/mali%20_2100_E_.pdf.

UNSC Resolution 2199 (2015), UN SCOR, 7379th mtg, S/RES/2199 (2015) (12 February 2015). Retrieved from: http://www.un.org/en/ga/search/-view_doc.asp?symbol=S/RES/2199%20%282015%29.

Rome Statute of the International Criminal Court, opened for signature 17 July 1998, 2187 UNTS 90 (entered into force 1 July 2002). (*Rome Statute*).

Rosenberg Judgement (1946, September 30 and October 1). Judgement of the International Military Tribunal (1946). Retrieved from: http://avalon.-law.yale.edu/imt/judrosen.asp.

Second Protocol to the Hague Convention of 1954 for the Protection of Cultural Property in the Event of Armed Conflict, opened for signature 26 March 1999, 2253 UNTS 212 (entered into force 9 March 2004). Retrieved from: http://portal.unesco.org/en/ev.php-URL_ID=15207&-URL_DO=DO_TOPIC&URL_SECTION=201.html. (*Second Protocol*).

Statute of the International Criminal Tribunal for the former Yugoslavia, (1993), SC Res 827, UN SCOR, 48th sess, 3217th mtg, UN Doc S/RES/827 (25 May 1993) as amended by SC Res 1877(2009), UN SCOR, 64th sess, 6155th mtg, UN Doc S/RES/1877 (7 July 2009). (*ICTY Statute*).

Universal Declaration of Human Rights 1948, UN GA Res 217A (III), UN GAOR, 3rd sess, 183rd plen mtg, UN Doc A/RES/217A (III) (10 December 1948). (*UDHR*).

REFERENCES

Abtahi, H. (2001). The Protection of Cultural Property in Times of Armed Conflict: The Practice of the International Criminal Tribunal for the Former Yugoslavia. *Harvard Human Rights Journal*, *14*, 1 – 32.

Alderman, K. (2011). The Human Right to Cultural Property. *Michigan Journal of International Law*, *20*(1), 69-81.

Baker, R. W., Ismael, S. T. & Ismael, T. Y. (2009). Ending the Iraqi State, in Baker, R. W., Ismael, S. T. and Ismael, T. Y. (Eds.). (2009). *Cultural Cleansing in Iraq: Why Museums*

Were Looted, Libraries Burned and Academics Murdered. London, GBR: Pluto Press. Retrieved from http://www.ebrary.com.ipacez.nd.edu.au.

Balcells, M. (2015). Left Behind? Cultural Destruction, the Role of the International Criminal Tribunal for the Former Yugoslavia in Deterring it and Cultural Heritage Prevention Policies in the Aftermath of the Balkan Wars. *European Journal on Criminal Policy and Research*, *21*(1), 1-13. doi: 10.1007/s10610-013-9220-8.

Bokova, I. (2012, December 2). Culture in the Cross Hairs, *New York Times*. Retrieved from http://www.nytimes.com/2012/12/03/opinion/global/cultu-ral-sites-must-be-protected.html?_r=0.

Bokova, I. (2013). Fighting Cultural Cleansing: Harnessing the Law to Preserve Cultural Heritage. *Harvard International Review*, *36*(4), 40-45.

Brodie, N., (2015). Syria and its Regional Neighbors: A Case of Cultural Property Protection Policy Failure? *International Journal of Cultural Property*, *22* (2–3), 317–335.

Bugnion, F. (2004, 14 November). The Origins and Development of the Legal Protection of Cultural Property in the Event of Armed Conflict. *International Committee of the Red Cross and Red Crescent Resource Centre.* Retrieved from. https://www.icrc.org/eng/resources/documents/misc/65shtj.htm.

"Culture stands on the front-line of conflict - it should be at the front-line of peace building," Director-General states to UN Security Council. (2015, April 27). UNESCO. Retrieved from: http://whc.unesco.org/-en/news/1269.

Cultural Heritage. (undated). *United Nations Multidimensional Integrated Stabilization Mission in Mali.* Retrieved from: http://minusma.-unmissions.org/en/cultural-heritage.

Cultural Landscape and Archaeological Remains of the Bamiyan Valley (undated). *UNESCO: World Heritage List.* Retrieved from http://whc.-unesco.org/en/list/208.

Curry, A. (2015, September 1). Here Are the Ancient Sites ISIS Has Damaged and Destroyed. *National Geographic*. Retrieved from: http://news.-nationalgeographic.com/2015/09/150901-isis-destruction.

Coupland, R. (2001). Humanity: What is it and how does it influence international law? *International Review of the Red Cross*, *83*, 969-989.

Drazewska, B. (2015). The Human Dimension of the Protection of the Cultural Heritage from Destruction during Armed Conflicts. *International Journal of Cultural Property*, *22* (2-3), 205-228. doi: doi:10.1017/-S09407 39115000132.

Fast, L. (2015). Unpacking the principle of humanity: Tensions and implications. *International Review of the Red Cross* 1-21. doi: 10.1017/S1816383115000545.

Freeman, M. (1998). National self-determination, peace and human rights. *Peace Review* 10(2), 157-163. doi: 10.1080/10402659808426138.

Frigo, M., (2004). Cultural Property v. cultural heritage: A "battle of concepts" in international law? *International Review of the Red Cross* 854. Retrieved from https://www.icrc.org/eng/resources/international-review/-review-854-protection-cultural-property-armed-conflict/index.jsp.

Helm, T. (2015, June 21). Britain signs convention on protecting treasures in war zones. *The Guardian Online.* Retrieved from: http://www.theguardian.com/world/2015/jun/21/britain-signs-up-to-protect-cultural-treasures-war-zones.

Howe, Z. (2012). Can the 1954 Hague Convention apply to non-state actors? A study of Iraq and Libya. *Texas International Law Journal*, *47*(2-3), 403–426.

International Committee of the Red Cross (ICRC, 2015), *Customary IHL, Rule 38* Retrieved from https://www.icrc.org/customary-ihl/eng/docs/v1_rul_ru le38.

Isakhan, B. (2013). Heritage Destruction and Spikes in Violence: The Case of Iraq. (Chapter 13) In Kila, J., Zeidler, J. (Eds.) (2013). *Cultural Heritage in the Crosshairs*. Leiden, Netherlands: Brill.

Ishwara Bhat, P. (2001). Protection of Cultural Property Under International Humanitarian Law: Some Emerging Trends. *ISIL Year Book of International Humanitarian and Refugee Law*, *1*, 47-71. Retrieved from: http://www.worldlii.org/int/journals/ISIL YBIHRL/2001/4.html.

ISIL blows up Arch of Triumph in Syria's Palmyra. (2015, October 5). *Al Jazeera*. Retrieved from http://www.aljazeera.com/news/2015/10/isil-blows-arch-triumph-syria-palmyra-151005033238445.html.

Jachec-Neale, A. (2015), After Palmyra, what can the world do to protect cultural treasures? *The Conversation*. Retrieved from: http://theconv-ersation.com/after-palmyra-what-can-the-world-do-to-protect-cultural-treasures-46839.

Kasymov, S. (2011). The Right of Communities to Self-Determination. *Peace Review*, *23*(2), 221-227. doi: 10.1080/10402659.2011.571615.

Merryman, J. H. (2005). Cultural Property Internationalism. *International Journal of Cultural Property* 12, 11-39. doi:10.1017/S0940739105 050046.

Neely, B. & Simpson, C. (2015, June 29). National Museum of Iraq Director Discusses ISIS Destruction of Relics. *NBC News Online*. Retrieved from: http://www.nbcnews.com/ storyline/isis-terror/national-museum-iraq-director-discusses-isis-destruction.

'Nothing remains' of Bamiyan Buddhas. (2002, March 1). *BBC News Online*. Retrieved from http://news.bbc.co.uk/2/hi/south_asia/1849843.stm

O'Rourke, M. Raiders of the Lost Art: Why didn't we protect the National Museum and Library in Baghdad? (2003, April 17). *Slate.com*. Retrieved from: http://www.slate.com/ articles/arts/culturebox/2003/04/raiders_of_-the_lost_art.single.html.

Paroff, S. (2004). Another Victim of the War in Iraq: The Looting of the National Museum in Baghdad and the Inadequacies of International Protection of Cultural Property. *Emory Law Journal*, *53*(4), 2021-2054.

Pessendorfer, M. (2013). Respecting and Protecting Cultural Heritage in Peace Support Operations - A Pragmatic Approach. In Kila, J., Zeidler, J. (Eds.) (2013). *Cultural heritage in the crosshairs*. Leiden, The Netherlands: Brill 51 – 65.

Phuong, C. (2004). The Protection of Iraqi Cultural Property. *International and Comparative Law Quarterly*, *53*(4), 985-998, p 986. doi: 10.1093/iclq/53.4.985.

Prott, L. V. & O'Keefe, P. J. (1992). 'Cultural Heritage' or 'Cultural Property'? *International Journal of Cultural Property*, *1*, 307-320.

Romney, K. (2015, March 24). Despite ISIS Threat, Looted Antiquities Returning to Iraq. *National Geographic*. Retrieved from: http://news.nationalgeographic.com/2015/03/ 150324-iraq-artifacts-return-isis-baghdad-museum-islamic-state-archaeology/.

Schipper, F. & Frank, E. (2013). A Concise Legal History of the Protection of Cultural Property in the Event of Armed Conflict and a Comparative Analysis of the 1935 Roerich Pact and the 1954 Hague Convention in the Context of the Law of War. *Archaeologies*, *9*(1), 13-28. doi: 10.1007/s11759-013-9230-7.

Shaheen, K. & Black, I. (2015, August 19). Beheaded Syrian scholar refused to lead Isis to hidden Palmyra antiquities. *Guardian Online.* Retrieved from: http://www.theguardian.com/world/2015/aug/18/isis-beheads-archaeologist-syria.

Situation in Mali: Ahmad Al Faqi Al Mahdi surrendered to the ICC on charges of war crimes regarding the destruction of historical and religious monuments in Timbuktu (2015, September 26). *Website of the International Criminal Court.* Retrieved from: https://www.icc-cpi.int/en_menus/icc/press%20and%20media/press%20releases/Pages/pr1154.aspx.

Solf, W. A. (1986). Protection of civilians against the effects of hostilities under customary international law and under Protocol I. *American University Journal of International Law and Policy*, *1*(1), 117-135.

State Parties Convention for the Protection of Cultural Property in the Event of Armed Conflict with Regulations for the Execution of the Convention. (undated), *UNESCO.* Retrieved from: http://www.unesco.org/eri/la/-convention.asp?KO=13637& language=E.

Statement of The Prosecutor of The International Criminal Court, Fatou Bensouda, on The Alleged Crimes Committed By ISIS. (2015). *Website of the International Criminal Court.* Retrieved from https://www.icc-cpi.int/en_menus/icc/press%20and%20media/press%20releases/Pages/otp-stat-08-04-2015-1.aspx.

Stone, P. (2012). Human rights and cultural property protection in times of conflict. *International Journal of Heritage Studies*, *18*(3), 271-284. doi: 10.1080/13527258.2012.651737.

Thurlow, M. D. (2005). Protecting Cultural Property in Iraq: How American Military Policy Comports with International Law. *Yale Human Rights and Development Law Journal*, *8*, 153–187.

Toman, J. (2005). The Hague Convention – A Decisive Step taken by the International Community. *Museum International*, *57*(4), 7-31. doi: 10. 1111/j.1468-0033.2005.00538.x.

UN peacekeepers to protect world heritage sites from ISIS attacks. (2015, October 20) Russia Today. Retrieved from: https://www.rt.com/news/-318965-un-protect-heritage-sites/.

United Nations Institute for Training and Research (UNITAR) (2015). UNOSAT Confirms Destruction of Palmyra Temples in Syria. Retrieved from: http://www.unitar.org/unosat-confirms-destruction-palmyra-temples -syria.

United Nations Institute for Training and Research (UNITAR) (2014). Satellite-based Damage Assessment to Cultural Heritage Sites in Syria. Retrieved from http://unosat.web.cern.ch/unosat/unitar/downloads/chs/FINAL_ Syria_WHS.pdf.

Van Der Auwera, S. (2010). Peace Operations and the Protection of Cultural Property During and After Armed Conflict. *International Peacekeeping*, *17*(1), 3-16.

Van der Auwera, S. (2013). International Law and the Protection of Cultural Property in the Event of Armed Conflict: Actual Problems and Challenges. *Journal of Arts Management, Law, and Society*, *43*(4), 175-190. doi: 10.1080/10632921.2013.841114.

Watson, A., (2015, April 2). Islamic State and the 'Blood Antique' Trade. *BBC Online.* Retrieved from: http://www.bbc.com/culture/story/20150 402-is-and-the-blood-antique-trade.

In: International Human Rights and Justice
Editor: Doug Hodgson
ISBN: 978-1-63484-709-4

Chapter 9

The International Human Right to Freedom of Expression: A South African Constitutional Perspective

CM van der Bank*
Vaal University of Technology, Vanderbijlpark, South Africa

Abstract

Our entire social system is pervaded with a myriad of issues relating to freedom of expression, therefore freedom of expression has been established as a key freedom required for sustaining a democracy. However with every right comes responsibility and therein is the need for a limitation on the rights to freedom of expression so as to prevent the destructive and regressive effect it could have. In a system of democracy dedicated to openness and accountability, as ours is, the especially important role of the media, both publicly and privately owned, must be recognized. Freedom of expression is therefore a part of the very definition of self-government: the process of free discussion is required no matter whether the process leads to the truth or not. Freedom of expression is a tool for daily life in modern society.

African human rights, and more specifically freedom of speech, are still weak and indeed in certain areas of Africa in their infancy. Undoubtedly the prosecution of the most serious violations of human rights committed in Africa contributes to the protection and promotion of human rights on the continent. International prosecutions will serve as a deterrent element, and thus contribute to the eradication of the rampant culture of impunity in Africa.

Keywords: freedom of expression, prosecution, democracy and values

* Corresponding author: riana@vut.ac.za.

1. INTRODUCTION

Freedom of expression is a method of achieving a more adaptable and hence a more stable society, of maintaining the precarious balance between cleavage and necessary consensus (Baker, 1978).

John Manyarara describes press freedom as: "...*Press freedom in the region is like the English weather: bright and sunny when you emerge from the comfort of your home – but if you are initiated, you will carry an umbrella because you are likely to need it on your way back. Therefore, my survey of press freedom in the region will be like a weather forecast: the forecast is always correct, it is the bloody weather which keeps changing*" (Duncan and Seleoane, 1998). The barometer by which the extent of press freedom existing in a country can be measured with reasonable accuracy is that country's political climate.

Article 19 of the United Nations *International Covenant on Civil and Political Rights 1966* states as follows:

(1) Everyone shall have the right to hold opinions without interference.
(2) Everyone shall have the right to freedom of expression; this right shall include freedom to seek, receive and impart information and ideas of all kinds, regardless of frontiers, either orally, in writing or in print, in the form of art, or through any other media of his choice.
(3) The exercise of the rights provided for in paragraph 2 of this article carries with it special duties and responsibilities. It may therefore be subject to certain restrictions, but these shall only be such as are provided by law and are necessary:
   (a) For respect of the rights or reputations of others;
   (b) For the protection of national security or of public order (ordre public), or of public health or morals.

Section 16 of the *South African Constitution,* 1996 states:

(1) Everyone has the right to freedom of expression, which includes-
   (a) freedom of the press and other media;
   (b) freedom to receive and impart information and ideas;
   (c) freedom of artistic creativity; and
   (d) academic freedom and freedom of scientific research.
(2) The right in subsection (1) does not extend to-
   (a) propaganda for war;
   (b) incitement of imminent violence; or
   (c) advocacy of hatred that is based on race, ethnicity, gender or religion, and that constitutes incitement to cause harm (*South African Constitution*, 1996).

Freedom of expression is fundamental for democracy to succeed. It does, however, precipitate profound jurisprudential issues and complex problems that require dispassionate examination and a judicious weighing up of competing interests in a democratic body politic (Van der Westhuizen, 1994).

Chapter 2 of the *South African Constitution* 1996 contains no express hierarchy of rights and is affirmed by the Constitutional Court in *Khumalo and Others v Holomisa* 2002 (5) SA (CC0 (2002 (8) BCLR 771) nevertheless freedom of expression is a cornerstone of an authentic democracy since it is "*the indispensable condition of nearly every other form of freedom,*" without which other freedoms would not long endure and therefore *de facto* it must be ranked as a very important right (Carpenter, 1995) In this regard a distinguished American judge, Mr. Justice Cardozo, commented that "freedom of thought and speech are the matrix, the indispensable condition, of nearly every other form of freedom" (*Palko v Connecticut* 1937 302 US 319).

2. Censorship: Freedom versus Moral Responsibility

Censorship is a doubled-edge sword that has bred legal, political, and moral wrangling across the globe. Historically, the politicians, judiciary, powerful groups and the public at large were involved in guarding public morals and rooting out obscenity. In the past cultural values, politics and demography played a vital role in deciding what needed to be censored. Internet as an electronic global village has defined demography, therefore the global as well as indigenous standards were once analysed for censorship is now blurred because it is so wide. Censorship is used not only to address social ills but also to control public awareness and information. South Africa sometimes uses censorship to silence opposition or criticism. The promise of free speech has empowered people that live in mature democracies. However, there should be a self-imposed code of conduct so that the right of free speech does not infringe on other people's human rights.

The most serious attacks on freedom of expression are perpetrated by countries, which have struggling democracies, or non-democracies. Moreover, half of the world's population lacks an independent press (Newth, 2010).

South Africa is not individually classified by the OpenNet initiative, but is included in ONI's regional overview for Sub-Saharan Africa (ONI regional Overview: Sub-Saharan Africa: September 2009). Over the last century, as mass media expanded across the world and entered into most homes, many countries have used laws and regulation to limit children's exposure to, for example violence or sex. South Africa has a set of media regulations designed to protect children These include restrictions on broadcasters that bans content deemed unsuitable for children until after 9pm. In November 2013, the Protection of Personal Information Act was signed into law, enacting measures to protect users' online security, privacy and data. South Africa's regulations and acts have been vigorously criticised by many organisations that they are draconian and that they are unworkable. Censorship and control of media exists in every country in the world but it has varied greatly depending on the form of media.

3. The Nature of Freedom of Expression

Section 16(1) protects free expression as well as free speech (De Waal, Curie and Erasmus, 2002). Expression is a wider concept than speech and includes activities such as displaying posters, painting and sculpting, dancing and the publication of photographs. In principle, every act by which a person attempts to express some emotion, belief or grievance should qualify as constitutionally protected expression (De Waal, Curie and Erasmus, 2002).

Our entire social system is pervaded with a myriad of issues relating to freedom of expression. In the past a vast number of restraints inhibiting freedom of expression were adopted and used because of the oppressive nature of our body politic. The fact that South Africa is now functioning under a *Constitution*, which protects freedom of expression, implies that there will have to be changes, also in the area of freedom of the press, where the common law is not in step with the constitutional values of freedom, equality and human dignity.

4. The Limitation of this Right

Fundamental rights and freedoms are not absolute (Carpenter, 1995). Their boundaries are set by the rights of others and by the legitimate needs of society. In the *South African Constitution*, a general limitation clause- section 36- sets out specific criteria for the restriction of the fundamental rights in the *Bill of Rights*. The existence of a general limitation clause does not mean that rights can be limited for any reason. The reason for limiting a right needs to be exceptionally strong. The limitation must serve a purpose that most people would regard as particularly important (Meyerson, 1997). But, however important the purpose of the limitation, restrictions on rights will not be justifiable unless there is good reason for thinking that the restriction would achieve the purpose it is designed to achieve, and that there is no other way in which the purpose can be achieved without restricting rights. "*A free responsible press is one of society's greatest assets. The press is the artery through which a democracy's lifeblood flows, exposing corruption, dishonesty and maladministration. Thus the press has to be the watchdog, inciting the inert and curbing the over-eager. Effective freedom of press would be frustrated if freedom of expression is limited in such a way as to intimidate the media into not publishing*" (Klopper, 1987).

5. Strict Liability of the Press

In the past our courts construed defamation in our common law in a very wide manner, thereby restricting press freedom. Strict liability of the press is now rejected as unconstitutional since it impedes the free flow of information - a democratic principle (Burchell, 1998). Thus *bona fide* published untruths in the political sphere are defensible if it is of public interest. The press serves the public interest by making available information relevant to the community as well as criticism on all aspects of public, political and social activities (Burchell, 1993).

Through freedom of expression, the press helps to establish true democracy. The contentious issues are the extent to which freedom of expression should be permitted and the manner in which the courts ought to balance it against equally fundamental rights and considerations applying in a democratic society such as *inter alia* the right to reputation or dignity, privacy, political activity, fair trial, economic activity and property (Burchell, 1993).

It is not without significance that section 16 of the *South African Constitution*, after stating that 'everyone has the right to freedom of expression,' includes 'freedom of the press and other media' under the general rubric of freedom of expression, and places these facets of the right on an equal footing with the 'freedom to receive and impart information and ideas, freedom of artistic creativity, academic freedom and freedom of scientific research.' "*The press should not be placed in a privileged or superior position to that of the individual on the basis that the press constitutes an essential bastion of free expression in a democracy. They bear an obligation to provide citizens both with information and with a platform for the exchange of ideas which is crucial to the development of a democratic culture... If the media are scrupulous and reliable in the performance of their constitutional obligations, they will invigorate and strengthen our fledgling democracy* (*National Media Ltd v Bogoshi* 1998 (4) SA 1195 (SCA)).

6. DEFAMATION

The common law of delict requires a plaintiff in a defamation action for damages to show that a defamatory statement has been published with intent and knowledge of wrongfulness *(animus iniuriandi)*. In the pre-democratic era, the courts alleviated the plaintiff's burden by presuming the presence of both intent and unlawfulness when defamatory material directed at the plaintiff was published to communicate information and comment, while obviously crucial in a modern democracy, should be no greater than that of an ordinary citizen to communicate to balance the defamatory material. This need for substantially equal treatment of all who communicate with others has been recognised (*Pakendorf en andere v De Flamingh* 1982 3 SA 146 (A) 156B).

The Supreme Court of Appeal in *National Media Ltd v Bogoshi* 1998 (4) SA 1195 (SCA) has set broad, realistic standards of reasonableness, or reasonable care, for the media in regard to the publication of matter, which could be defamatory or impair other personality rights of the individual.

Hefer JA's judgment in *Bogoshi* constitutes the watershed decision in the revival of the common-law emphasis on freedom of expression, in particular of the print and electronic media. The court, in rejecting the concept of strict liability for the media, re-emphasised the vital role of media freedom in a democracy, affirmed that there was no closed list of defences excluding unlawfulness, and stressed that although a high degree of care is required of editorial staff, even the publication of some falsity may be in the public interest in special circumstances.

Publication in the press of false defamatory statements of fact will be regarded as lawful if, in all the circumstances of the case, it is found to be reasonable;... protection is only afforded to the publication of material in which the public has an interest (i.e., which it is in the public interest to make known as distinct from material which is interesting to the public (*Financial Mail (Pty) Ltd and Others v Sage Holdings Ltd and Another* 1993 (2) SA 451 (A)).

The decision in *Bogoshi (National Media Ltd and Others v Bogoshi* 1998 (4) SA 1195 (SCA) (1999 (1) BCLR 1)) relates both to the fault element of the delict of defamation and to the element of unlawfulness. Insofar as fault is concerned, the usual rule is that one will be liable for defamation only if one has *animus inuiriandi.* The focus in *Bogoshi* was thus the question of fault (negligence as opposed to strict liability).

A fault criterion of negligence is necessary not only to address freedom of expression but also to emphasise the imperative that the media should not be treated in a way which is substantially inferior to other defendants in defamation cases. In other words, fault is required for the liability of both the individual and the media defendant; intention is required for the former and negligence is sufficient for the latter. The distinction is more readily justifiable as a reasonable one than the now jettisoned distinction between intention-based liability for the individual and strict (no-fault) liability for the mass media. The press will thus not be held liable for the publication of defamatory material where it can show that it has been reasonable in publishing the material. Accordingly, the form of fault in defamation actions against the press is negligence rather than intention to harm.

However, fault need not be in issue at all if in the particular circumstances anterior inquiry shows that the publication is lawful because it is justifiable. *Bogoshi* indicates that the reasonableness of the publication might also *justify* it. In appropriate cases, a defendant should not be held liable where publication is justifiable in the circumstances – when the publisher reasonably believes that the information published is true. The publication in such circumstances is not unlawful. Political speech might, depending on the context, be lawful even when false provided that its publication is reasonable. It determines whether, on grounds of policy, a defamatory statement should not be actionable because it is justifiably made in the circumstances.

In *Holomisa v Argus Newspapers Ltd* 1996 (2) SA 588 (W) at 618E-F a judgement presciently foreshadowing *Bogoshi* as regards the availability of a defence based on absence of negligence, Cameron J held that a defamatory statement "*which relates to free and fair political activity*" is constitutionally protected, even if false, unless the plaintiff shows that, in all the circumstances of its publication, it was not reasonably made. The court in *Holomisa* did not, however, consider it correct to import into our law the so-called *Sullivan* principle *(New York Co v Sullivan* (1964) 376 US 254 (1964) 11 L ed 2nd 686) that defendant press members will not be liable for defamatory statements made of public figures unless the plaintiff can show that the statement was made with actual malice. Such a principle would give far too little protection to the right of dignity. The approach that is preferred is that adopted in both *Holomisa* and *Bogoshi* of reasonable publication.

Jonathen Burchell commenting on *Bogoshi* writes, *"The test of reasonableness or public (legal) policy is a supple criterion which can ensure that the law of delict is able to meet the needs of a changing society... The accommodation of freedom of expression under the unlawfulness inquiry is now firmly acknowledged by the Supreme Court of Appeal"* (Burchell, 1998).

The central reasoning of the Supreme Court of Appeal in *Bogoshi* confirmed that the media defendant bore a full burden of proof on a preponderance of probabilities rather than a mere evidential burden. The media defendant in a defamation action is often in the best position to know whether reasonable steps were taken to verify the information published and so to establish that the publication was reasonable. It would be unrealistic to expect the plaintiff to prove facts that he or she has very little chance of discovering.

It was with great relief that I read the judgment of Hefer JA in *Bogoshi* and I enthusiastically support the conclusions thereof. These conclusions in *Bogoshi* are momentous and signify a profound, beneficial change in direction of the common law.

Freedom of expression (including media freedom) at last received due recognition. A vital function of the press is to make available to the community information and criticism about every aspect of public, political, social and economic activity and thus to contribute to the formation of public opinion (Van der Walt, 1998).

However, without wishing to appear churlish, I want to focus on some blurred edges in the judgment. The central problem is whether a media defendant can rely on absence of knowledge of unlawfulness and negligence, i.e., whether reasonable mistake or ignorance could be a defence. Negligence of the defendant may well be a determinant of the unlawfulness of the publication.

The central issue is not whether a media defendant can rely on a defence of absence of knowledge of unlawfulness due to negligence, but whether such a defendant can rely on a defence of absence of knowledge of unlawfulness not due to negligence. Reasonableness of the publication also includes an inquiry into whether the person detrimentally affected by the publication was given an opportunity to reply, at least after publication. The fact that a media defendant, who has channels of reply available, has not granted the opportunity to a person detrimentally affected by one of its publications to reply to the allegations about him or her, after publication, will be a factor to be considered in determining the overall unreasonableness of the publication.

But the reasonableness inquiry is not completely open-ended: it involves the balancing of other rights against freedom of expression, and what is most important, in the context of freedom, equality and dignity. A right to reply (rebuttal) is plausible - it may provide a quick and effective remedy and, in most cases, would not interfere with any editorial discretion because very little editing appears to take place.

The question arises whether special principles should be invoked to protect the press, or for that matter individuals, when they make defamatory statements about a member of Government. The *Reynolds* decision in the Court of Appeal of England and Wales (referred to by Hefer JA in *Bogoshi*) was confirmed by the House of Lords (*Reynolds v Times Newspapers Ltd and Others* [1999] 4 All ER 609 (HL) [2001]2 AC 127).

The House of Lords declined to recognize a special defence of political speech. It differed in this regard from the Australian High Court decision in *Lange v Australian Broadcasting Corporation* (1997) 189 CLR 520 (1997) 145 ALR 1 (a case approved by Hefer JA in *Bogoshi*), finding that the common law should not develop 'political information' as a generic category of information, the publication of which attracts a qualified privilege irrespective of the circumstances. In *Lange v Atkinson* [1997] 2 NZLR 22 Lord Nicholls pointed out: *"One feature of all the judgments, New Zealand, Australian and English, stands out with conspicuous clarity: The recognition that striking a balance between freedom of expression and protection of reputation calls for a value judgment which depends upon local political and social conditions. These conditions include matters such as the responsibility and vulnerability of the press."*

7. Right to Dignity and Right to Freedom of Expression

Twenty-two years after the decision in *Pakendorf v De Flamingh* 1982 3 SA 146 (A) where strict liability of the press was held to apply, *Mthembi-Mahanyele v Mail & Guardian*

Ltd and Another 2004 (6) SA 329 held that strict liability has a negative impact on press freedom. There must be a balance between the right to dignity, including reputation, and the right to freedom of expression. Both rights were now given special protection in the *Bill of Rights*, and the question was whether a class of people (members of Government) had to lose the right to the protection of their dignity and reputation in the interest of public information and debate.

In *Mthembi-Mahanyele* the Cabinet Minister had asserted that words published by a certain weekly newspaper in its annual 'report card' on the performance of Government Ministers were defamatory of her. She pleaded that the respondents had acted recklessly, not caring whether the contents were true; and that they took no reasonable steps to establish whether the statement made was true. The Court had for reasons of convenience referred to Cabinet Ministers, but that could not be taken to mean that other members of Government, or parliamentarians or officials of State had to be treated differently (*Mthembi-Mahanyele v Mail & Guardian Ltd and Another* 2004 (6) SA 332).

In *The Citizen 1978 (Pty)Ltd & others v McBride[2011] JOL 27088 (CC)* judgment was handed down in the Constitutional Court on the issue of whether a person convicted of murder, but granted amnesty for the offence, could be called later a "criminal" and a "murderer" in comment opposing his appointment to a public position. McBride lost his drawn-out defamation case against The Citizen. McBride sued the paper after a series of articles and editorials questioned his suitability for the post of police in 2003. The articles were published in The Citizen in September and October 2003. He sued for damages for R3,6 million and demanded a front-page apology for alleged defamation and impairment of dignity. The Constitutional Court judgment ruled that amnestied killers can still be called "murderers."

Once it is accepted that freedom of expression is just another human right of no more or less importance than dignity and equality, for instance, then the crucial question becomes, in a clash between one person's dignity(in the sense of individual autonomy of the utterer of the racial insult) and another 's (in the sense of respect due to the victim of the insult, or his or her self-esteem), which is to triumph?

Freedom of expression in political discourse is necessary to hold members of Government accountable to the public and some latitude must be allowed in order to allow robust and frank comment in the interest of keeping of society informed about what Government did. Errors of fact should be tolerated, provided that statements were published justifiably and reasonably. That does not mean that there should be a licence to publish untrue statements about politicians. They too have the right to protect their dignity and their reputations.

As Burchell puts it: "*There are limits to freedom of political comment, especially in regard to aspects of the private lives of politicians that do not impinge on political competence. Politicians or public figures do not simply have to endure every infringement of their personality rights as a price for entering the political or public arena, although they do have to be more resilient to slings and arrows than non-political, private mortals*" (Burchell, 1998).

But where publication is justifiable in the circumstances the defendant will not be held liable. Justifiability is to be determined by having regard to all relevant circumstances, including the interest of the public in being informed; the manner of publication; the tone of the material published; the extent of public concern in the information; the reliability of the source; the steps taken to verify the truth of the information (this factor would play an important role too in considering the distinct question whether there was negligence on the part of the press, assuming that the publication was found to be defamatory); and whether the person defamed has been given the opportunity to comment on the statement before publication (*Mthembi-Mahanyele v Mail & Guardian Ltd and Another* 2004 (6) SA 332). In cases where information is crucial to the public, and its disclosure is urgent, it may be justifiable to publish without giving an opportunity to comment.

8. Freedom of Expression under Attack in South Africa

Freedom of expression is a fundamental human right guaranteed by the *Bill of Rights* providing greater public transparency and accountability as well as good governance and the strengthening of democracy. The key role of communication is in ensuring full respect for freedom of expression, in promoting the free flow of information and ideas, in assisting people to make informed decisions and in facilitating and strengthening democracy.

The South African Government's assault on media freedom over the last 18 months has also emboldened other African states to further clamp down on free speech. Only eight of Africa's 54 countries have any legislation guaranteeing freedom of expression (Kretzmann, 2011). In March 2013 the Parliamentary Committee tried to rush an attempt to complete the Protection of Information Bill but the Freedom of Expression Institute stood up and blocked the Bill in despair in the face of government pressure. The main demands are that the Bill should:

- Limit secrecy to core state bodies in the security sector
- Limit secrecy to strictly defined national security matters. Officials must give reasons for making information secret.
- Not exempt the intelligence agencies from public scrutiny.
- Not apply penalties for unauthorized disclosure at large.
- Allow for an independent body to be appointed by Parliament and not the Minister of Intelligence as the arbiter of decisions about what may be made secret.
- Not criminalise the legitimate disclosure of secrets in the public interest.
- Ensure that whistle-blowers who unlawfully and intentionally disclosed classified state information in contravention of the Act would be guilt of an offence and liable to a fine or imprisonment (for a period not exceeding five years), except where such disclosures reveal criminal activity, including criminal activity for ulterior purposes.

In contradiction with the preamble to this Bill, which states that the aim is to "promote the free flow of information within an open and democratic society without compromising the security of the republic," the Bill will not only hamper the collection and the disclosure of information, but also reward those who do with lengthy jail sentences. Any head of a state body, or duly authorized delegate of a state body, has the power to classify a document, a record or a non-physical item, as confidential, secret or top secret. A well-known example was when President Jacob Zuma was highly infuriated after the appearance of a Zapiro cartoon depicting him with a shower on his head during his rape trial. The cartoon, which was born from Zuma's own claim to have showered to diminish the risk of AIDS after intercourse with the HIV-infected plaintiff, resulted in Zuma initially suing the cartoonist for R20 million- an amount that has subsequently reduced to R2 million. If the new Act had been in place at that time, the Government would have been able to prevent the publication of the cartoon, withhold information from the press and censor any reference to his trial before it would allow going into print.

The right to freedom expression is fundamental to the existence and consolidation of democracy. Central to freedom of expression is freedom of the press. Sadly though, it is this critical aspect of democracy that is so frequently undermined and attacked by government.

The Bills remains deeply flawed. But for the first time, there is real light at the end of the tunnel. On a policy level, the once-yawning gap between the ruling party and civil society is all but bided. Now comes the hard part: to turn messy democratic success into good law (http://mg.co.za/article/2012-05-11-secrecy-bill-light-atend-of-tunnel).

CONCLUSION

The *Constitution* 1996 requires the government to respect the principle of democracy when dealing with citizens. Therefore, in a democratic system of government, the relationship between state and the citizen is not simply a power relationship. Rather than state power, the consent of the governed is the defining characteristic of the relationship.

> *In Holomisa Cameron J said: "Our Constitutional structure seeks to nurture open and accountable democracy. Party to that end, it encourages and protects free speech and expression, including that practised by the media. If the protection the Constitution affords is to have substance, there must in my view be some protection for erroneous statement of defamatory fact, at least in the area of 'free and fair political activity.'" (Holomisa v Argus Newspaper Ltd* 1996 2 SA 588 (W)).

In a system of democracy dedicated to openness and accountability, as ours is, the especially important role of the media, both publicly and privately owned, must, in my opinion, be recognised.

Our entire social system is pervaded with a myriad of issues relating to freedom of expression. Courts are obliged to consider the *Bill of Rights* and the values embodied therein, when assessing whether conduct is wrongful. The *Bill of Rights* is therefore a medium or prism through which the light of every aspect of the law of delict will eventually be refracted. Limitations on freedom of expression should only be justifiable when it can be shown that the non-limitation would probably cause specific harm.

Freedom to speak and write about public questions is as important to the life of our government as is the heart of the human body. Freedom of expression is therefore a part of the very definition of self-government; the process of free discussion is required no matter whether the process leads to the truth or not. In fact, this privilege is the heart of our government! If that heart be weakened, the result is debilitation; if it be stilled, the result is death. *It is reporting that puts the needs of society first and everything else; including the need for the media to make profit, last... Responsible reporting is reporting that reflects reality as it is not as journalists and those propping them up would like it to be* (Nel, 1998).

Reported Cases

Australia:

Lange v Australian Broadcasting Corporation (1997) 189 CLR 520.

England:

Reynolds v Times Newspapers Ltd and Others [1998] 3 All ER 961 (CA).

Reynolds v Times Newspapers Ltd and Others [1999] 4 All ER 609. [2001] 2 AC 127 (HL).

USA

Chaplinsky v New Hampshire (1942) 315 US 568.

New York Times Co v Sullivan (1964) 376 US 254.

Palko v Connecticut (1937) 302 US 103.

New Zealand

Lange v Atkinson and another (New Zealand) 1999 UKPC 46.

South Africa

Financial Mail (Pty) Ltd and Others v Sage Holdings Ltd and Another 1993 (2) SA 451 (A).

Holomisa v Argus Newspaper Ltd 1996 2 SA 588 (W).

Khumalo and Others v Holomisa 2002 (5) SA 401 (CC) (2002 (8) BCLR 771).

Mthembi-Mahanyele v Mail & Guardian Ltd and Another 2004 (6) SA 329.

National Media Ltd v Bogoshi 1998 4 SA 1195 (SCA).

Pakendorf en andere v De Flamingh 1982 3 SA 146 (A).

The Citizen 1978 (Pty) Ltd & others v McBride[2011] JOL 27088 (CC).

Electronic sources

http://mg.co.za/article/2012-05-11-secrecy-bill-light-at-end-of-tunnel access on 3 September 2012.

References

Baker, C. E. (1978). *'Freedom of Speech" Law Review*, *25* UCLA, 964.

Burchell, J. M. (1998). *Personality Rights and Freedom of Expression: the modern Actio injuriarum* Juta, Kenwyn.

Burchell, J. M. (1993). *Principles of Delict* Juta, Cape Town.

Carpenter, G. (1995). "Internal modifiers and other qualifications in Bill of Rights- some problems of interpretation" *SA Publiekreg.,* 260-282.

Carpenter, G. (1996). "Fundamental rights: is there a pecking order?" Codicillus xxxvi No 1, PP. Unisa, Pretoria.

Coetzee, J. M. (1990). *Censorship in South Africa,* Vol *17*, no 1 May 1990. 1-20.

Devenish, G. E. (1999). *A Commentary on the South African Bill of Rights* 2nd edition, Butterworths, Durban.

De Waal, J., Currie, I. & Erasmus, G. (2002). *The Bill of Rights Handbook* 3rd edition, Juta Kenwyn.

Duncan, J. & Seleoane, M. (1998). *Media and Democracy in South Africa* HSRC, Pretoria.

Klopper, H. B. & Strauss, Strydom en Van der Walt. (1987). *Mediareg* 4th edition, Van Schaik, Pretoria.

Kretzmann, S. (2011). South Africa Casts a Shadow over Freedom of Expression in the Continent http://allafrica.co/stories/201108020011.html.

Malley, I. (1990). *Censorship and libraries.* London: Library Association Publishing.

Manyarara, J. (1998). "Climate for Press Freedom" in Duncan J (ed) *Media and Democracy in South Africa* HSRC, Pretoria, 92-96.

Meyerson, D. (1997). *Rights Limited* 1st edition Juta, Kenwyn.

Nel, F. (1998). *Writing for the Media in South* Africa 2nd edition, International Thomson Publishing Johannesburg.

Newth, M. (2010). *The long history of censorship.* Retrieved on 11 August 2015 from http://www. Beaconforfreedom.org/lists.html?tid+415& art_id +475.

Van der Westhuizen, J. (1994). "Freedom of Expression" in Van Wyk D *Rights and Constitutionalism: The New South African Legal Order* Juta, Kenwyn, 264-291.

United Nations *International Covenant on Civil and Political Rights*, 1966.

Van der Walt, J. C. (1998) *Gedenkbundel: HL Swanepoel* at 68.

In: International Human Rights and Justice
Editor: Doug Hodgson

ISBN: 978-1-63484-709-4

Chapter 10

How Demanding Is the Right to Benefit from Scientific Progress?

Elizabeth Victor [*,†]
William Paterson University, Wayne, New Jersey, US

Abstract

The United Nations (U.N.) has long maintained that all persons have the right to share in scientific advancements and enjoy the benefits of scientific progress and its applications. The 2012 *Special Rapporteur* situates this right within the broader field of cultural rights, indicating that what it means to benefit from scientific progress will be context and location-specific. As the U.N. has presented it, the right to science, as it is called, is cast as a positive right—a right that entails actions on the part of some other persons or institutions (e.g., government, institution of education). The *Special Rapporteur* also frames this right as a bridging right—a right that is necessary for citizens to exercise other fundamental rights and liberties. This chapter will explore the limits of government and institutional action that ought to be taken toward enabling this right. I begin by critically analyzing the idea of progress in science, the kinds of science that can be measured by beneficial applications, and the implications of understanding the right to benefit from scientific progress as a positive, bridging right. Prima facie, this is a demanding right that resource-poor countries would be unable to meet. Moreover, the kind of scientific progress that benefits the citizens of resource-poor countries may not be the kind of science that researchers in developed countries pursue. I argue that a right to benefit from scientific progress entails a host of other, more fundamental positive rights be met—many of which are necessary for a decent human life, i.e., education/reasoning, personal security, health, etc. Thus, the right to benefit from scientific progress is a positive right that only obtains when more fundamental rights are satisfied. I argue throughout that a claim that a person has a right to benefit from scientific progress only makes sense if we conceive of this right as a bundle theory of rights.

---

[*] Corresponding author: Department of Philosophy, Atrium Building 113, William Paterson University, Wayne, NJ (USA) 07470, Email: victore@wpunj.edu.

[†] This research was supported (in part) by a Summer Stipend from the Research Center for the Humanities and Social Sciences at William Paterson University.

Keywords: applied science, development, global justice, human rights, scientific progress

INTRODUCTION

The *Universal Declaration of Human Rights*[71] specifies in Article 27 that "[e]veryone has the right freely to participate in the cultural life of the community, to enjoy the arts and to share in scientific advancement and its benefits" [1]. Additionally, Article 15 of the *International Covenant on Economic, Social and Cultural Rights*[72] recognizes that all persons have the right "[t]o enjoy the benefits of scientific progress and its applications...[and that] the benefits [are] to be derived from the encouragement and development of international contacts and co-operation in the scientific and cultural fields" [2]. In short, the U.N. system has long recognized the right of all persons to share in scientific advancements and that all persons have the right to benefit from scientific progress and its applications [1, 2].[73] Since these two proclamations, the United Nations system has issued a number of reports referencing the right of all persons to enjoy the benefits of science and its applications, scientific progress, and scientific knowledge,[74] the most recent of which was *The report of the special rapporteur in the field of cultural rights*[75] issued by Farida Shaheed on behalf of the Human Rights Council [3-5].

The 2012 *Special Rapporteur* sought to clarify what was entailed by this right, recognizing that its articulation has, up until this point, been largely defined by the normative associations with science as either good or a barrier to human flourishing. The *Special Rapporteur* considers "[t]he rights to science and culture [interlinked]...both relate to the pursuit of knowledge and understanding and to human creativity in a constantly changing world" [5]. While the *Special Rapporteur* recognizes that the right to science will be context and location-specific, since different states have different foci and aims particularly as they relate to their differences in cultural values, it ties the right to science (and culture) to other more fundamental rights. Among those specified are the right to science depends upon the right of individuals to engage in critical thinking (i.e., education), access to information, freedom of expression (and information dissemination), right of self-determination, which will entail the right to security, health, and the right to take part in public affairs [5].

As the U.N. has presented it, the right to benefit from scientific progress is cast as a positive right—a right that entails actions on the part of some other persons or institutions (e.g., government, institution of education). The *Special Rapporteur* also frames this right as a bridging right—a right that both depends upon other fundamental rights *and* is necessary for citizens to exercise related fundamental rights and liberties. As indicated by Audrey Chapman, there is a lack of consensus as to what this right entails [6]. Moreover, the

[71] Hereafter referred to as the "*Universal Declaration.*"
[72] Hereafter referred to as the "*ICESCR.*"
[73] Unlike the *ICESCR*, the *Universal Declaration* is not a legally binding treaty. When it was adopted by the United Nations in 1948, it was merely a non-binding, aspirational and programmatic document. However, with the passage of time and with its provisions being adopted in the constitutions of many UN Member states, most commentators would agree that its contemporary status is such that it now falls within the corpus of customary international law and, as such, is now legally binding on all countries and UN Member states.
[74] Different documents do not always separate or recognize these distinct rights. Thus different reports sometimes conflate one or all of these.
[75] Hereafter referred to as the "*Special Rapporteur.*"

Universal Declaration is limited in the sense that the Human Rights Committee does not have the power to compensate victims or order states to change their practices; its role being confined to making non-binding recommendations under the *International Covenant on Civil and Political Rights*.

In this chapter, I explore the limits of government and institutional action that ought to be taken toward enabling this right. I begin by critically analyzing the idea of progress in science, the kinds of science that can be measured by beneficial applications, and the implications of understanding the right to benefit from scientific progress as a positive, bridging right. Prima facie, this is a demanding right that resource-poor countries would be unable to meet. Moreover, the kind of scientific progress that benefits the citizens of resource-poor countries may not be the kind of science that researchers in developed countries pursue.

I argue that a right to benefit from scientific progress entails a host of other, more fundamental positive rights be met—many of which are necessary for a decent human life, i.e., education/reasoning, personal security, health, etc. What this means is that rather than the right to enjoy the benefits of scientific progress fulfilling other rights, I will argue for a more dynamic approach to understanding the "right to science" as articulated by the *Universal Declaration* (specifically Articles 22 and 27), the *ICESCR*, and the *Special Rapporteur*. I will suggest that we should prioritize other fundamental rights both *as a means to* increasing the likelihood that citizens of resource-poor countries benefit from scientific progress and its applications. Thus, the right to benefit from scientific progress is a positive right that only obtains when more fundamental rights are satisfied. I suggest that the claim that a person has a right to benefit from scientific progress only makes sense if we conceive of this right as a bundle theory of rights.

KINDS OF RIGHTS

Rights are colloquially understood primarily as both moral rights and legal rights.[76] In either case, rights have rightholders (i.e., individuals or specific groups), specify some freedom, power, or immunity, and rights identify corresponding dutybearers who must act to make the right available [7]. Philosophical accounts of moral rights can be justified in either a top-down or bottom-up approach [8].[77] The top-down approach begins by articulating some over-arching moral principle or decision-making procedure, and then derives human rights from this more general principle or moral standard.[78] In contrast, the bottom-up approach begins with rights as they appear in our actual social life (e.g., rules of organizations, laws, policy), and then attempts to discern the kinds of abstract principles one needs to rely upon for those rights to obtain.[79] While contemporary philosophical accounts of rights prefer the top-down approach, international bodies such as the United Nations prefer bottom-up

[76] While legal rights are often reflective of socially endorsed moral rights, they need not be. For example, the impetus behind the civil rights movement in the United States was, in part, to address the gap between the recognized legal rights of minorities and socially endorsed moral rights.

[77] For a more detailed analysis of this general account see Griffin (2008), especially chapters 1-3.

[78] Common examples of this approach include the principle of utility, Kant's Categorical Imperative, or an idealized account of the social contract bringing parties together to reach an agreement.

[79] For example, many generally accepted human rights rely upon concepts such as freedom, justice, fairness, equality, etc. The bottom-up approach begins with human rights to see how the state or specific social institutions are guided by these more general or abstract moral principles.

approaches. The *Universal Declaration*, for example, does not begin with a metaphysical account, but attempts to articulate rights that all states, regardless of variations in culture or moral evaluations, agree are human rights. In this way, the *Universal Declaration*, along with other reports issued by the United Nations system, can be considered broadly bottom-up.

Of the rights specified in the *Universal Declaration*, we can identify a distinction between positive and negative rights, and whether a right is a stand-alone right or a bridging right. We might say that the freedom of thought, as mentioned in Article 18 of the *Universal Declaration*, is a stand-alone right whereas the right to freedom of expression depends upon the right to security; without security to our person, the freedom of expression rings hollow. Hence, the right to security (and freedom of movement, possibly) is a bridging right. Negative rights require that the dutybearer refrain from doing something, whereas positive rights require the dutybearer to perform some action they might otherwise not. The rights articulated in the *Universal Declaration* [1] include both negative and positive rights. For example, Article 13 of the *Universal Declaration* specifies, in part, that everyone has the right to freedom of movement within the borders of each state. In this case, all persons are specified as having a particular freedom, and this is a freedom from arbitrary interference with their lawful movement within a state's borders. Freedom from arbitrary interference makes this a negative right. In comparison, Article 25 of the *Universal Declaration* specifies, in part, that motherhood and childhood are entitled to special protection. This right applies to both a specific group (i.e., women that have children) and to all persons, insofar as all persons experience childhood. This right is also a positive right; it requires that states take action to ensure all mothers and children have access to assistance and protection.

Article 22 of the *Universal Declaration* indicates that "everyone, as a member of society, has the right to social security and is entitled to realization, through national effort and international co-operation and in accordance with the organization and resources of each State, of the economic, social and cultural rights indispensable for his dignity and the free development of his personality" [1]. As explained by the *Special Rapporteur*, this Article, in conjunction with Article 27 of the *Universal Declaration*, makes up what is referred to as the "right to science" [5]. While little has been written to clarify what exactly is entailed by this right, it is broadly cast as a positive right and a bridging right. The right to enjoy the benefits of scientific progress will entail that the state, or specific individuals within state-sanctioned institutions, will need to take action to ensure that citizens have access to technological advancements in such a way that they directly benefit, or otherwise improve their life. Moreover, this right will determine the extent to which individuals will have access to food security, clean drinking water, access to educational resources (specifically science and research-based education), or have access to potentially lifesaving medical interventions, medications, or procedures. Thus, this right acts as a bridge to these other fundamental rights.

How we interpret this 'benefit' and the degree to which we evaluate whether specific countries fulfill this right will depend upon a number of factors. These factors include (but are not limited to) the resources a country has, whether 'science' and 'scientific research' are taken to be inherently progressive, how research is funded (public vs. private funding), and the extent to which citizens need other fundamental rights (freedom of expression, health, education, for example) for this right to obtain. In the following sections, I will argue that the interpretations of this right have presented this right as a positive-bridging right. This interpretation makes fulfilling this right essential to other fundamental rights, and may mean that resource-poor countries face mounting obstacles to ensure all citizens have this right satisfied. I suggest that a 'bundle theory' of rights will help to reorient the broader discussion and help explain why the right to enjoy the benefits of science and its applications cannot be easily extricated from other fundamental rights, specifically the right to food security, health, and education.

INTERPRETATIONS OF ARTICLES 22 AND 27

As I have explained, the standard presentation by the U.N. system of the right to science is one that stresses on the one hand that states must secure the other fundamental rights necessary for individuals and groups to engage in critical thinking, pursue scientific endeavors, and engage in policy discussions. On the other hand, the right to science is explained (and justified) by appealing to the benefits that will be enjoyed by individuals and groups when scientific progress and technological progress are supplemented by states to address pressing problems, most commonly in the areas of food scarcity, medical care, basic health, sanitation, access to clean drinking water, and basic infrastructure development. Recognizing the ways in which the right to science both depends upon, and is necessary for, a host of related rights to obtain will entail that we recognize that they are a bundle or collection of rights. Appealing to a bundle theory of rights suggests that we cannot extricate any one or set of rights specified from the right we call 'the right to science.' Rather, we need to recognize that they are dynamically interrelated, and not mutually exclusive (as the literature implies).

The *Special Rapporteur* builds upon the work of theorists to confirm that the link between the right to science and "other human rights, such as the rights to health, water, housing, and education, as well as the right to development and the emerging right to a clean and healthy environment [is obvious]" [5, 6, 9]. The link between science and human rights within the United Nations system is mediated by the historically contingent association of scientific advances as dangerous or beneficial. These associations have shifted with each iteration and further articulation of the right of all persons to enjoy the benefits of scientific progress and its applications. This means that as science and scientific knowledge were viewed as a threat to human well-being (hydrogen bomb, biological weapons, for example), defense and military-related research will be given priority over other kinds of scientific advancements [6]. Relatedly, who benefits from scientific research will depend heavily upon the system of funding and intellectual property rights in a given country. If, as is the case in the United States, the private sector funds scientific and medical research, prices of products will often pass on the cost of research and development to consumers. Another consequence of private sector-funded research is that research priorities may not reflect the research interests of scientists or even the general public. Rather, research priorities will be determined in large part by market forces and projected demand [6, 10].

In contrast, within the United Nations system, the right to science has been equivocated with the right to technological innovation and privileges applied science. This too is a particular kind of value judgment that prioritizes some kinds of science over others. One effect of this could be that the kinds of science education and the direction of publically funded research fits this narrower definition of science. This effect will be reified and perpetuated with a definition of scientific progress that only allows for certain kinds of science to show up as beneficial or promoted as worthy fields of study.

DEFINING SCIENTIFIC PROGRESS BY ITS APPLICATIONS

The *Special Rapporteur* mentions that further discussion should, among other things, focus on determining what is meant by "benefit" and what is meant by "scientific progress" [5]. Clarifying how we define scientific progress will have a bearing on how we allocate resources toward science education, value some kinds of science over others, and this can have an influence on the aims of future research (e.g., allocating state funds toward "applied" instead of "pure" sciences). The *Special Rapporteur* indicates that the terms benefits and scientific progress "must be understood as knowledge that is testable and refutable, in all fields of inquiry, including social sciences, and encompassing all research…[it conveys] the idea of a positive impact on the well-being of people and the realization of their human rights" [5]. This is a very narrow definition of what counts as science, what counts as scientific progress, and what counts as social benefit. While it is the case that scientific research is sometimes coextensive with technological progress and direct positive impacts on human life, it need not be. Many advances in the social sciences and sciences do not yet have the ability to be tested (e.g., some aspects of particle physics, statistical mechanics, cosmology theories), or as is the case with the humanities, methodologies employed by certain sciences do not lend themselves to empirical testing or replication.

The *Special Rapporteur* goes on to indicate that working toward a definition of scientific progress "must be guided by instruments such as Limburg Principle 11, stressing that popular participation at all stages is 'indispensable to achieving progress in realizing economic, social and cultural rights'" [5]. While a recent study has indicated that mechanisms driving scientific progress include social interactions and peer disagreement, this is limited to sciences that do not experience high fragmentation [11]. What this means is that the social sciences and humanities, which are characterized by a high degree of fragmentation (broken into 'schools of thought,' defined by fundamentally different methods, etc.), do not lend themselves to as much social engagement and peer disagreement in part because such disciplines do not readily yield "signals received from a correct answer" [11]. This, in turn, limits scientific progress in these disciplines. Yet this particular study does not clearly identify what concept of scientific progress underlies this test.

There are three common ways to define scientific progress as: (1) the accumulation of scientific knowledge, (2) the accumulation of true scientific belief (Newton advanced scientific knowledge even as the underlying science did not accumulate true scientific beliefs about the world), or (3) solving problems or achieving a scientific goal (e.g., creating a water purification system, landing the Curiosity Rover on Mars) [12].[80] While scientific knowledge changes, to say that science *progresses* implies that we're moving toward something, or at least away from what some have called "primitive beginnings" [13]. This view of progress, as moving away from the primitive or toward something, results in scientific progress becoming disconnected from the accumulation of true scientific belief, except insofar as the

[80] These definitions are not mutually exclusive. Some scientific endeavors might be best explained in terms of all three definitions of scientific progress.

accumulation of true scientific beliefs are coextensive with the accumulation of knowledge or solving a problem. One consequence of the tendency to reduce scientific progress with either accumulation of scientific knowledge or solving specific problems is that it privileges some kinds of science over others; in particular, it often privileges applied over pure scientific endeavors.

The historical division between the 'pure' and 'applied' sciences often rests on different measures of scientific progress. More concretely, the pure sciences (e.g., physics, quantum mechanics, and cosmology) do not always have easily articulated goals that solve problems in the world. For example, the development of cosmological simulations has taken decades and cost millions of dollars, and yet accurate models of the Earth's beginning may not have any direct bearing on the challenges faced by climate change. In contrast, applied sciences often arise out of the empirically-based problems specific groups experience or those faced by persons more generally. To take a recent example, the development of an Ebola vaccination was the result of a Herculean effort coordinated across many countries combining resources. Scientific progress in this case looks very different, and is measured in human lives saved. Both examples offered could be counted as progressing science, when we define scientific progress as an accumulation of knowledge; however, the applied science example clearly solved an immediate problem that was facing countless individuals and researchers. The tendency to privilege scientific progress as problem-solving through applied science could be interpreted as a desire to link scientific progress with social progress [14]. The challenge, then, is defining social progress robustly enough to capture all kinds of science, regardless of the rate of progress, and to resist the urge to privilege science that merely solves problems.

INSTITUTIONAL CONSTRAINTS

The cost to ensure that the rights upon which the right to science relies can present a challenge to many developing countries. The *Special Rapporteur* uses the example of a Venezuelan Supreme Court decision, which "found that the failure of the Venezuelan Institute for Social Security to ensure a regular and consistent supply of the drugs needed to by HIV-positive persons covered by it constituted, inter alia, a violation of the right to enjoy the benefits of scientific progress" [5]. If citizens have a right to life-saving pharmaceutical therapies, it would not be much of a stretch to recognize that all persons have a right to life-saving medical interventions more generally. However, with the rising cost in healthcare, life-saving therapies, even when technologically possible, become a budgetary impossibility for resource-poor countries and developed countries alike. In one contemporary case, Pauline Talty successfully petitioned the Australian Government for a three million dollar bowel transplant to save her life [15]. Compared to countries that have far smaller budgets, this kind of lifesaving therapy would decimate their resources or unfairly distribute the goods to a few citizens leaving the rest with minimal medical support.

Similarly, the *Special Rapporteur* indicates that electricity and other infrastructure development (sewer, clean water, internet access, e.g.,) constitute necessary rights to fulfill the right to science. Many of the world's countries are facing mounting obstacles and mounting demands to fulfill, even minimally, the right to science. The *Special Rapporteur* suggests that some of these costs might be mitigated by modifying intellectual property rights, loosening access to peer-reviewed journals through the establishment of more journal repositories and encouraging open-access publishing, and delinking research and development costs from product prices [5]. However, there will still be highly specialized skills and scarce medical resources that will require travel and heightened cost compared to receiving benefits in one's home country.

Conclusion

I have argued that the U.N. system understands the right to science to be a positive right—a right that entails actions on the part of some other persons or institutions (e.g., government, institution of education). The U.N. *Special Rapporteur* also frames this right as a bridging right—a right that both depends upon other fundamental rights *and* is necessary for citizens to exercise related fundamental rights and liberties. I have suggested that the dynamic interrelation between the necessary conditions to obtain the right to science is best understood as a bundle of rights. We cannot easily separate the right to education, access to information, health, security, etc. from the right to science.

One consequence of conceptualizing the right to science as a bundle of rights is that it will suggest long-term policy solutions instead of focusing science and scientific research on short-term problem-solving. Moreover, we need to attend to the manner with which individuals, policy-makers, and the U.N. system presents scientific progress. Specifically, attention should be paid to how one definition of scientific progress (i.e., scientific progress as problem-solving) can problematically close down or exclude sciences that do not operate by that definition of progress. Finally, it might encourage policy-makers to shift their focus away from immediate budget items to engage in a more robust conversation about the long-term benefits of shifting scarce resources into science education. Such shifts in focus might help identify the ways in which states can prioritize other fundamental rights both *as a means to* increasing the likelihood that citizens of resource-poor countries benefit from scientific progress and its applications.

References

[1] *Universal Declaration of Human Rights*. (1948). 151st Meeting, held on Monday, 22 November 1948 (A/C.3/SR.151). *General Assembly, 3rd Session, 3rd Committee.* Paris: United Nations.

[2] *International Covenant on Economic, Social and Cultural Rights*. (1966). *993 U.N.T.S. 3, G.A. Res. 2200 (XXI), 21 U.N. GAOR Supp. (No. 16 at 49, U.N. Doc. A/6316).*

[3] UNESCO. (2009). *The right to enjoy the benefits of scientific progress and its applications.* Paris: UNESCO.

[4] Müller, A. (2010). Remarks on the Venice statement on the right to enjoy the benefits of scientific progress and its applications (Article 15(1) (b) ICESCR). *Human Rights Law Review, 10*(4), 765-784. Doi:10.1093/hrlr/ngq033.

[5] Shaheed, F. (2012). *Report of the special rapporteur in the field of cultural rights: The right to enjoy the benefits of scientific progress and its applications.* United Nations General Assembly, Human Rights Council. Paris: United Nations.

[6] Chapman, A. R. (2009). Towards an understanding of the right to enjoy the benefits of scientific progress and its applications. *Journal of Human Rights*, *8*(1), 1-36. Doi:10.1080/14754830802701200.

[7] Nickel, J. W. (2007). *Making sense of human rights* (2nd Ed.). Malden, MA: Blackwell Publishing.

[8] Griffin, J. (2008). *On human rights.* New York, NY: Oxford University Press.

[9] De Schutter, O. (2011). The right of everyone to enjoy the benefits of scientific progress and the right to food: From conflict to complementary. *Human Rights Quarterly*, *33*(2), 304-350. doi:10. 1353/hrq.2011.0020.

[10] Timmermann, C. (2014). Sharing in or benefiting from scientific advancement? *Science and Engineering Ethics*, *20*(1), 111-133. Doi:10. 1007/s11948-013-9438-3.

[11] Balietti, S., Mäs, M. & Helbing, D. (2015). On disciplinary fragmentation and scientific progress. *PLoS ONE*, *10*(3), 1-26. doi:10. 1371/journal.pone.0118747.

[12] Mizrahi, M. & Buckwalter, W. (2014). The role of justification in the ordinary concept of scientific progress. *Journal for General Philosophy of Science*, *45*(1), 151-166. Doi:10.1007/s10838-014-9243-y.

[13] De Langhe, R. (2014). A comparison of two models of scientific progress. *Studies in History and Philosophy of Science*, *46*(1), 94-99. Doi:10.1016/j.shpsa.2014.03. 0020039-3681.

[14] Douglas, H. (2014). Pure science and the problem of progress. *Studies in History and Philosophy of Science*, *46*(1), 55-63. Doi:10.1016/j.shpsa. 2014.02.0010039-3681.

[15] Miller, N. (2009, November 14). Intestinal fortitude required. *The Age*. Retrieved from http://www.theage.com.au/national/intestinal-fortitude-required-20091113-ieta.html.

In: International Human Rights and Justice
Editor: Doug Hodgson

ISBN: 978-1-63484-709-4

Chapter 11

Descent, Filiation and the Rights of Children among the Fantse of Ghana

Alex J. Wilson*
Centre for African and International Studies, University of Cape Coast,
Cape Coast, Ghana

Abstract

Human rights documents enjoin State Parties to ensure that children grow up in a family environment so that they can develop their personality to the fullest. Furthermore, they direct that the responsibility for upbringing of children should be borne by both parents. However, Britwum, Atuguba, Dadzie, Bruce-Catheline, Kuma and Minka-Premo (2004) argued that although the cultural practices of the Akan of Ghana assign responsibilities to fathers to ensure the maintenance of their children, some indigenous practices such as mode of reckoning descent promote parental neglect on the part of fathers. Some authors including Christensen (1954) and Wilson (2011) confirm that the Fantse (a sub-group of the Akan) place a high value on men who socialize and maintain their children as well as those of their sisters. Hence there are social control mechanisms that make men responsive to the maintenance and upbringing of children. Policy-makers have realized that though Ghana has a strong legal framework, there is a need to strengthen the implementation of the laws at the community level and engage all stakeholders and structures at that level in order to ensure that child welfare policies are effective. Considering that Ghana's legal systems are conditioned within the framework of legal pluralism where national laws operate alongside the local customary laws and that laws are more effective when they are in line with the cultural values of a people; policy-makers will be interested in the underlying cultural practices that promote children's rights in Ghana. This chapter examines the literature on the cultural practices of the Fantse and argues that to a greater extent, the cultural values of the Fantse of Ghana ensure the rights of children. It concludes that when the core of Fantse culture is upheld, it will help to overcome the problem of child neglect and the abuse of children's rights. Based on this, it recommends that researchers delve deep into indigenous cultural

* Corresponding author: ajwilson@ucc.edu.

practices of the various ethnic groups in Ghana in order to educate people and help enforce the laws and policies on children's rights for national development.

Keywords: child rights, complementary filiation, descent, family, Fantse, filiation, Ghana, human rights, personhood

INTRODUCTION

International conventions on the rights of the child including the United Nations *Convention on the Rights of the Child* (*UNCRC*), the *African Charter on the Rights and Welfare of the Child* (*ACRWC*) and the United Nations *Vienna Declaration and Programme of Action 1993* adopted by the World Conference on Human Rights demand the fullest enjoyment of the rights of the child within the framework of healthy family systems. In furtherance of these rights, the national laws of Ghana on the rights and welfare of children prescribe modes of ensuring that these rights are upheld. However, some reports indicate that, in Ghana, the responsibilities for caring for children have become increasingly reserved for mothers only, although the cultural practices assign responsibilities to fathers to ensure the maintenance of children (Britwum, Atuguba, Dadzie, Bruce-Catheline, Kuma and Minka-Premo, 2004; Brown, 1994). Britwum et al. and Brown maintain that among the matrilineal Akan of Ghana (made up of the Asante, Akyem, Brong, Fantse, Kwahu and many others) indigenous practices, such as the mode of reckoning descent, make children and their fathers members of different lineages and thereby prevent children from benefiting from the lineages of their fathers. They noted that this promotes parental neglect on the part of fathers. Hence, in spite of the customary and statutory laws that protect children's rights, many children with Akan background are denied their rights, especially their rights to inheritance and succession. Therefore, Britwum et al. argued that this situation undermines child maintenance responsibilities assigned to fathers and increases mothers' stake in ensuring the survival of their children into adulthood. Furthermore, they argue that the capacity of indigenous child maintenance institutions to ensure compliance with child maintenance awards and the use of social pressures and various methods of appealing to the conscience of members of the community help to improve fathers' sense of responsibility towards their children. Hence, they recommended that these indigenous methods should be explored. They noted that a number of institutions, including the Department of Social Welfare (DSW), Commission on Human Rights and Administrative Justice (CHRAJ), Legal Aid Board (LAB) and the Police, exist to ensure that children's wellbeing prevails. With all these legal provisions and institutions, one would expect that the rights of the child would be upheld to the highest level in Ghana. Hence, Britwum et al. call for more research on the rights of children.

In this chapter, I examine the rights of children in the context of the family among the Fantse of Ghana. I argue that Fantse cultural values uphold children's rights. The indigenous culture vests the rights of children in the family system and spells out how personhood, descent and filiation should help condition the rights of the child. Moreover, the situation where children's rights to enjoy a smooth childhood is seen only in terms of a child's relationship in the nuclear family tends to obscure the rights that children derive from a typical African family system. Also, the situation where children's rights are examined in line with those that they obtain from their parents conceals the extent to which the Fantse uphold children's rights. This underrates the rights that children derive from their father's lineages.

JUSTIFICATION

The literature on the rights and welfare of Ghanaian children are replete with a number of chilling revelations which call for research on children's rights in Ghana. A critical examination of laws and policies governing the welfare of children shows that Western cultures have often become the modes for making, interpreting and implementing the laws and policies. For instance, the *Children's Act 1998* of Ghana replicated Britain's *Children's Act 1989* and hence the two bear a close resemblance (Takyi, 2014). Nonetheless, individual rights as exist in Western societies have little meaning to traditional societies like that of the Fantse where communitarianism provides mutual support for group action (Saha, 2007; Wilson 2011). In practice, traditional institutions shape local organization and have always sustained societies in spite of efforts made by state institutions to control the traditional ones (Kendie & Guri, 2010). In rural and peri-urban communities, traditional and informal structures continue to play important roles in addressing child protection issues instead of Social Welfare Officers since the latter are not readily accessible to community members (Casey, 2011). In spite of the important role of the family and other cultural institutions in the care and socialization of children, the state does not focus on the family and customary structures that impact on children in the enactment of laws (GNCRC, 2014). The Child, Family and Welfare Policy of Ghana shows that even though Ghana has a strong legal framework, strengthening the institutions at the community level by engaging all stakeholders will help to effect the policies on the rights of children in the best interests of the child. It is expected that everyone in the Ghanaian community will be mindful of the rights of children so that the partnership and co-operation among members of the society for the best interests of the child will prevail. Unfortunately, institutional challenges make the implementation of laws difficult. For instance, the human resources for service delivery do not meet the expectations as implementation of the laws are more of top to bottom approach (Kuyuni & Mahama, n, d). Likewise, parents and other members of the communities do not cooperate with the agencies tasked to implement the law; hence the agencies do not receive adequate notifications of violations of children's rights (GNCRC, 2014). Meanwhile, considering that imported concepts and worldviews cannot be used to explain the needs and experiences of people in developing societies, where laws must be conceived and implemented in their cultural framework, indigenous knowledge should be used to address some of these problems (Wilson, 2012). Therefore a better understanding of the indigenous social, political and legal systems will help to ensure that children's rights are upheld. By limiting ideas in this chapter to the Fantse, I expect that other authors will replicate the ideas in this chapter for other ethnic groups so that a holistic cultural-based approach can be adopted for ensuring the existence of children's rights in Ghana.

METHODOLOGY

This chapter developed out of a PhD dissertation on the Fantse which examined matrilineality and inheritance in five Fantse communities, including Apewosika (in Cape Coast), Baafikrom (near Mankesim), Dago (in the Gomoa West District), Kormantse (in the Mfantseman District) and Mankesim (Wilson, 2011). Some of the findings influenced four months of research that I conducted in Apewosika in the Cape Coast metropolis in 2014 to gather information on childhood and the rights and responsibilities associated with it. In both studies, qualitative research design was adopted for ethnographic study. I spent three months in the field for an in-depth study. I collected data through participant observation and interviews. In addition, the first research also used focus group discussions. Among the findings were that though the Fantse are matrilineal, children enjoy a number of rights from their fathers. These rights are conceived in the principle of reciprocity whereby the rights that a person enjoys must be provided for by another person or entity as a duty. In addition, rights have corresponding duties which a person must perform in the course of life. As a result, children have to perform certain duties for their fathers in a father's life time or after his death. In addition to the primary data, I used secondary data on a number of themes and built my conceptual framework with triangulation of concepts such as descent, filiation, complementary filiation and personhood from the ideas of Meyer Fortes.

STUDY AREA

The Fantse are one of the Akan-speaking groups. They live in parts of the Central and Western regions of Ghana (Wilson, 2007). Their family system is double unilineal with more rights and obligation conferred on the matrilineage (Christensen, 1954; Hagan, 2000; Wilson, 2007; 2011; 2012). Their worldview about children is that they are gifts from the Supreme Being to a couple, clan and the community; hence, children belong to their mothers only when they are in the womb but once they are born, they belong to the entire community. The father of a child serves as his or her spiritual force and hence provides him or her with his or her personality. Children are weak and need the support of adults in the community. Finally, they have different perceptions about childhood construction including the child as a fetus, as an unmarried person, as a son or daughter of a person or linage and as a member of a generation.

EXAMINATION OF THE RELEVANT LITERATURE

As I noted earlier, the literature is replete with a number of problems associated with the rights of children. It also produces a number of ideas that are in line with human rights among the Fantse and therefore provides a solid base for articulating my arguments. Issues that I examine in this chapter include indigenous knowledge systems and human rights; the concept of childhood, the principle of natural law and the age of reason in the classical context of human rights. I also examine international documents and national laws on human rights.

Indigenous Knowledge and Institutions

In contemporary times, indigenous socio-political, economic, religious and legal institutions influence the lives of people in local organization. They have always sustained societies in spite of the efforts of contemporary state institutions to control the traditional ones (Kendie and Guri, 2010). Thus, in order to make contemporary laws more effective, they should be based on the culture of a group (Filey, 1975; Wilson, 2012). Since culture is dynamic, the indigenous knowledge systems can be studied and incorporated into contemporary ideas to make human rights more understandable.

Although the indigenous Fantse knowledge system is replete with ideas of human rights, very little use is made of those ideas. For instance, customary laws enjoin parents and communities to ensure the well-being of their children. Moreover, nuclear family exists as an appendage of a mega family (Agorsah, 2012, Awedoba, 2005; Wilson, 2011). Thus, the mega family becomes very important in ensuring that the rights of children are upheld since the family is the most important traditional social and political organization (Wilson, 2012).

Concept of Childhood

Attempts to universalize the concept of childhood have led to the misunderstanding of the worldview of children and generated interpretational fallacies because childhood is socially constructed and wide variations exist for this definition (Boakye-Boaten, 2009; Helman, 2007). The contentions associated with the definitions vary because of the political claims of culture and identity, the increasing rate of globalization and the changing roles of children within the socio-cultural and political construct of modern societies. Meanwhile, global trends have affected indigenous societies by transforming their institutions and social structure. Boakye-Boaten noted that children are social beings whose world is constructed within a historical and a cultural frame of reference; therefore, childhood should be understood within a socio-cultural context. These observations of Boakye-Boaten accede to the problems associated with definitions of childhood and also lay bare the difficulties that the society is expected to encounter as a result of the definitions. This calls for a re-examination of childhood and children's rights within the cultural context of the Fantse – issues which this chapter will address.

Conception of Human Rights from Antiquity

The United Nations *Universal Declaration of Human Rights 1948* developed from the principles of natural law and age of reason which postulated that human rights involve moral claims that human beings have, simply because they are humans (Hayden, 2001). Natural law theory holds that higher laws of nature prescribe the right conduct of people and make them act in ways which ensure the required moral and political order. This theory identifies what human beings are and how they ought to be treated. Moreover, it conceives rights and freedom as moral issues where freedom is not absolute. This calls for minimal constraints in upholding everybody's rights by noting that rights accompany the freedom to choose one's way of life. Furthermore, rights are inalienable. This means that society confers rights.

Therefore, only the society can take them away from its members. These notions coincide with the principle that government exists to protect the natural rights of its subjects. The principles of natural law, which had existed as part of the law of the Supreme Being however, became secularized as the ideas of natural law metamorphosed into right of reason. Consequently, philosophers began to argue that human beings can deduce rights from wrongs. It will, therefore, be noted that aspects of the principles of natural law, the age of reason and universal human rights prevail among the Fantse, through the concept of personhood, which this chapter examines.

International Documents on the Rights of the Child

The United Nations *Convention on the Rights of the Child 1989* (*UNCRC*) and the *African Charter on the Rights and Welfare of the Child 1990* (*ACRWC*) have the most influence on the child rights laws of Ghana. They have many things in common and few differences. Among the rights and freedoms recognised in the documents are the rights of children to know their parents and be cared for by them, as far as possible (Article 9 of the *UNCRC*) and the right to an identity, including a name, family ties and nationality (Article 8 of the *UNCRC*). A major issue raised in both documents is that in all actions concerning the child undertaken by any person or authority, the best interests of the child shall be the primary consideration (Article 4.1 of *ACRWC*). In addition, the *ACRWC* entreats State Parties to respect the duties of parents and legal guardians so that the latter provide effective guidance and directions to enable children to enjoy their rights subject to the national laws and policies (Article 9.3). Finally, governments must respect the duties of parents to provide guidance and direction in the enjoyment of these rights and help families to create an environment where children can grow and reach their potential (Articles 4 and 5 of the *UNCRC* and Article 9.3 of the *ACRWC*).

The *UNCRC* and the *ACRWC* encourage adults to listen to the opinions of children and involve them in decision-making. They recognize that the degree of a child's participation in decision-making must be commensurate with the child's level of maturity. It entreats parents to guide their children in matters of religion without necessarily placing them in a rigorous religious tradition. Children are to enjoy rights to health (Article 14 of the *ACRWC*). Therefore, it is worthy of note that these human rights instruments do not make governments directly responsible for the welfare and rights of children but rather helps families in those endeavors. Considering that the family is the important unit of social organization, it is prudent to examine the strengths of the indigenous Fantse family in helping to uphold the rights of the child.

The promulgation and ratification of the *UNCRC* provided for a uniform set of rights for all of the children of the world and provided the opportunity for instituting legislation, policies and structures for realizing the rights enshrined therein. The two documents are similar as they both highlight the rights and welfare of children. However, they also have differences in their approach. The *UNCRC* accedes to universalism, but it is more in tune with Western history and culture. Furthermore, it does not contemplate duties. The *ACRWC* provided a similar situation for African countries. However, the *ACRWC* was designed to reflect the history, values, traditions, and development of Africa (Achilihu, 2010). It combines African values with international norms by promoting internationally recognized individual rights and redefining rights in terms of reciprocities in line with indigenous African cultures; including describing rights in terms of reciprocal obligations. It proclaims collective rights and individual duties. Hence, in the *ACRWC*, the promotion and protection of the rights and welfare of the child also implies the performance of duties on the part of everyone. Nonetheless, the *ACRWC* attempts to strike a balance between the competing claims of rights between the individual and society. It is worthy of note that the two documents do not seek to oppose each other but rather complement each other. These differences are worth noting.

National Laws on the Rights of Children in Ghana

Under the *Constitution of the Republic of Ghana* (Ghana, 1992), the country operates a pluralist legal system. Thus, the laws of Ghana comprise the *Constitution*; enactments of parliament; orders, rules and regulations; and the common law, which includes customary law (Article 11). The main statutory laws that deal with the rights and welfare of children are the *Constitution* and the *Children's Act 1998*, (Act 560). Others are the *Criminal Code 1960* (Act 29), as amended in 1998, the *Matrimonial Causes Act 1971* (Act 367), *Wills Act 1971* (Act 360), *Intestate Succession Law 1985* (PNDC Law 111 and as amended by PNDC Law 264), the *Courts Act 1993* (Act 459), the *Human Trafficking Act 2005* (Act 694) and the *Domestic Violence Act 2007* (Act 732) (Britwum et al., 2004).

The 1992 Constitution of the Republic of Ghana

Fundamental rights and freedoms of children are provided for in Article 28 of the *Constitution*. Others include the right to education (Article 25), which states in part that basic education shall be free, compulsory and available to all children; cultural rights and practices of the people of Ghana (Article 26) and those that seek to protect and promote the rights of disabled children (Article 37). Article 26(2) of the *Constitution* states explicitly that all customary practices which dehumanize or are injurious to the physical and mental well-being of a person are prohibited.

In order to make the rights of the child more applicable, the *Constitution* enjoined Parliament to enact a law that would ensure that the natural parents of children up to the age of 18 would enjoy special care, assistance and maintenance necessary for children's development (Article 28). This culminated in the enactment of the *Children's Act 1998* which also set out a number of rights that ensured the well-being of children.

The Children's Act 1998 (Act 560)

The *Children's Act* sets out a number of rights that ensure the well-being of children. It relies on the welfare principles of the *UNCRC* and the *ACRWC*, especially the centrality of the concept of the best interests of the child in all matters concerning the child (Section 2). It also upholds the rights of children to grow up in a family and enjoy life as members of a family. It aims at assisting children, including orphans in need of care and protection. It charges parents and other legally liable persons to exercise proper guardianship by supplying children under their care with the necessities of health, life, education and reasonable shelter. It spells out the conditions under which one can foster (a customary form of adoption where children are voluntarily handed over by their natural parents to another person to raise without legal process) a child and the responsibilities of a foster parent. Finally, it outlaws the abuse of foster children (Appiah, n, d).

Among the rights enshrined in the *Children's Act 1998* are the child's rights to a name and nationality, grow up with his or her parents, have access to parental property, participate in social activity, and so forth. Under the Act, a court may order maintenance cost against a father so that he maintains the mother of his child (Section 51). This order may be awarded during the pregnancy period of the mother. Likewise, the Act protects children from exploitative labor (Sections 12 and 87), cruel, inhuman or degrading treatment or punishment including any cultural practice which dehumanizes or is injurious to their physical and mental wellbeing (Section 14) and forced betrothals, dowry transactions and marriage (Section 13). Again, it states that a child has a right to a reasonable portion of the parents' estates and that no person shall deprive him or her of a reasonable provision out of the estates of his or her parents (Section 7). Finally, a child is capable of forming his or her views, has the right to express an opinion, to be listened to and to participate in decisions affecting him or her (Section 11).

In furtherance of these rights, the Act charges parents to maintain their children and provide them with basic necessities of life including food, shelter, clothing, health, basic education, good guidance, care, assistance and maintenance for the child among other things (Sections 6 and 8). It charges the State to ensure the welfare of families so that families will be able to pursue the welfare of children. However, it is rather unfortunate that members of the various communities in Ghana do not support the agencies charged with the implementation of the rights of the child under the *Children's Act 1998*.

Other Statutory Laws

Aside from these laws, there are other statutory laws that uphold children's rights. Interestingly, some of these laws were enacted prior to the coming into effect of the *Constitution*. Among them are the *Criminal Offences Act 1960* (Act 29) and the *Intestate Succession Law 1985* (PNDCL, 111). Sections 71, 91 and 92 of the *Courts Act 1993* as amended in 1998 criminalized the abandonment or exposure of a child to danger, abduction of a child and a range of sexual offences that can render a child vulnerable to HIV infection. The *Intestate Succession Law 1985* (PNDCL 111) prescribes the way a person's property will be devolved when he or she dies intestate. It governs the devolution of property to a deceased person's children, whether born in wedlock or outside it. It states among other things that a child is entitled to a portion of his or her deceased parent's property if the parent dies intestate (Sections 3-5).

Other laws enacted after the *Children's Act 1998* to support the rights and welfare of the child are the *Human Trafficking Act 2005* (Act 694) and the *Domestic Violence Act 2007* (Act 732). The *Human Trafficking Act* seeks to prevent, reduce and punish human trafficking. It also provides for rehabilitation and re-integration of victims, including children into their families or communities which support their welfare. The *Domestic Violence Act 2007* (Act 732) provides for protection from physical abuse, sexual abuse, economic abuse and emotional, verbal or psychological abuse. It addresses issues such as sexual harassment and intimidation by inducing fear in other persons, especially children. The Act identifies the procedures under which neighbors and officials may assist a child to file a complaint. In addition, the Act deals with the receipt of a complaint and how arrest can be effected by the police. Furthermore, there is provision for protection orders where a person or institution may be authorized by a law court to take custody of a child.

Customary Laws

Customary law is defined under the *Constitution* as "the rules of law which by custom are applicable to particular communities in Ghana" [Article 11(3)]. The customary laws are local in nature and differ from one place to another. However, there are some similarities. Customary laws have been in existence since the precolonial days and are amended by traditional political institutions from time to time. Statutory laws are sometimes enacted to redefine the spirit and letter of customary laws. The customary laws define kinship relations – consanguinal and affinal. For instance, they define marriage in terms of relationships which lead to procreation and the development of the domestic group. Moreover, they define marriage exchange (prestations such as bridewealth and bride service) and the rights and duties contingent upon the marriage exchange between the couple (Wilson, 2011). They also define the concept of personhood, descent, filiation and complementary filiations and the rights and responsibilities associated with these are clearly stated in the customary laws. Lastly, they define the roles of married people and their respective descent groups (consanguine) and how these rights and obligations generate into duties towards the socialization of children to make them worthy of taking up their roles in their communities.

Implementation of the Laws on Children's Rights

The implementation of children's rights involves some problems. Some authors including Britwum et al. (2004) and Kuyini and Mahama (n, d) maintain that some traditional values, beliefs and customs conflict with the demands of national laws and prevent the implementation of the protective aspects of the laws. For example, Indigenous Ghanaian culture makes the engagement of children in work acceptable as it is seen as part of the children's contribution to family survival. Ironically, the *ACRWC* supports this as it couches it as a child's responsibility to his or her family. Kuyini and Mahama maintain that although parents contribute to their children's survival and expect children to do the same perhaps through child labor and other contributions, child rights laws challenge some of these long-held beliefs, values and practices. They argue that the dilemma about these values and orientations is more likely to be stronger when the laws are perceived to be countering the normality of life. Moreover, the laws transcend the indigenous values, beliefs and attitudes of child-rearing. Furthermore, when the dilemma is viewed in the context of the evidence that attitudes and ways of doing things that are value-laden are the most difficult to change, then the agencies have to do more work than usual in order to implement aspects of the laws that protect children in Ghana.

Secondly, some parents and members of the communities do not cooperate with the law enforcement agencies because they castigate those who report issues of violation of the rights of children. Therefore, many people prefer to use the traditional institutions for conflict resolution rather than report instances of abuse. These alternative dispute resolution methods enable people to perpetrate crimes with impunity as those institutions are not mandated to deal with crimes. Thirdly, a lack of resources inhibits the effective implementation of government policies, especially those of the social services sector (Kuyini and Mahama, n, d; UNICEF-Ghana, 2000).

Conceptual Frameworks

The title of this chapter calls for frameworks that catalogue concepts such as descent, filiation, complementary filiation and personhood. Fortes (1967; 1970; 1997) amplifies all these. Therefore, I triangulated these concepts to explain the extent to which the principles of human rights are embedded in Fantse cultural beliefs and practices. The four concepts chosen are inter-related. They examine the nature of relationships that develop out of kinship (Fortes, 1970). However, realizing that Fortes highlighted much more on descent, filiation and complementary filiation and mentioned the concept of personhood, casually I will support Fortes' ideas of personhood with that authored by Schnepel (1990), which dilates Fortes' works. I will also link the ideas to my work on personhood (Wilson, 2012) which I supported with those of Gyekye (1992, 1996) and Wiredu (2001).

Descent

Descent is the genealogical connection which a society recognizes between a person and any of his or her ancestors through a parent and subsequently a grandparent (Fortes, 1970). "It is an association of people of both sexes comprising all the recognized descendants by an accepted genealogy of a single named ancestor in a putatively continuous…line" (Fortes, 1969; p. 37). Fortes noted that society establishes descent by tracing a pedigree; however, it is not essential to establish pedigree in order to claim or demonstrate descent from an ancestor. Furthermore, he noted that a person's position establishes a pedigree by counting successive steps of filiation. In effect, the relationship associated with descent extends to an offspring and its offspring. Thus descent is generational.

In many African societies, descent is nominally unilineal and associated with terms like lineage and clan. A lineage traces descent over a short period while a clan traces it over a relatively long period. Therefore, a lineage is a subset of a clan. Fortes (1997) described lineages and clans as the most important social organization because they unite people for common social purposes and interests by identifying them exclusively with one another. Their memberships are clearly defined. All the members of a group have the same form of pedigree and all their pedigrees converge in a single common ancestor or group of ancestors.

Descent dovetails into the politico-jural domain (Fortes, 1970). This means that indigenous political systems are organized around the lineages and clans. An individual has no legal or political status unless such a status is couched within the framework of the lineage or clan. In segmentary lineage systems, descent provides the link between the internal domestic domain and the external political and jural aspects of unilineal descent groups. This means that descent conditions a person's place and statuses in the external politico-jural domain of his or her community.

Clans and lineages are corporate entities. They have legal and jural rights, including ownership of property, compelling entities which are related to them to perform some duties for them and obligations, such as ensuring the welfare of their members and performing religious duties (Fortes, 1970). Because of the social, political, economic, jural and legal functions of lineages and clans, they have structures of authority which they use to govern in order to maintain their perpetuity (Fortes, 1997). In indigenous African societies, descent determines citizenship.

Mindful of the rule that in African societies descent is mostly unilineal and double unilineal, Fortes (1970) suggested that for analytical purposes, the application of the term 'descent group' should be limited to groups which recruit membership by jurally acknowledging one line of descent only. The line defined by the other parent's connection to his or her lineage is described in terms of filiation and extended to complementary filiation.

Filiation

Filiation is the relationship that exists between a person and his or her offspring (Fortes, 1969). It signifies the relationship created as a result of being the legitimate child of one's parents. It is associated with specific moral and affective ties and cleavages between successive generations that arise from giving birth and exercising responsibilities of child-rearing. The relationship associated with filiation falls within the nuclear family. It is generally bilateral because almost all, if not all, societies give jural recognition to the parenthood of both mother and father.

Though filiation is universally bilateral, in indigenous African societies the concept does not provide equal social weighting on both parents because of the unilineal descent system; hence the term 'complementary filiation' develops out of filiation so that descent mediates in explaining the relationship between descent and complementary filiation. Thus, examination of complementary filiation helps to reckon the relationship which develops with the descent group with less social weighting while descent works for the group with more social weighting (Fortes, 1969). In order to distinguish between the dominant lineage and the less dominant ones, terminologies such as matrifiliation and partrifiliation develop as the basis for explanation.

Filiation may confer title to status (which means rights and capacities) in the politico-jural domain (Fortes, 1969). It creates a package of jurally, ritually, and morally validated credentials for the rights and duties, privileges and claims that constitute status for its bearers. Fortes noted that, based on the principle of patrilifiliation, an Asante enjoys some rights and privileges from his or her father's clan and chiefdom. Filiation falls in line with descent when descent is viewed as 'cumulative filiation' or as 'successive steps of filiation.'

Complementary Filiation

So far as descent provides the connecting link between the internal domestic domain and the external political and jural domain of unilineal descent groups, clear lines have to be established between filiation and complementary filiation. To do this effectively, Fortes' suggestion that the application of the term "descent group" should be limited to groups which recruit membership by jurally acknowledging one line of descent only should be considered. This resonates with the idea that only one mode of filiation (parent) is associated with unilineal descent groups. In the double unilineal system, both lines of descent are acknowledged; however, the acknowledgement goes with specific action. For instance, property devolves to both lineages but society identifies the particular property which devolves to each of the descent groups. This eventually results in differential weighting for the two groups; however, the difference is less than what prevails in a unilineal descent system. With the unilineal descent rule, the "dominant line" which confers descent on a person also confers membership and status to a person in the primary unit of the politico-jural domain. This allows complementary filiation to provide the essential links between a person's offspring and members of his or her lineage if that lineage does not determine the descent of his or her offspring (Fortes, 1997). Thus, the principle of descent counterbalances the principle of complementary filiation. This helps to draw a distinction between the descent group which serves as the dominant corporate unit and the group which has less influence on a person's social and political life.

Personhood

The major idea of Fortes (1967, 1969, 1970, 1997) on personhood is that it has two aspects – a person's internal orientation and a person's relationship with members of the society. That of a person's internal orientation is about his identity. Under the former, a person knows himself to be the person he is supposed to be; he or she assumes a moral responsibility for his or her conduct and has self-control over himself or herself. The latter aspect involves a person's relations with other people. Under this view, Fortes identified *personne morale* in which a person is not just a passive bearer of personhood but is aware of his or her social and moral obligations and always reflects on what the society expects of him or her (Schnepel, 1990). Fortes noted that society is not only a social order but also a moral order. This implies that members of the social order must assume moral responsibility for their conduct (Fortes 1967). Thus, a person becomes an individual as well as a social being. Therefore, he or she has to display his or her statuses in the socially prescribed and accepted ways and act in line with the norms and values of his or her society and culture. Fortes noted that a person - sole or corporate - must be identifiable from the outside. As a person, he or she has to internalize his or her statuses, the expected roles, rights and responsibilities and display them in socially prescribed and accepted ways.

Human Rights

Society uses sanctions derived from the politico-jural domain of kinship to legitimize rights and obligations. The rights and obligations arise from the politico-jural domain, or in descriptive terms, from the total social structure. Descent confers rights and duties, capacities and claims on members of the group. It distributes these rights among the various segments or classes. The rights, duties, etc. remain relatively fixed over a period of time so that the social system can maintain itself to enable a society to achieve its ends. Interestingly, privileges, rights and loyalties are divided along the lines of filiation and complementary filiation and thus enable one group to have the sanction of law to effect rules while the other group relies on religion and morality to effect an action (Fortes, 1997). Furthermore, Fortes noted that a cluster of moral and contingent rights, duties and claims connects the submerged line with religious sanctions.

Summary of Fortes' Ideas

The summary of the ideas put forward by Fortes (1967, 1969, 1970, 1997) are that descent and filiation develop from kinship. Whereas filiation is the relationship between a parent and his or her children, descent develops among a group of people and is reckoned by a pedigree. Besides, while filiation develops from both parents, descent develops from one of the parents. Thus, filiation exists within the domestic frame while descent is intergenerational. Similarly, the rights associated with filiation are not intergenerational but those associated with descent are.

Descent comes in many forms including unilineal, double-unilineal, bilineal and ambilineal. The unilineal descent and double unilineal descent systems explain the African concept of family. In the unilineal system, descent is reckoned through only one parent at a time from generation to another. Thus, a person has two clearly defined lineages – matrilineage (reckoned through the female line) and patrilineage (reckoned through the male line). However, it should be noted that no society is absolutely matrilineal or patrilineal. Therefore, a matrilineal society simply means that a greater percentage of reckoning descent goes through the female line while a minimal proportion of other rights and obligations are effected through the male line and vice versa. Similarly, double unilineal descent does not mean that descent is reckoned on equal bases, but because the percentages of reckoning are closer as compared to the unilineal descent.[81]

The unilineal descent system makes filiation more in tune with one of the lineages of the parents. For instance, society expects people who belong to matrilineal societies to have greater connection with their mothers and their mother's lineage and vice versa. Hence, a person's filial ties with a mother are expected to be greater if that person belongs to a matrilineal society, and vice versa. With this, the relationship with the other parent becomes complementary; meaning that filiation and descent have greater linkages while complementary filiation develops with less linkage to a lineage. Thus, while filiation becomes

[81] For the purposes of this article, I speculate that in unilineal descent, the percentages are about 80 percent and 20 percent while that of the double unilineal descent is about 55 percent and 45 percent. This claim is just hypothetical.

associated with descent, complementary filiation develops out of the roles and duties of the other parent who is presumed to have less descent and subsequently less filial ties. With the concept of complementary filiation, Fortes underscored the roles of both parents of a child in ensuring the existence of the rights of the child and legitimizing the child's social standing within the kinship system.

The distinction between filiation and complementary filiation is often apparent in the difference between relations with a grandparent based on the criterion of successive filiation (Fortes, 1969). In matrilineal societies, matrifiliation automatically confers membership by descent and, subsequently, citizenship to a person in indigenous states (chiefdom) at birth, while patrifiliation ensues only from acknowledged paternity. Patrifiliation becomes associated with complementary filiation and does not establish right to citizenship in the juridical sense. However, it is a prerequisite for determining status as a free citizen and distinguishing such a person from those who have slave ancestry. A person whose paternity is unknown is socially and ritually defective and jurally incomplete. This may prevent his or her eligibility for a lineage and political office. However, in special circumstances, patrifiliation may serve as the basis for acquiring quasi-citizenship in one's father's chiefdom. This occurs when a person voluntarily accepts a distinctive political obligation and pays levies imposed or performs military roles to his or her father's chiefdom.

Application of the Concepts

Fortes' works have been criticized in anthropology. However, I will not dilate on the criticisms. I will rather attempt to bring out some ideas which tend to create opposing views and consider them within the Fantse descent system. There is no gainsaying about the assertion by Fortes (1970) that filiation which is generally bilateral works with the Fantse. However, the Fantse give jural recognition to the parenthood of both mothers and fathers and, hence, although filiation will be expected to be bilateral, it cannot be said that it is totally bilateral, considering that there is gender division of functions between parents. Likewise, Fortes should not be faulted excessively because he also noted that filiation in African societies does not provide equal social weighting on both parents and the parents' kin connection. Furthermore, as children grow up, they also begin to uphold the principles of descent, filiation and complementary filiation.

Fortes' assertion that rules of complementary filiation help to explain features of double unilineal descent systems (Fortes, 1997) is laudable as it applies to the Fantse. It determines the statuses that are ascribed to a person and the expected roles and responsibilities that such statuses confer on a person. Moreover, it determines the privileges conferred by law and those conferred by religion and morality on the part of parents. Furthermore they help to assign religious and political offices and the concomitant authority to both the matrilineage and the patrilineage of a person and the entire community. The affinal relationship between the couple leads to conception and, hence, the beginning of personhood for the child. From there, filiation develops as the parents provide him or her with their emotional and physical needs. As children grow, parents socialize them and help them to develop affection to the members of the mega family. As children develop successive succession, they extend the filial ties a step or more further into the lineages of their parents.

Fortes' concepts work within the framework of the domestic group as well as the politico-jural domain from conception through childhood to adulthood, to provide the basis for understanding human rights. In order to apply the concepts, I have developed a graphical presentation (see Figures 1 and 2). For the purposes of this analyses, I begin from marriage and creation of the family of procreation. Figure 1 represents the relationships at birth through adolescence while Figure 2 represents when the child grows up and enters into marriage. In Figure 1, personhood merges with filiation and childhood because both childhood and personhood begin from conception (Wilson, 2012). The natural bonds between the parents, especially the mother, and the fetus begin immediately after conception. The child's connection to descent and complementary filiation are weak as he or she relates more with his or her parents; except in situations where he or she is fostered by relatives of any of the parents.

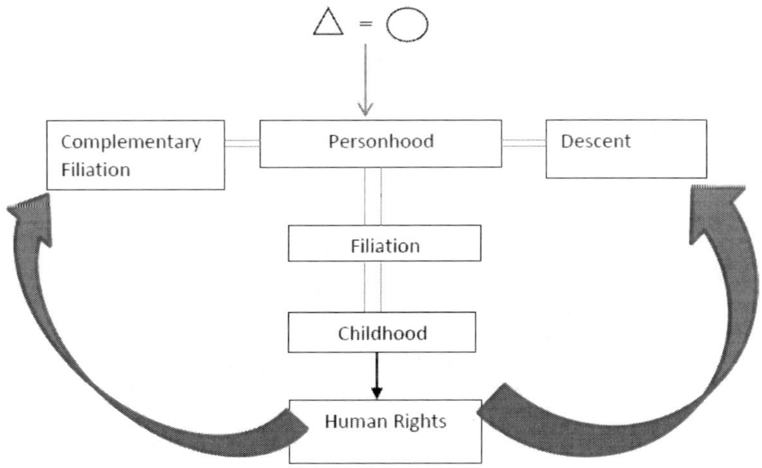

Figure 1. Relationship between personhood filiation and childhood in pursuit of Human Rights.

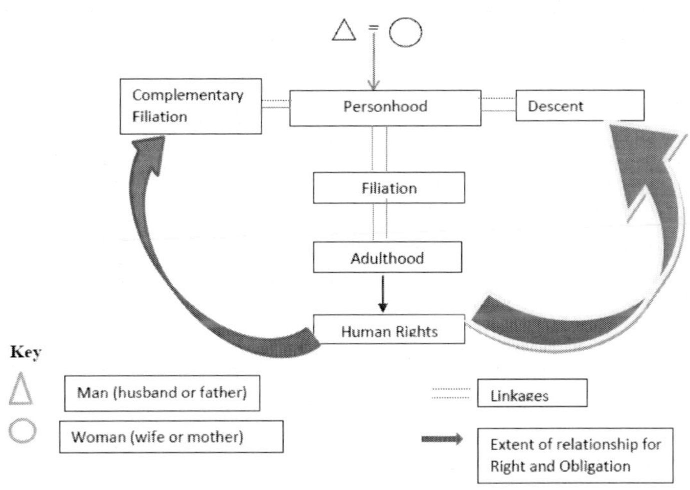

Figure 2. Relationship between personhood filiation and adulthood in pursuit of Human Rights.

Figure 2 represents adulthood (which to the indigenous family occurs at marriage), where the young adult draws clear lines between his matrilineage and patrilineage. The filial relations get connected to descent and complementary filiation with relatively more rights and obligations to both the matrilineage and patrilineage. However, more rights and responsibilities are obtained from the matrilineage as the father transfers some of his responsibilities to his child's matrilineage at marriage by ensuring that the matrilineage participates actively in the marriage ceremony of his child.

For purposes of social organization during adulthood, the young adult is more in tune with his or her matrilineage. His or her father's matrilineage does not wean itself from the child (adult son or daughter). Its members continue to guide him or her and ensure that he or she performs his or her duties in the matrilineage so that when his or her father dies, his or her matrilineage will be called upon to participate in the funeral. The matrilineage therefore supports the young adult to perform a befitting burial for the father. Thus, when the child marries, he or she becomes more in tune with descent while upholding the filial relation with his or her father and extending that relationship to the patrilineage. Therefore, descent is considered in terms of step-by-step filiation to establish the associated pedigree. Filial bonds move steps further into communal bonds and, hence, the concepts are very important for explaining rights and obligations in indigenous African societies such as that of the Fantse.

Personhood among the Fantse

Personhood is about what a person is made up of and the moral expectations of him or her from members of a community (Gyekye, 1996; Wilson, 2012; Wiredu, 2001). Among the Fantse, and for that matter the Akan, a person is made up of three elements – *bogya*[82] (blood), transmitted by his or her mother; *honhom* or *sunsum* (spirit), transmitted by a father and *kra* (soul) transmitted by the Supreme Being (Gyekye, 1995, 1996; Sarpong, 1974; Wilson, 2007, 2012; Wiredu, 2001). The *bogya* is believed to give rise to a person's *honam* (biological body); the spirit is believed to be associated with a person's personality and aspects of the character. It gives rise to *egyabosom*[83] (a patrilineal cult associated with a father's patrilineage). The soul is believed to give rise to *nkrabea* (destiny). The *bogya* and the *sunsum* constitute the material component of a person which comprises all the genetic factors responsible for biologically inherited characteristics, while the *kra* constitutes the non-material part of a person. A person relates to his or her mother and mother's lineage by virtue of the *bogya* and his or her father by virtue of the *egyabosom.* The basic function of the patrilineage is religious; however, the *asafo*, a group with socio-politico religious and military functions, also develops from it. A person is a creature of the Supreme Being and has aspects of the attributes of the Supreme Being and his or her parents in him or her. Though the attributes of the Supreme Being may be minimal, they are the foremost principles that confer human rights on him or her.

[82] This is spelled and pronounced in Twi (one of the Akan dialects) as *mogya*. All the authors to whom this is attributed, including Wilson (2007, 2012) who wrote about the Fantse, used *mogya*.

[83] In Twi this is known as *ntorɔ*.

The Concepts and Human Rights

Some principles underlying classical concepts of human rights that have influenced international human rights documents since time immemorial can be replicated in indigenous Fantse concepts of human rights. Among the principles which resonate with the concepts in indigenous Fantse worldviews about human rights are natural law and age of reason. For example, the principles which identify the composition of human beings, confer human rights on them and prescribe the right conduct of people for upholding human rights (Hayden, 2001) resonate with the ideas of Fortes (1967; 1970) on the moral aspects of personhood, where a person acknowledges his or her self-identity, assumes a moral responsibility for his or her conduct and relates very well with other members of the society. Thus, from all indications, personhood falls within the concept of natural rights.

Personhood explains the concept of human rights among the Fantse (Wilson, 2007, 2012) within the politico-jural domain and hence the community. As explained earlier, it confers a number of statuses on an individual. As a creature of the Supreme Being, he or she has aspects of the attributes of the Supreme Being as well as those of his or her parents in him or her. Though the attributes of the Supreme Being may be minimal, they are the foremost principles that confer human rights on him or her. By merely being a creature of the Supreme Being, he is endowed with rights (Gyekye, 1996; Wilson, 2012; Wiredu, 2001). These principles are in line with the principles of natural law and the age of reason. Just as natural law and rights of reason perceive a person as a creature of the Supreme Being and prescribe the nature of rights in classical context, personhood also perceives the composition of a person and contextualizes rights and obligations that a person enjoys and is expected to perform by merely being human among the Fantse. Similarly, personhood conceive rights and duties as moral obligations. However, whereas natural law conceives inalienability of rights in terms of what the state must provide, personhood conceives the inalienability of rights as something that members of the state must ensure with the state as the overseer.

Descent, filiation, complementary filiation and personhood generate a system of rights and obligations for individuals in a community as human rights are conceived in terms of reciprocities. However, because filiation serves as the starting point for reckoning rights and obligations, the onus for ensuring that children enjoy their rights from both parents' lineages develops from filiation (see Figure 1). Through descent and complementary filiation, the kin groups ensure that parents perform their duties for children to enjoy their individual and communal rights.

Fortes' argument that the concept of personhood serves as an assemblage of statuses and the starting point for inquiring into rights and obligations applies to the Fantse because personhood and filiation prescribe the principles underlying children's rights. Through the filial ties, descent and complementary filiation emerge to ensure that children enjoy their rights. Through descent and complementary filiation, members of the community contribute their quota to ensure the existence of human rights. As the clans come together for social and political action in the community, their collective efforts aim at ensuring that people perform their duties so that human rights, especially children's rights, prevail for everyone to enjoy. The concepts determine the rights and obligation of children (Wilson, 2012). In Fantse culture, children have basic rights. Because of the worldview that personhood develops from conception and evolves through childhood to adulthood, children begin to enjoy their basic human rights at the foetal stage and continue to be treated as such until they pass through various stages of life where some of the rights are gradually taken away from them and replaced with responsibilities.

Structures and Institutions for Addressing Children's Rights

Fortes' concepts help to develop structures and institutions for addressing children's rights among the Fantse. He noted that a person has to display his or her statuses in the socially prescribed and accepted ways and act in line with the norms and values of his or her society and culture. Among these institutions are the descent system, the age grade system and the chieftaincy institutions. However, all these develop from the descent groups which warrant further examination.

The dynamics associated with recruitment of members of a clan define the nature of solidarity among their members for common social and political actions and set the rules for human rights. Membership is open to females and their sons and daughters automatically. Furthermore, clans may incorporate strangers into their fold after all the necessary negotiations and rituals have been performed (Wilson, 2007; 2011). This includes integrating sons, daughters and slaves into a man's lineage. The clans serve as corporate entities and mobilize their members for political action. Though sons and daughters are not members of their fathers' lineages, nothing debars them from siting in a meeting or functions organized by their fathers' descent groups.

Clans mobilize their members for political action. They have chieftain positions and a representation on the council of elders which governs a community. They have legal and jural rights and obligations; own properties; have totems and political insignia, including a stool (major symbol of political office). Furthermore, they have structures of authority which exist in perpetuity and confer citizenship (Fortes, 1997). They also deliberate on issues and present resolutions on matters affecting them and their communities. Finally, they perform rituals, including installation for political officers and funerals for their members. Once every member of a community is incorporated into a clan, the clan, and for that matter descent promotes participation in communal affairs including social, political, economic and religious ones.

DISCUSSIONS: STRUCTURES AND INSTITUTIONS FOR ADDRESSING CHILDREN'S RIGHTS AMONG THE FANTSE

From all indications, children's rights work within the cultural framework of the Fantse, national laws and international laws on the rights of the child and also resonate with the principles of natural law. For example, the relationship between the cultural belief of the Fantse and the principles of natural law is that a child is a gift from the Supreme Being to the parents and the community; hence, it has natural rights. Just as the principles of natural law contend that human beings are creatures of the Supreme Being and ought to be endowed with fundamental rights, the principles of personhood expound the composition of a person (of blood, spirit and soul), the provider of these entities, the moral expectations of him or her from members of the community and why he or she should be endowed with human rights. In addition, natural law, the age of reason and personhood presuppose that government should safeguard the rights of people. The difference between the two is that whereas the state in the classical world exists outside the family, in indigenous African political systems, including that of the Fantse, the state subsists on the clan (family). Therefore, the state charges clans to ensure that everyone enjoys his or her basic human rights.

The Fantse maxim goes that a child belongs to its mother only when it is in the womb; however, once it is born, it belongs to everybody. The Fantse principle is that a person belongs to a descent group and, hence, the maxim that *Nyame bɔɔ nyimpa no ɔdze no too ebusua mu* (Lit: When the Supreme Being created human kind He placed him or her in a family). However, in the Fantse family system, the composite family, which is typically the composition of the members of a household, is an appendage of a lineage. Once descent is double unilineal, both the matrilineage and the patrilineage have roles to play in maintaining human rights. Hence, the descent group socializes a child and makes him or her fit into the society and ensures that he or she operates within the rights outlined by the society. Therefore, the concepts help to invoke the child's rights from both the descent groups and the community in the maxim, "I am because we are and we are because I am" which Mbiti (1990) explains as one does not exist solely on one's own.

The matrilineage and patrilineage have to work together, through their respective members who are linked to a child through filiation, to ensure that children enjoy their human rights. Thus, filiation operates as the forerunner to link descent and complementary filiation in order to maintain children's rights. Once society assigns differential roles to mothers and fathers and these extend to their respective lineages, one lineage serves as a check on the other, while the chieftaincy institution serves as the overall overseer and final arbiter in matters of human rights abuses. There is, therefore, no gainsaying that both parents and their lineages have roles to play in maintaining the rights of the child.

The reports that the mode of reckoning descent makes some fathers shirk their responsibilities (Britwum et al., 2004; Brown, 1994) should be seen as deviant behavior as people misinterpret the laws to favor themselves to the detriment of others. This has to be corrected through education and enforcement of laws. Hence, I shall explain how the mode of reckoning descent makes fathers more responsible to ensure their children enjoy the rights within the framework of the Fantse culture, national laws and international documents. Recalling earlier arguments that the national laws rely on the welfare principles of the *UNCRC* and the *ACRWC* and uphold the principle of the "best interests of the child," I shall examine how Fantse cultural beliefs and practices condition this principle and make it functional. My discussions will focus on the elements outlined by Fortes (1967; 1969; 1970, 1997). These elements work within the domestic family, age grades and chiefs. It is worthy of note, however, that once these institutions develop first of all in filial ties and extend to descent and complementary filial groups, clans (especially the matrilineages) are mandated to ensure that first and foremost, children enjoy the following rights which typically exist in the national and international laws, but fathers and their lineages are partners in this effort.

Right to Identity

This right, including right to a name and citizenship, is so important that the Fantse culture makes it a shared value where all the entities associated with personhood have either secular or religious roles to play in order to ensure that children enjoy this and other rights which they require for their personal and social growth and development. Considering that the Fantse, and for that matter the African, religious life is woven into the culture, society performs rites and rituals to name a child and confer a number of associated rights and obligations on him or her.

A Fantse child is named and outdoored on the eighth day after birth. His or her day of birth within the week naturally gives him or her a first name, the *kradzin* (lit-soul name). *Kradzin* presupposes that on that day he or she departs from the spiritual world as the Supreme Being commissions him or her with a destiny to shape his or her life in the physical world. This shows a person's connection with the Supreme Being. A father has the right and prerogative to provide his children with other names. This links the child to his or her father's descent group and gives him or her some privileges in that group. A child's mother does not give him or her a name. However, through the mother, a Fantse child gets citizenship of her hometown and, consequently, the indigenous state.[84] If the child's mother is not a Fantse and does not hail from a matrilineal society, then his or her father incorporates him or her into his descent group. Though when this happens, the person cannot hold any political office in his or her father's descent group when he or she becomes an adult but he or she may be accorded a chieftain position through achievement (Arhin, 1985).

The symbolism associated with the rituals of naming sets the conditions for explaining children's rights. On the day of naming the child, his or her father presents a number of specified items to the mother and child to show his love and support to them. To the mother, the gifts renew the bond of marriage while those to the child show that his or her father has accepted him or her as the father's and therefore is ready to take responsibility of everything that entails his or her rights and welfare. Thus, the father accepts the responsibility to provide for the needs and human rights of the child. He is obliged to bear the cost of every liability that arises out of nurturing the child until the child is capable of bearing such cost (Wilson, 2011). Thus, in relation to the situation where a parent may apply to a family tribunal to establish the fatherhood of a child as outlined in Section 40 of the *Children's Act 1998*, this piece of legislation recognizes these rites and ritual as one of the ways by which a father establishes his claim for the parentage of a child under Section 41.

The daily activities also signify that the parents and members of the community will work together to support the neonate to enjoy his or her rights. The parents of the child commit themselves to provide for the child's needs and also affirm their commitment to their older children and the entire community that they would raise the children to become responsible citizens. Members of the community support this affirmation by also showering gifts to the mother and the neonate. In addition, they offer pieces of advice to the parents urging them to grow in love and support the newborn child and older ones to be a worthy citizen. The child's right to identity is accompanied by some cultural practices that enumerate other rights including the rights to nurturance, growth within a family, socialization and healthcare. Therefore, the activities of the day serve as a platform for giving identity to the child, setting the pace for the actual beginning of his or her nurturance and socialization as a member of the human race and re-inculcating values of family life, including the importance of raising children in a family set up to help them to fulfil their rights within the context of "the best interests of the child" clause as exists in numerous human rights documents.

[84] The concept of hometown to the Fantse is not where a person is born, but rather where the mother hails from.

Rights to Nurture and Growth within a Family

Human beings have longer childhood dependence than other primates because their offspring are weak and defenseless (Odetola, 1985). Hence, society craves the indulgence of members of the respective lineages and the associated kin groups to accord children the right to be nursed (Wiredu 2001). From birth to the eighth day, society considers the child as a stranger from the spiritual world who must be treated with special care and given special protection so that he or she remains in the physical world. Most often, the child lives with his or her mother in the mother's lineage home, since women often give birth around the abode of their lineage members in other to benefit from the support of members, especially that from her mother and mother's sisters. A mother of a neonate does not do any household chores. Members of her lineage and other close relatives help her to recover from the strains of pregnancy and childbirth and encourage her to take her medication. This enables her to breastfeed the child constantly and take good care of him or her, all in the interests of the child.

A Fantse parent and any of his or her relatives should have access to a child who does not live with him or her. If such a parent is deprived of such access, he or she may lodge a complaint with his or her lineage head. The head is supposed to contact the head of the party who is preventing him or her from getting access to his or her child. If this fails then the matter must be reported to traditional authorities (chiefs). Thus if this cultural practice is followed, a parent does not need to apply to a family tribunal to gain access to his or her child as stated in Sections 43-46 of the *Children's Act 1998*.

A parent, especially a father, has to maintain a child. This role extends to members of the father's lineage especially, if the father is not capable of maintaining the child or if he is dead. This fulfils the interests of the child better than the provision in Section 51 of the *Children's Act 1998* which places the onus of maintenance on governmental agencies which do not often have the resources to maintain the child and have to raise the child in a makeshift family environment such as children's homes. All these support the spirit and letter of international human rights documents and national laws that the child must grow up in a family environment. The child does not only grow up in the family but is nurtured and given an identity to participate in the group's activities.

Fantse communities recognize the importance of ensuring that children grow up in the family and so even where a child is born out of marriage, society encourages the couple to regularize the marriage. If this becomes difficult, the lineages of the couple may permit them to live together in order to allow the child to grow until they decide to regularize the marriage. It is worthy of note, however, that though society allows this to take place, it often frowns upon such relationships when their regularization takes unduly long to occur. If, for any reason, the couple does not want to marry, then societal norms demand that the child is cared for by the mother until such time the father wants the child to live with him. During this period the father is given unrestricted access to the child so that the child and the father develop natural filial bonds. Similarly, when the woman marries or remarries, her new husband is encouraged to take good care of the woman's children (those born in the previous marriage) for the adage goes that *wo na nya kun a nna woso enya egya* (lit: once your mother gets a [new] husband, you also get a [new] father). The new husband has to play the role of a father to the children and vice versa.

Right to Socialization/Education

Human beings need more intelligence levels than other primates and hence have to be socialized (Odetola and Ademola, 1985). Parents and other members of the community are expected to socialize a child. Among the Fantse, socialization comes in two forms – moulding the child's character and personality and bearing the associated costs (Personal communications with Egya Abbiw on March 7, 2015). Because the character and personality are associated with the spiritual entity of personhood, which is obtained from fathers, the onus of socialization falls on a father (Wilson, 2011). Fathers delegate childcare and socialization of children at the early stages of life to the mother. Fathers are expected to provide the necessary conditions for the development of the child. Hence, the award of maintenance costs against a father so that he maintains the mother of his child (Section 51 of the *Children's Act 1998*) conforms to Fantse culture.

Like other African children, a Fantse child is trained to conform to the tenets of the culture as he or she follows the prescribed paths set by the custodians of the culture (Boakye-Boaten, 2009). As children attain adolescence, their mode of socialization changes according to their gender. At this stage, there is segregation by gender for effective socialization (Hagan, 1983). Males socialize males and vice versa. Where a father is not readily available to socialize his male children, a father's brother or mother's brother fills the gap. Fathers have prerogatives to train their children as well as step-children.

The domestic roles of the child increase gradually with age. This ensures that the child performs certain roles for the family and community as enshrined in the Preamble of the *ACRWC*. It is worth noting that in Fantse culture, the child performs these duties based on its abilities. Thus, even the duties assigned to the child should be guided by the "best interests of the child" clause in the *UNCRC*. Therefore, the child needs the support of members of the family, especially parents and members of the kin group to perform its duties.

Rights to Healthcare

Every child has a right to health care. As childhood among the Fantse begins from conception, health rights of children too begin at conception. The fetus' rights are linked to the reproductive rights of its mother. Hence, the various transitional rituals that pregnant women go through and the support that they receive from members of their families and communities provide avenues for both mothers and children to enjoy their rights to healthcare. The Akan consider maternal death as a taboo so they make efforts to support and protect expectant and nursing mothers. This helps to protect children from neonatal deaths. If a woman dies during pregnancy, the fetus is taken out of the womb in order to ensure that it is also dead before the deceased is buried. This helps to buttress the point that the fetus is considered as a human being and has a right to life.

The health of a child is dear to a father because the Fantse believe that diseases are caused by natural or supernatural entities (Opoku, 1978). If it is the supernatural, then the father, as the one who provides the child with a spirit and is his spiritual guardian, should be the best person to intervene for the healthcare of the child. If it is a natural disease, then the father should provide the means for healthcare. A husband's responsibility is to provide for the health needs of the wife, especially when she is pregnant. Thus, Christensen (1954) noted that when a woman tells her husband that she is pregnant, the husband takes her to a medicine man and provides all the resources needed for making pregnancy safer. This helps to improve the reproductive health of the woman as well as the health of the fetus and, subsequently, the child. With the support from members of the community, the child's rights to health becomes everybody's responsibility; however, the onus falls more on fathers than anyone else.

Responsibilities of Children

Among the Fantse, personhood and filiation set the conditions for rights and obligations of children. The Fantse proverb goes that *nyea w'ahwɛ wo ma wo se etutu no, wo so hwɛ no ma ne se ntutu* (Lit: As somebody has taken care of you to grow teeth, take care of that person so that he also loses his or her teeth). In context, this means one should reciprocate the gesture that his parents took care of him or her in childhood when one becomes an adult. These obligations run through a person's lifetime; hence, the worldview that one is a child of someone till one dies. The *ACWRC* recognizes the importance of the responsibilities for the proper socialization of children and captures it in its Preamble. However, society is also aware that an offspring will not be able to reciprocate all the benefits of childhood from his or her parents. For example, nurture and socialization will be difficult to reciprocate; however, parents benefit from these as they shape the attitudes of their offspring who tend to appreciate the need to reciprocate the kind gestures of their parents when the offspring become adults.

Through filiation, both parents can exact a number of duties from their children if the children are able to perform those duties. For example, before and during adolescence children can run errands for their parents and contribute labor to support the family's economy. Even after marriage, sons are expected to provide farm labor for their parents while daughters may help their mothers to sell their wares. The sons do this with alacrity as they mobilize their age mates to provide farm labor for their parents (Awedoba, 2005). Whereas a mother and members of the matrilineage exact rights *in personam* (the rights of a family to exact responsibilities from its own members) from the offspring, a father has rights *in personam* over his children in his lifetime but not after his death. Instead, a father's lineage has rights *in rem* (the rights that a corporate group exact on those who are not members of the group to perform a responsibility for the group) over the offspring after the death of the father where the clan of a father calls on the child to give his or her father a befitting burial (Wilson, 2011).

In many indigenous Fantse communities, laws on performance of funerals consider the extent to which a father played his role in the maintenance of his children. If a father took good care of his children in his lifetime, the children will reciprocate this gesture in their adulthood and give the father a befitting burial. However, if the father did not, then the burial will fall short of normal societal expectations. This creates a check on the father for the fulfilment of the child's rights in Section 47 of the *Children's Act 1998* which states that a father is duty-bound to supply the necessities of health, life, education and reasonable shelter for his children.

As stated earlier, complementary filiation goes beyond filial ties to the lineage and clan of a father. Otherwise, it would be expected that a father's lineage should have no power to exact rights *in rem* from a man's offspring. However, with classificatory filiation, where a society perceives a man and all his siblings as a father to his offspring, the siblings of a man who in most cases are not members of his lineage and clan can exact rights *in rem* from the offspring. Therefore, in addition to the rights *in personam*, complementary filiation brings about rights *in rem* which a father's lineage exacts from their offspring. For example, in old age the offspring are under obligation to provide for their father's needs or upon the death of a father, a father's lineage calls on the offspring to perform a befitting burial for a father.

Similarly, if a father dies, his children will have to be catered for by his siblings or members of his lineage until they are in a position to fend for themselves. The father's lineage is also under obligation to perform marriage rites for the offspring when they get to marriageable age and want to marry. All these ensure that offspring are provided for up to a reasonable age. Furthermore, it helps to fulfil the requirement "in the best interests of the child" which international human rights documents like the *UNCRC* and the *ACRWC* advocate. After marriage, a person's matrilineage becomes responsible for his or her rights and privileges. The element of personhood that fathers contribute (the spirit) links the offspring to their fathers and the latter's lineages permanently.

Factors Militating Against Rights of Children

A major shortfall in children's rights among the Fantse is the inheritance system which does not consider the rights of children as exist in patrilineal societies and also as provided for in the national laws and international documents. Fantse culture sets rules concerning the management of the deceased and his or her estates. The basic rule is that upon the death of a person, the corpse and any property left behind automatically belong to its descent group. Hence, the clan has the sole right and obligation to organize funerals for its deceased members. Until the coming into effect of the *Intestate Succession Law 1985* (PNDCL 111), succession and inheritance were administered as per the rules in customary laws. Among the Fantse, the major rule of succession is that males inherit from males and vice versa and inter-generational alliance must be considered; that is, siblings must be considered first before mothers' children (Christensen, 1954; Sarbah, 2004; Wilson, 2011). Though clans organize funerals, marriage and filiation give the clans the rights *in rem* to demand from the widow and offspring who do not belong to the deceased's clan, that they contribute to the ritual objects and participate in the funeral. Unfortunately for the children and the widow, they do not have inheritance rights from the husband and father because of the rules governing inheritance and succession. This has always been a case for rights of children.

Once children do not have inheritance rights from their father, it is repugnant to justice. As far back as 1935, the Judicial Committee of the Privy Council of the then Gold Coast held in *Abusatu Balogun and Anor v Amodi Balogun and others* (1935) 2 WACA 290, 306 that customary laws should be allowed to operate, provided that they are not repugnant to justice (Wilson, 2011). It must be noted that the indigenous law was not made to be repugnant but social change and the abuse of rights and privileges made it so. Under customary law, land and immoveable properties belonged to lineages. People had usufruct rights on the land. Hence, members of the lineage used it in their lifetime and it passed to the lineage upon death. With the social change brought about first by colonialism, people acquired land on leasehold and could dispose of it by will to whoever they pleased. As a result land devolved to offspring.

The abuse of privileges set in when successors failed to use the property acquired for the upkeep of a deceased's children. Under customary law, whoever succeeds a deceased person is under an obligation to take care of the children and widow. The rules of descent and succession are that the successor is the father of the surviving children and, hence, should do everything within his means to ensure that he serves the best interests of the children. Under indigenous culture, such abuses were reported to the indigenous institutions such as the family and chieftaincy. Unfortunately, colonialism created a situation where people felt that alternative dispute resolution mechanisms which were more popular should be used instead of reporting to government agencies. This situation persists after so many years of independence and, hence, people remain reluctant to report cases of abuse. Though Section 16 of the *Intestate Succession (Amendment) Law 1991*, PNDCL 264 and Sections 7 and 15 the *Children's Act 1998* criminalize the situation where children are deprived of portions of their deceased fathers' estates, many will not waste their time on seeking redress from the law courts.

RECOMMENDATIONS

Though the family systems within which the concepts work have undergone considerable social change, it is also on record that in spite of the changes introduced, the systems have continued to exist, taking into consideration the framework of the culture. Moreover, the African family systems which the colonial and neocolonial institutions (including the church, national laws and international human rights instruments) are seeking to change have been commended for saving the face of the family institution worldwide (Refer to United Nations documents on the declaration of 1994 as the International Year of the Family and the *Africae Munus* document of the Roman Catholic Church). This shows that whatever laws are introduced, they can never work unless it is couched within the framework of the culture. For example, when Christian missionaries attempted to organize marriage ceremonies outside the framework of the family, it did not work and, hence, the churches therefore made the indigenous ceremony a precondition for church marriages (Wilson, 2011). It is worthy of note that it is still the practice in many, if not all, churches. Similarly, though the *Intestate Succession Law* (Ghana, (1985), PNDCL 111) identifies sharing a person's estate into 16 portions and distributing them to the various stakeholders, the Fantse system is more in tune with the *ebusa* system (one where farm produce and property are divided into three portions for distribution to the parties involved in a contract). The cultural framework identifies the strengths of this system, considering that there are three major stake-holders in the estate of a person and so it uses the *ebusa* system conveniently to apply the law, though the law does not make mention of *ebusa* (Wilsn, 2011). In some situations, even though the law does not make room for anyone to live with the sons and daughters of a deceased, the matrilineage negotiates with the patrilineage so that a room is given to the successor of the intestate person if there are enough rooms in the estate. Where there are not enough rooms, arrangements are made for peaceful co-existence of the matrilineage and the patrilineage.

There is no denying that rights of the child as presented in this chapter do not encounter any shortfalls on the part of members of Fantse societies. Societies have their own share of social deviance that make fathers irresponsible and hence prevent children from enjoying their legitimate rights from fathers and their lineages. For example, some men refuse to accept responsibilities for a woman's pregnancy and hence fail to take good care of their children and ensure that these children enjoy their rights. Moreover, some parents may abuse the role of children in providing labor to support the family economy as part of their socialization process. In such situations, the International Labour Organization suggests that the jobs should not be risky for the children and also should not affect their education in adverse ways. Indigenous culture ensures that children work within their ability.

Considering the abuse that children from broken homes go through, it would be in the best interests of the child to decide where it would prefer to live as stated in the law but, unfortunately, the indigenous culture does not accord children such rights. There are newspaper reports about children living with their mothers being sexually abused by their step-fathers. When this happens, mothers find it difficult to report their husband's attitudes to their children to law enforcement agencies for fear of reprimand from family members (Britwum et al., 2004; Kuyini and Mahama, n, d). Furthermore, when children from broken homes leave the homes of their mothers for that of their fathers, they often live with their step-mothers who at times abuse them physically. These practices are not in the best interests of the child. However, because the indigenous Fantse culture upholds the view that lineages in marriage should handle such cases, it becomes difficult to report such cases to the law enforcement agencies. Therefore, it becomes difficult to implement the law to the letter. This clearly shows that a law operates better if it aligns with the culture of a people.

Conclusion

This chapter has examined how Fantse culture resonates with human rights documents. Using concepts developed by Fortes on African family systems such as filiation, descent, complementary filiation and personhood, it has been argued that these concepts serve as the bases for explaining indigenous Fantse ideas on human rights. Fantse culture upholds principles in universal human rights documents, though their applications should rather be conceived in relativistic terms. Some customary practices of the Fantse are in line with the rights enumerated in the *UNCRC* and the *ACRWC*. Moreover, the rights that one enjoys during one's childhood transform into obligations when one grows up and has to take care of one's children and parents (Wilson, 2012). Though the national laws of Ghana, particularly the *Children's Act 1998*, serve as a vital legislative reform for the protection of children's rights in Ghana, a better understanding of the concepts of personhood, descent and filiation resonates with legal and human rights concepts and therefore helps to educate people about the social systems and the ways to better ensure the implementation of this legislation.

References

Achilihu, S. N. (2010). *Do African children have rights? A comparative and legal analysis of the UNCRC*. Boca Raton, FL: Universal Publishers.

Agorsah, (2012). *Marry me in Africa*. Bloomington, IN: Author House.

Appiah, E.M. (n,d). Protecting the rights of children in Ghana: The legal framework and ancillary matters. Retrieved from www.cepa.org.gh/researchpapers/Protecting69.pdf.

Arhin, K. (1985). *Traditional rule in Ghana: Past and present.* Accra, Ghana: Sedco Publishing Limited.

Awedoba, A. K. (2005). *Culture and development in Africa: With special reference to Ghana* (2nd Ed.). Legon, Ghana: Institute of African Studies.

Boakye-Boaten, A. (2009). Changes in the concept of childhood: Implications on children in Ghana. *AFROEUROPA- Journal of Afroeuropean Studies*, 3(1). Electronic Version.

Britwum, A. O., Atuguba, J. R. A., Dadzie, C., Bruce-Catheline, W., Kuma, E. & Minka-Premo, S. (2004). *Child maintenance and plural legal systems in Ghana.* GTZ Legal Pluralism Gender Pilot Project (Family Law Focal Area).

Brown, C. K. (1994). *Gender roles in household allocation of resources and decision-making in Ghana: Family and development programme.* Accra, Ghana: University of Ghana.

Casey, S. (2011). *Final report of the mapping and analysis of Ghana's child protection system.* Kowloon, Hong Kong: Child Frontiers Ltd.

Christensen, J. B. (1954). *Double descent among the Fanti.* New Haven: Human Relations Area Files.

Filey, A. C. (1975). *Interpersonal conflict resolution.* Glenview, IL: Scott, Foresman & Co.

Fortes, M. (1967). Totem and taboo [Presidential Address]. *In Proceedings of the Royal Anthropological Institute for 1966*, (pp. 5-22). London: Royal Anthropological Institute of Great Britain and Ireland. DOI: 10.2307/3031711.

Fortes, M. (1969). *Kinship and the Social Order: The Legacy of Lewis Henry Morgan.* Oxford: Routledge.

Fortes, M. (1970). Descent, filiation and affinity. In M. Fortes (Ed.), *Time and social structure and other essays*, (pp. 122-124). London: Athlone Press.

Fortes, M. (1997). The structure of Unilineal descent group. In R.R. Grinker & C.B. Steiner (Eds). *Perspectives on Africa: Reader in culture, history, and representation*, (pp. 11-23). Oxford: Blackwell Publication.

Ghana, (1985). *Intestate Succession Law, PNDCL 111.* Accra, Ghana: Assembly Press.

Ghana, (1991). *Intestate Succession (Amendment) Law.* Accra, Ghana: Assembly Press.

Ghana, (1992). *Constitution of the Republic of Ghana.* Accra, Ghana: Assembly Press.

Ghana, (1998). *Children's Act, Act 560.* Accra, Ghana: Assembly Press.

Ghana, (2005). *Human Trafficking Act, Act 694.* Accra, Ghana: Assembly Press.

Ghana, (2007). *Domestic Violence Act, Act 732.* Accra, Ghana: Assembly Press.

GNCRC, (2014). *Report to the UN Committee on the Rights of the Child 2014.* Accra, Ghana: GNCRC.

Gyekye, K. (1992). Person and community in African thoughts. In: K. Wiredu and K. Gyekye (Eds), *Person and community: Ghanaian philosophical studies 1*, (pp. 193-206). Washington, DC: Council for Research Values in Philosophy.

Gyekye, K. (1995). *An essay on African philosophical thought: The Akan conceptual scheme* (rev. ed.) Philadelphia: Temple University Press.

Gyekye, K. (1996). *African cultural values: An introduction.* Accra, Ghana: Sankofa Press.

Hagan, G. P. (1983). Marriage, divorce and polygyny in Winneba. In C. Oppong (Ed.), *Female and male in West Africa.* Boston: Allen and Unwin.

Hagan, G. P. (2000). *"Divided we stand" A study of social change among the Efutu of Coastal Ghana.* Trondheim: Norwegian University of Science and Technology.

Hayden, P. (2001). Introduction to part one. In P. Hayden (Ed.), *The philosophy of human rights*, (pp. 3-10). St. Paul, MN: Paragon House.

Helman, C. (2007). *Culture, Health and Illness* London: Holder Education.

Kendie, S. B. & Guri, B. Y. (2010). Indigenous institutions and contemporary development in Ghana: Potentials and challenges. In M.S. Subramanian & B. Pisupati. (Eds.), *Traditional knowledge in policy and practice: Approaches to development and human well-being*, (pp. 52-71). Tokyo: United Nations University Press.

Kuyuni, A. B. & Mahama, F. K. (n, d). Implementing child rights and protection law in Ghana: Case study. Retrieved from http://www.eshare. edgehill.ac.uk/3328/pdf.

Mbiti, J. S. (1990). *African religions and philosophy* (2nd rev. ed.). Oxford; Portsmouth, NH: Heinemann.

Organization of African Unity (OAU), *African Charter on the Rights and Welfare of the Child*, 11 July 1990, CAB/LEG/24.9/49 (1990).

Odetola, T. A. & Ademola, A. (1985). *Sociology: An introductory African text*. London: Macmillan.

Opoku, K. A. (1978). *West African traditional religion*. London: F.E.P. International.

Saha, S. C. (2007). Saharan state-building and ethnicity. In S.C. Saha (Ed.), *The politics of ethnicity and national identity*, (pp. 139-172). New York: Peter Lang.

Sarbah, J. M. (2004). *Fanti customary laws: A brief introduction to principles of native laws and customs of the Fanti and Akan Districts of the Gold Coast.* Bristol: Thoemes Press.

Sarpong, P. K. (1974). *Ghana in retrospect: Some aspects of Ghanaian culture*. Tema, Ghana: Ghana Publishing Company.

Schnepel, B. (1990). Corporations, personhood, and ritual in tribal society: three interconnected topics in the anthropology of Meyer Fortes. *JASO*, *21*(1), 1-32.

Takyi, E. (2014). Child Labour in Ghana: Ecological Perspective. *Developing Country Studies.*, *4* (10), 35-44.

UNICEF, (1991). *Plan of action for implementing the World Declaration on the Survival, Protection and Development of Children in the 1990s*. New York: UNICEF.

UNICEF-Ghana, (2000). *A situation analysis of children and women in Ghana*. Accra, Ghana: UNICEF.

United Nation General Assembly, *Universal Declaration of Human Rights*, 10 December 1948, 217 A (III).

United Nations General Assembly, *Convention on the Rights of the Child*, 20 November 1989, United Nations, Treaty Series, vol. *1577*, p. 3.

United Nations General Assembly, *Vienna Declaration and Programme of Action*, 12 July 1993, A/CONF.157/23.

Wilson, A. J. (2007). Women's power in the socio-political organization of the Fante of Ghana: The case of *Asafo* companies. *UMOJA*, *2*(1), 1-12.

Wilson, A. J. (2011). Mothers' wealth: Matrilineality and inheritance among the Fantse of Ghana. A PhD dissertation presented to Ohio University.

Wilson, A. J. (2012). Personhood, human rights and health among the Akan and Igbo of West Africa. *African Identities*, *10*(4), 439-453.

Wiredu, K. (2001). An Akan perspective on human rights. In P. Hayden (Ed.), *The philosophy of human rights*, (pp. 298-338). St. Paul, MN: Paragon House.

BIOGRAPHICAL SKETCH

Alex J. Wilson (PhD) is a senior lecturer at the Centre for African and International Studies, University of Cape Coast, Ghana. He was an adjunct lecturer in the Colleges of Nursing at Korle Bu and Pantang, Ghana. He obtained his PhD in Inter-Disciplinary Studies with majors in Anthropology and Cultural Studies from Ohio University in Athens OH, USA. He holds a postgraduate diploma in African Community Health, also awarded by Ohio University. His research interest is in indigenous African knowledge systems, especially social, political, health and educational systems. He is the author of 'Personhood, Human Rights and Health among the Akan and Igbo of West Africa,' published in Volume 10 Issue 4 of *African Identities* (a journal).

In: International Human Rights and Justice
Editor: Doug Hodgson

ISBN: 978-1-63484-709-4

Chapter 12

SUBORDINATION AND SUPER-ORDINATION: DISCOURSE ANALYSIS OF MEDICALIZATION OF PREGNANCY AND CHILDBIRTH IN GHANA

Alex J. Wilson [*] ***and Douglas Frimpong-Nnuroh***
Centre for Africa and International Studies, University of Cape Coast,
Cape Coast, Ghana

ABSTRACT

Though the policy on free antenatal and postnatal care services in Ghana was expected to motivate women to receive maternity care from skilled providers, patronage of the services is low. Instead of addressing this problem, some officials attribute the situation to factors including superstition. Using post-colonial theory to digest the literature on medicalization, medical pluralism, and pregnancy and child-birth, to support the role of culture in health-seeking behaviour, this chapter argues that the targets set for achieving Millennium Development Goal (MDG) Five encourage medicalization; which also promotes super-ordination of biomedicine and subordination of ethnomedicine. Hence, biomedical practitioners overlook the need to improve upon their services and respect for client's rights to choose service providers. The chapter concludes that this super-ordination results in resistance to maternity care from biomedical services and forestalls the achievement of MDG Five. The authors recommend the re-examination of the essence of culture in healthcare for addressing the power relations associated with medical pluralism.

Keywords: reproductive health, medicalization, millennium development goals, making pregnancy safer, human rights, post-colonialism, Ghana

[*] Corresponding author: ajwilson@ucc.edu.gh.

Introduction

Many authors and policy-makers criticize indigenous African cultural practices for failing to encourage birth-giving in health facilities; and hence creating difficulties for achieving the United Nations Millennium Development Goal (MDG) Five – improving maternal health. Many policy-makers overlook the essence of rights-based care for maternal health as they tout the availability of facilities and expert care-givers as the way to achieve MDG Five. By so doing, they tend to present Western cultures as 'superior' and desirable and indigenous African cultures as 'inferior' and undesirable. They attribute the health-seeking behaviour of indigenous people to superstition and postulate that such behaviours militate against the processes of making pregnancy safer and achieving MDG Five. Such attitudes smack of the subordination of indigenous African cultures and super-ordination of Western and elite African cultures. The discourse is heightened as reports on healthcare providers deviate from the principles of rights-based healthcare promotion to imposition of standards of healthcare delivery. The reports negate the essence of improving healthcare delivery for achieving MDG Five. Furthermore, they downplay the value of participation of clients as exists in the new order of reproductive health and rather project the old order of Maternal and Child Health and Family Planning (MCH–FP), where clients were mere recipients of maternity services.

Objectives and Methodology

This chapter uses secondary materials to bring to the attention of health workers their responsibilities in the face of clients' right to choose healthcare regimes that they want. While not undermining the efforts that are being made to achieve the MDGs on healthcare or being oblivious of the extent to which medicalization has helped to prevent maternal morbidity and mortality, this chapter uses the cultural interventions outlined by the World Health Organization's Making Pregnancy Safer (MPS) initiative (WHO, 2010) to tease out the discourse associated with medicalization of pregnancy and childbirth in the healthcare system of Ghana. It postulates that medicalization, as practised in Ghana, has the tendency to subordinate clients and argues that achieving MDG Five does not depend solely on birth-giving in healthcare facilities but more importantly providing people with better alternatives based on best practices of care. It examines the existing literature of the Ministry of Health (MoH) of Ghana and the World Health Organization (WHO), using post-colonialism as a theoretical framework, to explain the discourse associated with subordination and super-ordination. Considering that clients of healthcare services replicate some indigenous cultural practices in their health-seeking behaviour, the chapter examines how pregnancy and childbirth are embedded in the medical systems of Ghana and how they influence the achievement of MDG Five. It is worth noting that though diverse cultures exist in Ghana as a result of a multiplicity of ethnic groups, there are also more common practices as a result of interactions among the various ethnic groups, thereby creating what can be termed Ghanaian culture. Therefore, where necessary, the authors mention practices that are attributable to specific ethnic groups.

FOCUS ON MAKING PREGNANCY SAFER (MPS) INITIATIVE

The MPS initiative of the WHO focuses on evidence-based interventions which target the major causes of maternal and new-born mortality and morbidity. It underscores the importance of infrastructure, availability of professional maternity care providers, improvement in services delivery as well as positive community actions to ensure that women and their new-borns have access to skilled care. Specifically, it emphasizes the important roles of women, their partners and families in developing their capacities for making healthy choices to improve maternal and new-born health. It notes that the critical link between healthcare providers and the community throughout pregnancy, childbirth and postpartum periods provides the continuum of care and access to a skilled attendant when obstetric and neonatal complications arise and helps to make pregnancy safer (WHO, 2010; WHO, ICM and FIGO, 2004).

The MPS initiative is, therefore, congruent with the worldview of Ghanaians on pregnancy. This is because indigenous Ghanaian cultures perceive pregnancy as a bio-social issue and highlight the important roles of members of the family in maternity care. For instance, pregnant women receive more support from members of their families and community, especially Traditional Birth Attendants (TBAs). They go through the various transitions during pregnancy with their relatives who offer support because it is incumbent upon the relatives to provide avenues for them to enjoy their reproductive rights (Wilson, 2012). Furthermore, if a pregnant woman dies, her family members go through rituals to cleanse themselves from the calamity which has befallen their relative and to guard against the recurrence of maternal deaths within the clan and the entire community. Thus, Ghanaian cultural values have the potential for upholding the MPS initiative and achieving MDG Five.

MEDICAL SYSTEMS OF GHANA

Medical pluralism – mainly biomedical and ethnomedical practices – exists in Ghana. The basic principle underlying biomedical practice is that diseases are caused by physiopathological agents (Sofowora, 2008). The development of biomedicine in Europe and its spread to other parts of the world during the Enlightenment Period contributed to its acceptance throughout the world (Geest and Finkler, 2004). The people of the then Gold Coast (now Ghana) also benefited from it as missionaries and colonizers established clinics to offer services to the people they wanted to 'civilize' and also to save themselves from contracting infectious diseases like yaws (Headrick, 1981). In effect, biomedical services were limited to Europeans and only extended to Africans in order to reduce the high rate of mortality among the former. Since the introduction of biomedicine in Ghana, it has been practised alongside ethnomedicine - a situation referred to as "medical pluralism" (Twumasi, 1979).

On the other hand, ethnomedicine combines knowledge and practices based on past experiences of a group of people used in diagnosing, preventing and eliminating a disease. The practice of ethnomedicine differs from one society to another because of cultural differences. In Ghana, it is an aspect of indigenous cultural practices which explains the rationale for illness and misfortunes. A major worldview associated with ethnomedicine is that diseases and misfortunes among humans do not occur by chance; but, rather, as a result of a lack of harmonious relationships with the human environment (Appiah-Kubi, 1981). For instance, the degradation of water bodies, land and air as well as the destruction of the relationship between a person and his or her religious environment may result in illness.

Consequently, the causes of diseases may be natural (ordinary) and/or unnatural (extraordinary). The natural diseases are those that are explicable while the unnatural ones are inexplicable – those which may be caused by the supernatural including displeasure from ancestors, witchcraft, spirits, deities and divinities (Opoku, 1978; Sofowora, 2008). Hence, indigenous healthcare providers use magico-religio concepts, acts, and symbolism in their healing practices. Furthermore, they use physical cures and treatments, some of which have scientific validity (Twumasi, 1979). However, the indigenous Ghanaian worldview of religion and health is that science works through the magnanimity of the Supreme Being.

Thus, medical pluralism has been essential in the healthcare delivery system of Ghana. Traditionally, healthcare has been part of the indigenous religious systems. The introduction of biomedical services by missionaries supported the indigenous worldview of illness as a spiritual phenomenon. In contemporary times, biomedical service providers collaborate with religious groups to provide holistic healthcare. Christian mission hospitals and other major healthcare facilities have chaplaincies. Moreover, churches provide spiritual support for the sick. Furthermore, new Christian movements perform healing services for their adherents (Sackey, 1999). This demonstrates the extent to which religious worldviews have been embedded in the healthcare delivery systems and also how indigenisation continues to accommodate social change. Therefore, the omission of religious worldviews in healthcare delivery in Ghana will not achieve optimum uptake of service delivery.

MDG FIVE IN FOCUS

The MDGs are a range of economic and social indicators that the world aims at achieving by 2015. Africa has made substantial progress towards achieving many of them, especially MDG Five. However, many reports show that it still has the world's highest maternal mortality ratio in the world. Many African countries cannot reduce maternal mortality by two-thirds of the levels they had attained in 1990 (Easterly, 2009: UN Millennium Project, 2005). Noting that maternal mortality and morbidity result mainly from the inability of the healthcare system to manage complications associated with childbirth, UN (2014) advocates integrated maternal and child health interventions that focus on strengthening health systems, reducing adolescent birth rates and increasing access to skilled birth attendants, antenatal visits and contraceptive use in order to speed up the progress of attaining MDG Five. Efforts at achieving the MDGs in Ghana, especially MDG Five, are on course – though there are some challenges. For instance, the Campaign on Accelerated Reduction of Maternal Mortality in Africa (CARMMA) listed on its website that Ghana is among 44 African countries which have adopted CARMMA's strategies.

Whereas about 77% of women in Ghana make four or more antenatal visits, only about half (55%) of all deliveries are assisted by trained personnel (20% and 9% assisted by trained and untrained Traditional Birth Attendants (TBAs) respectively) (Dako-Gyeke, Aikins, Aryeetey, Mccough and Adongo, 2013; Ghana Demographic Health Survey (GDHS), 2008).

Furthermore, about 54% of births are delivered in health facilities while 45% occur at homes. In Northern Ghana, about 71% of pregnant women deliver at home and 25% in a hospital or clinic. Though government policies encourage women to receive maternity care from skilled providers, many pregnant women seek care from sources other than the formal health sector (Dako-Gyeke et al., 2013; Kwapong, 2008; Sackey, 2002). Therefore, achieving MDG Five has not been easy.

PREGNANCY AND CHILDBIRTH

Two paradigms exist for pregnancy and childbirth – biological and cultural (Jónsdóttir, 2012). The biological process includes the changes that occur in the pregnant woman's body. The cultural aspects are the norms that affect the outcome of pregnancy. Both paradigms influence women's health-seeking behaviour during pregnancy and childbirth. They also influence individuals' and societies' (including service providers') attitudes towards pregnant women. Fathalla (2004) states, "Pregnancy and childbirth are a privileged function of women, essential for the survival of [human] species" (p. 7) Furthermore, maternity is considered as a bio-social function and not a disease; hence, society should not equate maternal mortality to mortality caused by diseases but uphold the obligation to prevent maternal deaths as well as deaths that can be attributed to diseases.

Fathalla (2004) projects the indigenous Ghanaian worldview that pregnancy is not a disease but part of the developmental process that a woman should go through in her lifetime. Pregnancy is an unstable condition which is potentially perilous and may be associated with illness, mishaps and, eventually, death. A pregnant woman is considered to be in the profane state. She becomes pure after childbirth when the necessary rites have been performed to re-integrate her into normal social life.

Therefore, providing care for pregnant women is multifaceted and requires a holistic approach to care, including medical, psycho-social, economic and spiritual support (Dako-Gyeke et al., 2013) as is evident in the ethnomedical practice in Ghana. The psycho-social care is often religious, including observance of taboos and performance of rituals. Society expects her to suppress her wishes for the sake of the unborn child. It is worthwhile to note that because pregnancy is not considered as a disease, maternal mortality is considered unnatural and must be prevented from occurring. When it occurs, the various ethnic groups have elaborate rituals that must be performed for the deceased as well as the surviving close relatives.

MEDICALIZATION OF PREGNANCY AND CHILDBIRTH

Medicalization is the process whereby society defines non-medical conditions and treats them as medical problems (Conrad, 1992). It makes behaviours or social conditions take on medical meanings and hence medical practices are used for controlling problematic social experiences. For instance, physiological events which occur in womanhood, such as menstruation and menopause, which indigenous cultures view as natural human developmental process is viewed by biomedicine as pathological (Airhihenbuwa, 2007).

Medicalization of pregnancy has been part of the biomedical system since biomedicine was introduced to the health systems of Ghana. The *Declaration of Alma-Ata* adopted on 12 September 1978 at the World Health Organization-sponsored International Conference on Primary Health Care and the International Conference on Population Development (ICPD) plan of action entrenched medicalization of pregnancy. The *Declaration of Alma-Ata* introduced the Primary Health Care (PHC) programme and made MCH–FP major components of healthcare. The ICPD called for a paradigm shift from MCH–FP to reproductive health and called for deliveries in health facilities under the supervision of qualified health practitioners. This call projected attendance at antenatal, natal and postnatal clinics and, hence, increased medicalization of pregnancy and child-birth. However, reproductive healthcare emphasizes human rights-based care and advocates participation of all individuals irrespective of their age and gender, families and communities (UNFPA, 2004). This development empowers clients to participate in decision-making based on informed choices about their reproduction instead of the situation under the MCH–FP where clients were seen as mere recipients of services. The discourse associated with the call by the ICPD Action Plan for a paradigm shift is that, in Ghana, the human rights-based care has been negated. Thus, the Action Plan presents a two-pronged situation which emphasizes the need for clients to participate in reproductive healthcare delivery system, and yet it does not accept rights-based decision-making influenced by indigenous Ghanaian culture – a clear indication of subordination of ethnomedicine and indigenous cultural practices.

Discourse Associated with Pregnancy and Childbirth

The foregoing discussion presents a number of discourses because the increased management of pregnancy in healthcare facilities results in the replication of Western biomedicine and standardization of healthcare practices. For instance, biomedicine projects the biological paradigm of pregnancy to overshadow the cultural paradigm. Furthermore, increased management of pregnancy without a corresponding awareness of rights-based care for patients has brought about subordination and hence a discourse. Biomedical practice copes with Christianity but not indigenous religions of Africa. For instance, in many healthcare facilities, including the public ones, daily activities begin with Christian prayers while indigenous religion will not be accepted in the facility.

Aspects of this discourse associated with post-colonialism are portrayed in both national and international health where the uneven relations of Western knowledge distort everything about traditionalism and determine what is scientific and acceptable. Furthermore, traditional medical practitioners and their clients have been stereotyped negatively by some policy-makers, academics and healthcare providers even though the traditional system can claim some successes in healthcare delivery. Repeated failure of aspects of biomedicine has led people to turn to the use of traditional medicine (Hountunji 1997). There are concerted efforts to side-line ethnomedicine but the extent to which it flourishes in Ghana demonstrates the degree to which Ghanaian cultures support it. This has culminated in the enactment of the *Traditional Medicine Practice Act 575 2000* to regulate ethnomedical practice so as to encourage collaboration between biomedical and ethnomedical practices.

THEORETICAL FRAMEWORK

Subordination and super-ordination in African societies are best described in post-colonial theory propounded by Said (1979), Fanon (2004) and Spivak (2006). Post-colonialism helps to identify the power relations. It generates a discourse about situations where everything that is advanced, good and civilised is measured in terms of the Western construct and empowers members of the downtrodden societies to resist such relations (Cesaire, 2000). For instance, it criticizes the situations where every aspect of traditional African cultures and scientific knowledge have been trampled upon, fear cunningly instilled in Africans, thereby swaying Africans from their useful ways of life (Nketsia, 2013). Instead, it advocates a knowledge base strengthened by a symbiotic relationship between traditional African and modern knowledge where traditional knowledge shapes the modern and modern knowledge helps to fulfil traditions. Thus, it despises a relationship where the two systems exist in a relationship defined by subordination and super-ordination.

Post-colonial discourse also highlights the politics associated with the inequalities among women whereby privileged women who often represent underprivileged women tend to fight for their own interests and thus re-present the underprivileged (Spivak, 2006). They do this by creating the impression that men often subordinate women so efforts should be made at fighting against domination by men. By so doing, they overlook the subordination of women by fellow women and make the downtrodden more invisible. Attacking men alone for violence against women often creates suspicion and negates the complementary roles which men and women play in order to make pregnancy safer.

Post-colonialism advocates a deliberate destruction of Africa's colonial past, reinvention of its peoples and culture and resistance to misrepresentation and subordination. Furthermore, it calls for a proactive deconstruction of the knowledge system based on colonialism and its tenets, and reconstruction of a system based on the indigenous African systems. With regard to women, it calls for a new orientation that recognizes the class structures that exist among them. It also underscores the need for advocacy for the downtrodden by empowering women to fight for their rights.

Thus, the advocacy of post-colonialism, that once discourse subdues a group, it requires a critical analysis to reveal, depoliticize and reduce the effect of the inherent power relations associated with an existing knowledge system, has been adopted for this chapter. The theory has the potential to make women who feel threatened by medicalization become empowered to enable them resist standardization in the health delivery systems of Ghana. This realization strengthens the need for the critical discourse analyses required for deconstructing issues of medicalization of pregnancy and childbirth, as will be discussed in this chapter.

APPLICATION OF THE DISCOURSE TO MEDICALIZATION OF PREGNANCY AND CHILDBIRTH

The discourse created in the medical systems of Ghana calls for rejecting Western master-class ideologies so that Africans may develop through reconnecting with indigenous knowledge systems. In the following discussion, this chapter examines the discourse associated with the subordination of women in Ghana through medicalization of pregnancy and childbirth and how the health systems have denied women the power to decide on their reproductive health needs in the sub-themes identified below.

Culture: 'Tradition' and 'Modernity' as Discourse

Calhoun, Light and Keller's (1997) definition of culture as "The integrated way of thinking, understanding, evaluating, and communicating that makes possible a shared way of life" (p. 93) offers the framework for understanding healthcare systems because health is part of the cultural practices of a group and is influenced by the group's worldviews about well-being, how it assesses health situations and how it communicates these to other people. Furthermore, the ICPD Action Plan, which served as a precursor for MDGs Four and Five, encourages the use of cultural and symbolic meanings to support rights to reproductive health (Anderson, 2005a). Similarly, the MPS initiative encourages cultural institutions such as the family and community to collaborate with health professionals to ensure safe pregnancy. The use of indigenous culture brings about choice and hence alternatives for individuals and countries to become empowered. Consequently, best practices for pregnancy and childbirth based on indigenous Ghanaian cultural practices ensure participation, make maternity and pregnancy safer and help to achieve the targets set under MDG Five.

In health matters, the concept of the 'other' in post-colonialism has been replicated under the guise of medical pluralism. In Ghana, pluralism conceived within the binary of biomedicine and ethnomedicine creates power relations with biomedical practitioners having more power than ethnomedical practitioners. Both colonial and post-independence laws and the social and health structures give biomedical practitioners more power. International organizations rely on these Western ideas and influence national laws, including those associated with healthcare. At the moment, biomedical practitioners and their cohorts continue to influence the laws on healthcare practices. The knowledge base of biomedical practice is attached to scientific knowledge which has Western paradigms; hence, the unequal power relations. At times, in reaction to the subordination of ethnomedicine, many people resist biomedical practice. There are also situations where clients of biomedical facilities tend to hide their health problems from professionals (Riley, 1994). This negates the collaboration between healthcare providers and members of the community; contrary to what the MPS initiative advocates.

In Ghana, both biomedical and ethnomedical practitioners do not explain their practices to clients as should be the case. Ethnomedical practice depends on the adage among the indigenous people that "clients value healing and not the healing process." Biomedicine cannot rely on this premise; otherwise, it cannot be deemed scientific. If it does, it also becomes shrouded in mystery just like ethnomedicine. In an environment where medical practitioners do not feel obliged to explain health-delivery mechanisms, clients are likely to adopt alternatives which are readily available and culturally friendly but equally shrouded in mystery. This discourages deliveries at healthcare facilities under the supervision of qualified personnel. Therefore, MDG Five will not be readily achievable.

Most often, knowledge about, and the use of, modern contraceptives have been used as a mark of development and enlightenment. However, though many women knew about modern contraceptives and the contraceptives were readily available in the market, only a few actually used them (Adanu et al., 2012; GSS et al. 2009). Besides, those who had ever used modern contraceptives were more than those who were using them at the time the research was conducted. Moreover, those who used traditional contraception, including abstinence, withdrawal and breastfeeding, were more than those who used the modern methods. Furthermore, of those who did not use contraceptives, only 0.5% mentioned prohibition in any form. Of the rest, 42.3% did not have partners, 19.9% desired pregnancy, 11.4% disliked use, or feared the side-effects, of the contraceptives, 13.4% did not know of contraceptives or refused to use them, while others offered economic reasons.

Even though the reports show that there has been little or no improvement in the provision of information on modern methods of contraception to support informed choice over the past five years and there are misconceptions about the side-effects of modern contraceptives, it cannot be said that women use the traditional methods because of misinformation. This demonstrates that in Ghana, modernization as a development paradigm for healthcare does not really work under the framework which is being used. Hence, the efforts at reducing fertility and achieving MDG Five through modern contraception are not receiving the much-needed response.

Development Paradigms as Discourse

Development paradigms have been constructed around westernization and modernization and made development agencies call on Africans and Asians to eschew their cultural practices that are not in tune with European culture. However, development takes place within the framework of a culture, including the philosophy and worldview upon which the value-systems, cosmology, institutions and structures of society are based. This provides the powerhouse for members of the society to help them to articulate their positions and interact with the rest of the world in order to ensure that society survives (Awedoba, 2005; Nketsia, 2013; Riley, 2005). The UN *Declaration on the Right to Development 1986* perceives development as a dynamic process which involves a number of parameters, including the cultures through which individual and societal well-being improves steadily. Hence, anyone who uses values and paradigms that perceive his or her culture as inferior becomes an instrument for denigrating his own self and community (Nketsia, 2013). Furthermore, Nketsia noted that culture informs the politics and economics that conceive, inform and condition development.

The dynamic process that is required for development built around the culture of the people who aspire to develop is missing in biomedical practice in Ghana. For instance, recalling that biomedical services were limited to Europeans and extended to Africans in order to reduce the high rate of mortality among Europeans, coupled with the description of ethnomedicine as one which does not have a scientific basis and therefore dwells on superstition, a discourse is created that makes it amenable for resistance. The superstitions associated with indigenous medicine are only based on the aspects that are inexplicable. Though science helps to explain the worldview of people, the power relations associated with the oft-given explanation make biomedical practitioners in Ghana feel reluctant to explain the science behind their practice. As noted earlier, this makes many people resist deliveries in biomedical facilities with skilled birth attendants. It is worth noting that neither biomedicine nor ethnomedicine can single-handedly meet the health needs of the people of Ghana; hence, the need for integration of the two in order to make pregnancy safer and achieve MDG Five.

Millennium Development Goals and Discourse

Though the MDGs have brought the international community together to share common ideas and set common goals, the arbitrary nature of the means adopted to measure progress on health issues results in domination to the extent that European modes of measuring empowerment are used. This situation makes African countries look worse than they really are and makes their successes portrayed as failures (Easterly, 2009). A typical example is the common refrain in the literature and reports that African countries are bound to fail in achieving the MDGs, especially MDG Five, even though there are no reliable data for African countries on the MDGs. For instance, targets set for reducing maternal deaths include the need for deliveries to be assisted by skilled birth attendants (90% globally and 60% in countries with high maternal death rates), high level of use of biomedical facilities and an increase in the use of contraceptives among women (Odoi-Agyarko 2003). These targets give the impression that people everywhere will use biomedical services. However, as noted earlier, of the number of people who receive antenatal care in biomedical facilities, only a few actually used biomedical facilities for deliveries (Adanu et al. 2012; Dako-Gyeke et al. 2013). Coupled with the impression highlighted earlier under "'Tradition' and 'Modernity' as Discourse" that knowledge of contraceptives has no correlation with their use and, hence, the knowledge and use cannot be used to measure empowerment, this is worth noting for achieving MDG Five.

The West sets performance standards for all countries in the world. These standards tend to control developing countries which are isolated from discussions and the standards are presented as if all countries have to achieve the MDGs before it becomes possible for the world to develop. Furthermore, the MDGs represent what is feasible at the global level, based on global trends observed in the 1970s and 1980s, and not necessarily at the national level; hence, they fail to identify the appropriate policies and necessary inputs for the various countries to achieve the targets (Vandemoortele, 2014). Globalization exhibits Western imperialism (Robertson, 1992) and entrenchment of the capitalist ideology. It creates a discourse as the Western world identifies avenues for determining the health needs of developing countries and finds ways to make money and test medicines which it has manufactured. Thus, Vandemoortele cautions that development is a process of collective self-discovery and, hence, the MDG targets cannot be reduced to a series of standard interventions called best practices. His suggestion, that the global targets should rather widen the policy space to make underprivileged groups benefit immensely from the targets in order to improve upon their own lifestyles, is worth noting for achieving MDG Five.

Discourse Associated with Human Rights on Health

Healthcare is a human development as well as a human rights issue. Various resolutions on human rights emphasize the sovereignty of the individual and need for States Parties to create the necessary conditions for the attainment of the rights to development in which the human person is the central subject of development (David, 2011). The 1993 World Conference on Human Rights reiterated that development should be linked to democracy and peace so that people can participate in developing policies on their welfare. Furthermore, the UN *Declaration on the Right to Development 1986* emphasizes voluntary participation.

Hence, participation of clients in healthcare is important for human development. Within an international human rights context, Article 25(1) of the UN *Universal Declaration of Human Rights 1948* provides in part that everyone has the right to a standard of living adequate for their health and well-being and for that of their family including medical care and social services while Article 25(2) states that motherhood and childhood are entitled to special care and assistance. Article 12 of the UN *International Covenant on Economic, Social and Cultural Rights 1966* relevantly states that States Parties recognize the right of everyone to the enjoyment of the highest attainable standard of physical and mental health and obligates them to take steps for the reduction of the still-birth rate and infant mortality. Article 12(2) of the UN *Convention on the Elimination of All Forms of Discrimination Against Women 1979* requires States Parties to ensure to women appropriate services in connection with pregnancy, confinement and the post-natal period. At the regional human rights level, Article 16 of the *African Charter on Human and Peoples' Rights 1981* provides that every individual shall have the right to enjoy the best attainable state of physical and mental health and obliges States Parties to take the necessary measures to protect the health of their people and to ensure that they receive medical attention.

The World Health Organization outlines rights-based approaches to health and recommends the integration of acceptable principles and practices including human dignity and accessibility to health (Wilson, 2012). Furthermore, advocacy for rights to health now combines ensuring availability of facilities with efficiency of services rendered and aims at bridging the gaps between the core and periphery. For instance, in considering the gaps between advanced and developing countries, advocates aim at ensuring that people in both developing and advanced countries function within their own social and political context (Gruskin et al., 2005). Therefore, the negative impact of development would be felt more if rights-based activities do not conform to the right to practise one's culture.

Health-seeking behaviour is influenced by a number of factors relating to a person and his or her dignity as a member of the human community. This includes personal preferences, the facilities and services available and the socio-cultural environment (Iyalomhe and Iyalomhe, 2012). A person's preferences may be influenced by his or her personal background, culture and history. Other relevant socio-cultural factors which affect the perception of health and well-being include religion, availability of relatives in the hospital or connection with hospital staff, family decision, marital status, position in the family, educational status and also, more importantly, the nature of the illness. The MPS initiative upholds these. Therefore, the situation where medicalization emphasizes the role of the individual at the expense of the collective function of the group has reduced the level of participation in reproductive health delivery to individual participation at the expense of the communal value systems that African cultures uphold. This has also made it difficult to uphold the roles of families and communities in maternity care as noted by the MPS initiative and has also made it more difficult to achieve MDG Five in Ghana.

Among women's rights is the right to reproductive health including making informed choices about one's sexuality, relationships and service providers. Since culture influences a group's decisions on reproductive health (Helman, 2007; Wilson, 2012), reconsidering issues of medicalization and childbirth is best undertaken within the framework of indigenous Ghanaian worldviews and cultures in relativistic principles. Unfortunately, in their quest for health and maternity care, women have been overtly or covertly subordinated because medicalization follows a 'scientific' basis that should be replicated to provide the same results whenever a procedure is applied and, hence, is more in tune with universal human rights rather than relativistic terms. Therefore, other ways of accessing healthcare may not be acceptable to policy-makers and international development agencies, thus making the chances of achieving of MDG Five slim.

By relying on medical 'experts' to define their experiences, pregnant women cede matters concerning their reproductive health to members of the medical profession. Biomedical practitioners often treat pregnant women as if the women do not know anything about their own reproduction. They do not even accept requests from 'patients' to be treated according to the patient's past experiences (Dako-Gekye et al., 2013). Their attitudes to 'patients' are conditioned by the fact that pregnancy changes the body system; hence, pregnant women need help to enable them respond to those changes. Furthermore, they assume that women are oblivious to these changes and consider that only health professionals have the requisite knowledge to transmit to the women.

The indigenous Ghanaian perception about pregnancy as part of womanhood and motherhood makes it imperative for all adults, especially women who have many children, to have foreknowledge about major aspects of health implications associated with the statuses. This calls for collective participation of members of the community in reproductive healthcare. Unfortunately, there are situations where some health officials refuse to accord 'patients' the respect they deserve. For instance, health workers give 'patients' orders and insult them when they please. They even extend such practices to relatives of patients. Furthermore, as biomedical facilities fail to provide avenues for family members and members of the community to support expectant and nursing mothers, they limit the level of acceptability of biomedical facilities in meeting the health needs of the community. This prevents people from seeking professional care. Therefore, attainment of MDG Five is more difficult.

A major human rights discourse is the dichotomy between universalism and relativism. Universalism is about the parameters within which rights work for all nations while relativism conceives rights within the socio-cultural, historical and philosophical systems of a group. Universalism questions many aspects of indigenous African ways of life for focusing on groups instead of the individual. For instance, the situation where African communal values place human rights within the context of the collective has often been attacked. However, relativism in the African context defines rights in terms of both individual and collective rights by emphasizing clear-cut boundaries between the two. In both situations rights go with responsibilities (Gyekye, 1992; Wilson, 2012; Wiredu, 2001). Furthermore, the notion of collective responsibility does not exonerate a person from individual responsibility (Bannerman-Richter, 1982; Gyekye, 1992). The individual is held responsible for his or her actions and in some situations, especially where the offence is about breaking of taboo, a social group dissociates itself from the offender (symbolically) before the individual is sanctioned.

Individual and collective rights and responsibilities are important for discussions on reproductive health because reproductive health embodies both the individual and shared group responsibilities. An individual's reproductive health status affects the community. The community has a stake in the reproductive health of all persons. Moreover, community-based health education is integral to ensuring the health of individuals and groups (Anderson, 2005b). Therefore, conditioning rights in terms of individualism with no regard for the collective is not good enough for ensuring community health. Furthermore, the achievement of the MDGs is more of a collective responsibility that goes beyond nations to the entire world.

Feminist Discourse

Another discourse in the universalists-relativists debate that tends to reconstruct African womanism in terms of Western feminist ideas is the situation where rights-based health has been conceived in individual choice and negates the collective choice which is typical of Africans (see Gyekye, 1992; Wilson, 2012; Wiredu, 2001). African women exert their collective reproductive rights when they perform rituals and take vital decisions that affect their reproduction. This enables them to enjoy support from indigenous women's groups. Unfortunately, these decisions, including those that members of a woman's natal family take, are considered as subordination because the decision is not conceived within the context of individual choice as advocated by universalism. Once the Western world conceives family life in terms of conjugal relations, the erroneous impression created is that if a woman's reproductive rights are not vested in her person then it is probably vested in her husband. Hence, some policy-makers are oblivious of the right to collective decision-making that African women have within their lineages and other social and political groups which provide the platform for educating women and shielding them from the potential powers of their husbands to control their reproduction. Thus, many policy-makers do not use the indigenous Ghanaian knowledge base which is potent for raising awareness to make pregnancy safer and to achieve MDG Five.

At times feminist literature subordinates women as it creates the impression that women's rights have been ceded to men. For instance, Hartmann (1995) and Fathalla (2004) argue that African women do not have reproductive rights because the rights are vested in their husbands. However, Wilson (2012) debunks these as typical modernist and structuralist arguments which project women as uninformed and men informed. Another erroneous impression created is that sex is a man's business yet in many Ghanaian societies, wives have rights to sexual satisfaction from their husbands in return for fidelity on the part of the woman (Wilson, 2012). This makes sexual relations matters a collective issue of mutual rights and obligations between spouses. This calls for critical observation and further probing into the discourse to establish the realities on the ground to help educate members of the society in order to make pregnancy safer and achieve MDG Five.

At times gender activists ignore some unseen feminist discourses where women subordinate fellow women. As noted earlier, this situation is very common in medicalization in Ghana where health workers, especially nurses, treat less educated women as if they have no knowledge about their own reproductive system and no right to determine the service providers they want or influence the service they want and, therefore, coerce them to accept the type of knowledge system that is produced by medicalization. Thus, the biomedical system does not offer the necessary support for empowerment of clients. Hence, some women have become disillusioned by the use of medicalization in managing their previous births and feel that they need to take control of their reproductive rights and give birth in the way that they feel empowered and supported (Jónsdóttir, 2012). The discourse here is similar to what Spivak (2006) identifies in subaltern women who although being represented by fellow women, the representatives do not speak for them but rather misrepresent them. This has stalled the achievement of MDG Five.

CONCLUSION

This chapter has examined one of the major problems that militates against achieving MDG Five in Ghana – medicalization of pregnancy and child-birth. It argues that though the ICPD Action Plan and MDG Five uphold the rights to healthcare, medicalization of pregnancy and child-birth has limited the efforts at making pregnancy safer and achieving MDG Five to the availability of health facilities and existence of healthcare service providers. As a result, inherent power relations exist where biomedical practice overshadows ethnomedical practice. These relations have made biomedical practitioners overlook the right of clients to choose service providers and thereby made it difficult for Ghana to achieve MDG Five. To conclude, until policy-makers and healthcare service providers accept that clients are rational in choosing service providers, service providers will continue to package anything as service and expect clients to accept it. However, because clients have the alternative of ethnomedical practice, if service providers do not offer the best of service, clients will refuse to participate in biomedical service delivery. Thus, efforts at reducing maternal deaths and, hence, achieving MDG Five will be futile.

The way forward is strong collaboration between biomedical and ethnomedical services; for example, one between TBAs and midwives. Though there are calls for private-public partnership (PPP) in the healthcare delivery system, the picture does not include the type of collaboration where midwives work with TBAs in the same facility. It is on record that this has produced very good results in some localities in Ghana and, hence, the need for re-examining all its potential to help achieve the best. There are other examples where midwives applied indigenous knowledge systems which clients are more familiar with (ARHR n.d.). The reports indicate that these efforts increased the rate of attendance to clinics for all maternity services. Hence, there is no gainsaying that collaboration results in mutual benefits instead of a power structure that subordinates ethnomedical practice. Furthermore, collaboration validates the cultural-based care where family and community members are crucial in making pregnancy safer for achieving MDG Five.

Secondly, a rights-based approach to healthcare should be vigorously pursued with a blend of universalism and relativism. While universalism aims at providing healthcare institutions and building structures that encourage people to speak up, relativism encourages the use of the beneficial aspects of cultural practices of Ghana for reproductive healthcare. Moreover, both universalism and relativism strengthen a rights-based approach to indigenous knowledge systems because any new idea that is transmitted to a person is first internalised within the framework of his or her culture. Furthermore, a cultural group is used to its indigenous institutions so a critical re-examination of the strengths and weaknesses of these institutions helps to improve upon people's capacity to call for better services. This helps to empower the downtrodden in the community to speak out about their health-seeking behaviour.

Thirdly, rights-based forms of medicalization call for professionalism, education on the relationship between service providers and clients and the rule of law. These call for regular public forums to bring clients and service providers together so that that they can find better ways of relating. At the moment, there are many policies on progressive healthcare delivery which have the potential for resolving conflicts between clients and service providers; however, the policies do not encourage the use of alternative dispute resolution mechanisms, the use of which the social systems of Ghana encourage. If the system does not admonish service providers when they go wrong, clients will be unwilling to report recalcitrant ones. Hence, there is the need for effective supervision and monitoring by a working complaints unit which investigates complaints of clients and acts upon them.

Finally, it must be reiterated that neither biomedicine nor ethnomedicine has been able to solve all health problems by itself (Sindiga 1995). However, Western knowledge has accepted certain concepts that it had earlier rejected from indigenous knowledge systems. For example, the practice of prolonged breastfeeding was once considered to be outmoded and discouraged in Europe but now it has once again been acknowledged as a healthy way of caring for children and recommended for achieving MDG4. Therefore, there is a need for effective integration of medical systems in order to make pregnancy safer and help Ghana to achieve MDG Five.

References

Adanu, R. M., Seffah, J., Anarfi, N., Lince, N. & Blanchard, K., (2012). Sexual and reproductive health in Accra, Ghana. *Ghana Medical Journal*, *46*(2), 57-65.

Airhihenbuwa, C. O. (2007). *Healing our differences: The crises of global health and the politics of identity.* Lanham, MA: Rowman and Littlefield.

Anderson, B. A. (2005a). Speaking with one voice. In B.A. Anderson (Ed.). *Reproductive health: Women and men's responsibility.*, (pp. 4-7). Sudbury, MA: Jones and Bartlett.

Anderson, B. A. (2005b). Reproductive health: Advocacy in action. In B.A. Anderson (Ed.). *Reproductive health: Women and men's responsibility.*, (pp. 1-2). Sudbury, MA: Jones and Bartlett.

Appiah-Kubi, K. (1981). *Man cures, God heals: Religion and medical practice among the Akans of Ghana.* Totowa, NJ: Allanheld Osmun.

ARHR (undated). *The White Ribbon Alliance Atlas of Birth.* http://www.mamaye.org.gh/sites/default/files/evidence/Ghana%20Atlas%20of%20Birth%202012.pdf.

Awedoba, A. K. (2005). *Culture and development in Africa: With special reference to Ghana.* Legon: Institute of African Studies.

Bannerman-Richter, G. (1982). *The practice of witchcraft in Ghana.* Elk Grove, CA: Gabari.

Calhoun, C., Light, D. & Keller, S. (1997). *Sociology.* New York: McGraw Hill.

Cesaire, A. (2000). *Discourse on colonialism.* New York: Monthly Review Press.

Conrad, P. (1992). Medicalisation and social control. *Annual Review of Sociology*, *18*, 209-252.

Dako-Gyeke, P., Aikins, M., Aryeetey, R., Mccough, L. & Adongo, P. B. (2013). The influence of socio-cultural Interpretations of pregnancy threats on health-seeking behavior among pregnant women in urban Accra, Ghana. *BMC Pregnancy and Childbirth.*, *13*(211), 1-12. doi:10. 1186/1471-2393-13-211.

David, W. L. (2011). The human right to development. In L. Keita (Ed.). *Philosophy and African development: Theory and practice*, (pp. 37-56). Dakar, Senegal: CODESRIA.

Easterly, W. (2009). How the millennium development goals are unfair to Africa. *World Development*, *37*(1), 26–35.

Fanon, F. (2004). *The wretched of the earth*. New York: Grove.

Fathalla, M. F. (2004). *Reproductive rights and wrongs: The case for maternal mortality as a reproductive wrong*. Abuja, Nigeria: MacArthur Foundations.

Geest, S. der. & Finkler, K. (2004). Hospital ethnography: Introduction. *Social Science and Medicine*, *59*, 1995–2001.

GHS (Ghana Health Service). (2007). *Reproductive health strategic Plan 2007-2011*. Accra, Ghana: Reproductive and Child Health Department, MOH.

Gruskin, S. & Tarantola, D. (2005). Health and human rights. In S. Gruskin, M.A. Grodin, G.J. Annas and S.P. Marks (Eds.). *Perspectives on health and human rights*., (pp. 3–58). New York: Routledge.

Gruskin, S., Grodin, M. A., Annas, G. J. & Marks, S. P. (2005). Introduction. In S. Gruskin, M.A. Grodin, G.J. Annas & S.P. Marks (Eds.). *Perspectives on health and human rights*, (pp. xii-xx). New York: Routledge.

GSS (Ghana Statistical Service) and GHS (Ghana Health Service) (2009). *Ghana maternal health survey*, 2007. Maryland: Ghana Statistical Service/Ghana Health Service/Macro International.

GSS, GHS and ICF Macro (2009). *Ghana demographic health survey 2008*. Accra, Ghana: GSS, GHS and ICF Macro.

Gyekye, K. (1992). Person and community in African thoughts. In K. Wiredu & K. Gyekye (Eds.). *Person and community: Ghanaian philosophical studies 1*, (pp. 193-206). Washington, DC: Council for Research Values in Philosophy.

Hardee, K., Gay, J. & Blanc, A. K. (2012). Maternal morbidity: Neglected dimension of Safe motherhood in the developing world. *Global Public Health: An International Journal for Research, Policy and Practice*, *7*(6), 603-617.

Hartmann, B. (1995). *Reproductive rights and wrongs: The global politics of population control*. Boston, MA: South End Press.

Headrick, D. R. (1981). *The Tools of empire: Technology and European imperialism in the Nineteenth Century*. New York and Oxford: Oxford University Press.

Helman, C. G. (2007). *Culture, health and illness*. London: Holder Education.

Hountunji, P. J. (1997). Introduction. In P.J. Hountunji (Ed.). *Endogenous knowledge research trails*, (pp. 1-42). Dakar: CODESRIA Books.

Iyalomhe, G. B. S. & Iyalomhe, S. I. (2012). Health-seeking behaviour of rural dwellers in Southern Nigeria: Implications for healthcare professionals. *International Journal of Tropical Disease & Health*, *2*(2), 62-71.

Jónsdóttir, O. V. (2012). *Medicalisation of childbirth in Western society: can women resist the medicalisation of childbirth?* Retrieved from http://skemman.is/stream/get/1946/11156/27462/1/Mannfr%C3%A6%C3%B0i_BA_ritger%C3%B0_-_Oddn%C3%BD_Vala_J%C3%B3nsd%C3%B3 ttir.pdf.

Kwapong, O. A. T. F. (2008). The health situation of women in Ghana. *Rural and remote health*, *8*, 963. retrieved from: http://www.rrh.org.au.

Nketsia, N. K. (2013). *African culture in governance and development: The Ghanaian paradigm*. Accra, Ghana: Ghana Universities Press.

Odoi-Agyarko, H. (2003). *Profile of reproductive health situation in Ghana*. Geneva: WHO.
Opoku, K. A. (1978). *West African traditional religion*. London: F.E.P. International.
Organization of African Unity (OAU), *African Charter on Human and Peoples' Rights ("Banjul Charter")* 27 June 1981 CAB/LEG/67/3 rev. 5, 21 ILM 58 (1982).
Riley, M. (1994). "The new mat is woven over the old one": Ghanaian indigenous communication forms and their potential as facilitators in health education programs. PhD. Thesis. Simon Fraser University.
Riley, M. (2005). Indigenous resources in a Ghanaian town. In K. Ansu-Kyeremeh (Ed.). *Indigenous communication in Africa: concept, application and prospect*, (pp. 141-158). Accra, Ghana: Ghana Universities Press.
Robertson, R. (1992). *Globalisation: Social theory and global culture*. London: SAGE Publication.
Sackey, B. M. (1999). Women and health-seeking behaviour in religious contexts: Reproductive and antenatal care in Ghanaian religious movements: A case study of the Twelve Apostles Church. *Research Review New Series*, *15*(2), 65 91.
Sackey, B. M. (2002). Faith healing and women's reproductive health. *Research Review New Series*, *18*(1), 5-11.
Said, E. (1979). *Orientalism*. New York: Knopf Doubleday Publishing
Sindiga, I. (1995). African ethnomedicine and other medical systems. In I. Sindiga, C. Nyaigot-Chacha & M. P. Kanunah (Eds.). *Traditional medicine in Africa*, (pp. 16-28). Nairobi, Kenya: East African Educational.
Sofowora, A. (2008). *Medical plants and traditional medicine in Africa*. Ibadan, Nigeria: Spectrum Books.
Spivak, G. C. (2006). Can the Subaltern speak? In B. Ashcroft, G. Griffiths & H. Tiffin (Eds.). *The Postcolonial studies reader*, (pp. 28-37). London: Routledge.
Twumasi, P. A. (1979). History of pluralistic medical systems: A sociological analysis of the Ghanaian Case. *A Journal of Opinion*, *9*(3), 29-34.
United Nations (UN), *Universal Declaration of Human Rights 1948* 10 December 1948 217 A (III).
United Nations (UN), *International Covenant on Economic, Social and Cultural Rights 1966* 16 December 1966 United Nations, Treaty Series, vol. 993, p. 3.
United Nations (UN), *Convention on the Elimination of Discrimination Against Women* 18 December 1979 United Nations, Treaty Series, vol. 1249, p. 13.
United Nations (UN), *Declaration on the Right to Development 1986* 4 December 1986 A/RES/41/128.
United Nations (UN) (2014). *The Millennium Development Goals Report 2014*. New York: United Nations. http://www.un.org/millenniumgoals/2014%20MDG%20report/MDG%202014%20English%20web.pdf.
United Nations Millennium Project (2005). *Investing in development: A practical plan to achieve the Millennium Development Goals*. London: Earthscan. http://www.unmillenniumproject.org/documents/MainReport Complete-lowres.pdf.
United Nations Fund for Population Activities (UNFPA) (2004). *Program of action adapted at the International Conference on Population and Development, Cairo in 1994*. http://www.unfpa.org/sites/default/files/event-pdf/PoA_en.pdf.

Vandemoortele, J. (2014). Post-2015 agenda: Mission impossible? *Development Studies Research: An Open Access Journal*, *1*(1), 223-232, DOI: 10.1080/21665095.2014.943415.

World Health Organization (WHO) (2004). *Making pregnancy safer – The critical role of the skilled attendant: A joint statement by WHO, ICM and FIGO*. Geneva: WHO.

World Health Organization (WHO) (2010). *Making pregnancy safer: Making individuals, families and communities to improve maternal and newborn health*. Geneva: WHO Press.

Wilson, A. J. (2012). Personhood, human rights and health among the Akan and Igbo of West Africa. *African Identities*, *10*(4), 439-453.

Wiredu, K. (2001). An Akan perspective on human rights. In P. Hayden (Ed.). *The Philosophy of human rights*, (pp. 298 – 338). St. Paul, MN: Paragon House.

Yamin, A. E. & Maine, D. P. (2005). Maternal mortality as human rights issue: Measuring compliance with international treaty obligations. In S. Gruskin, M. A. Grodin, G. J. Annas & S. P. Marks (Eds.). *Perspectives on health and human rights*, (pp. 469-472). New York: Routledge.

BIOGRAPHICAL SKETCH

Alex J. Wilson (PhD) is a senior lecturer at the Centre for African and International Studies, University of Cape Coast, Ghana. He was an adjunct lecturer in the Colleges of Nursing at Korle Bu and Pantang, Ghana. He obtained his PhD in Inter-Disciplinary Studies with majors in Anthropology and Cultural Studies from Ohio University in Athens OH, USA. He holds a postgraduate diploma in African Community Health, also awarded by Ohio University. His research interest is in indigenous African knowledge systems, especially social, political, health and educational systems. He is the author of 'Personhood, Human Rights and Health among the Akan and Igbo of West Africa,' published in Volume 10 Issue 4 of *African Identities* (a journal).

Douglas Frimpong-Nnuroh is a lecturer at the Centre for African and International Studies, University of Cape Coast, Ghana. He holds a master's degree in African Studies from University of Ghana, Legon and a second masters in Gender and Development from University of Bergen, Norway. His PhD is due from University of Amsterdam in June 2016. As an Applied Social and Cultural Anthropologist, the author's research interests cover family, gender and vulnerability, governance and democracy and care of children. He is the author of "Ghost Mothers and wet nurses: breastfeeding practices and care of children in crisis in Ellembelle Nzema" Research Review 2004.

INDEX

#

A

B

C

F

G

H

J

K

L

M

N

O

P

Q

R

S

T

Y

Z